THE
TUDOR
SOCIALITE

THE TUDOR SOCIALITE

A SOCIAL CALENDAR OF TUDOR LIFE

JAN-MARIE KNIGHTS

AMBERLEY

First published 2021

Amberley Publishing
The Hill, Stroud
Gloucestershire, GL5 4EP

www.amberley-books.com

Copyright © Jan-Marie Knights, 2021

The right of Jan-Marie Knights to be
identified as the Author of this work has been
asserted in accordance with the Copyright,
Designs and Patents Act 1988.

ISBN 978 1 3981 0129 6 (hardback)
ISBN 978 1 3981 0130 2 (ebook)

British Library Cataloguing in Publication Data.
A catalogue record for this book is available
from the British Library.

1 2 3 4 5 6 7 8 9 10

Typesetting by SJmagic DESIGN SERVICES, India.
Printed in the UK.

CONTENTS

INTRODUCTION

A royal family came to prominence more than five hundred years ago and occupied the national stage for just over a century. Some of its larger-than-life characters captivated their contemporaries and still fascinate us today. That family is the Tudors.

Flamboyant attire, hairstyles, rich jewels, mishaps, love affairs and scandals were as eagerly read about centuries ago as they are today. Royal proclamations and pamphlets – the Crown's earlier media channels – informed the public of royal news, betrothals, marriages and deaths.

We think we know them, these five monarchs who form part of our national consciousness: Henry VII the old miser; Henry VIII the fat, tyrannical king who married six women and beheaded two of them; Edward VI the sickly, dispassionate boy; Bloody Mary the religious fanatic; and Elizabeth I the Virgin Queen.

In cameos of the monarchs' private and public lives, meet instead the young Henry VII, survivor and clement victor of the Wars of the Roses, who encouraged poets and explorers to come to his court, laughed at tumblers and disliked bloodshed. Find his son, Henry VIII, ascending the throne as a vibrant, active seventeen-year-old, his head full of chivalrous playacting, a playboy prince who developed remedies and enjoyed studying the stars. Stop before his ten-year-old son, Edward VI, who held up his coronation progress to laugh at a tightrope walker and who enjoyed plays and martial events. Spare a thought for Mary I, who desperately sought the love of her father and husband. Finally, there is Elizabeth I, courageous in the face of persecution by her elder sister and the dangers of imminent invasion by Philip II's Spanish Armada.

This book tells you of their foibles and pastimes using the journals, letters and reports of those people who witnessed and recorded the Tudors' joys and sorrows, their triumphs and tragedies, against the backdrop of the times in which they lived.

BACKGROUND
THE COUSINS WHO WOULD BE KING

The Black Prince, eldest son and heir of Edward III, the victor of Poitiers who captured the French king Jean II, was greatly mourned when he died in 1376. When his ten-year-old son and heir, Richard, inherited the throne after the death of his grandfather Edward III in June 1377, he had a tough act to follow. But his mettle was soon proved when he rode out at fourteen years old, almost alone, to face the rebel Wat Tyler, who was leading the uprising against the new poll tax, which demanded a shilling to be paid by every person, rich or poor, above fifteen years of age.

The adult Richard II stood six feet tall, had long blonde hair and was brave in battle. His master cook's 1390 recipe book *The Forme of Cury* illustrates his 'fondness of good living'. Richard also inherited the notorious Plantagenet temper, exacerbated perhaps by the death of his beloved wife, Anne, in 1394. They were childless, and many regarded Richard's uncle John of Gaunt, Duke of Lancaster, and his son Henry of Bolingbroke after him, as next in the line of succession.

When a quarrel broke out between Henry and the Duke of Norfolk, Richard banished them both. When Henry's father died in 1399, Richard II unjustly confiscated his estate, dishonourably depriving Henry of his inheritance. Not one to take this lying down, while Richard warred in Ireland, Henry landed with a small force in Yorkshire and by popular acclaim was crowned Henry IV. Richard, forced to abdicate, was imprisoned in Pontefract Castle, where he was starved to death. The body, shown with neither 'mark nor scar', was buried at King's Langley. Although rumour said Henry slept uneasily, he reigned for fourteen years. His son peacefully ascended the throne and was crowned Henry V.

In the first year of his reign, Henry V, 'for love of Richard II', whom he had served in Ireland, moved Richard's body to Westminster to be buried beside Queen Anne 'as his desire was'. The boy 'foreshadowed the man'. When Henry was seven years old, 12*d* was paid out for 'a new scabbard of a sword' and '8*d* for harp strings'. This cultured warrior king of Agincourt, who took his harp on campaign, died of dysentery at Vincennes in 1422 aged thirty-five. He left his nine-month-old son to ascend the throne as Henry VI, and his young wife, twenty-one-year-old Katherine of Valois, to take a second husband, Owen Tudor. They had three sons: Edmund, Jasper and Owen.

Henry VI was crowned in England and France. In 1445, he married Margaret of Anjou after falling in love with her portrait. At the beginning of 1453 he suffered a mental breakdown and was unfit to govern, so the council appointed his cousin and presumptive heir, Richard, 3rd Duke of York, Protector of the Realm. Many, including Richard himself, felt he had a better right to the throne than Henry, being descended from John of Gaunt's older brother Lionel, Duke of Clarence, albeit through the female line, which had married into the line of Edward III's son Edmund, Duke of York.

The status quo changed in October 1453. Queen Margaret gave birth to Henry's son, Edward, which proved a surprise to Henry when he regained his wits on Christmas Day 1454. Margaret's hatred for Richard burned. Her attempts to deprive him of office and adherents so aggrieved him it led to the first battle of the Wars of the Cousins, now described as the Wars of the Roses: the white rose of York against the red rose of Lancaster. The first blood was spilt at St Albans on 22 May 1455. Henry himself commanded the royal army against Richard but he was captured at the town's market cross, his army defeated. His wits once again went astray.

Rather than being invited to take on the kingship as he had expected, Richard was merely reappointed Lord Protector, though promised the throne if his cousin died or resigned. Nevertheless, Margaret was furious. She had no intention of her son being disinherited. Richard, for his part, had no intention of waiting. Battles between the two factions raged up and down the country. Executions on both sides decimated the nobles. Yet, judging by the letters of the Plumpton and Cely families, the lives of merchants and ordinary people carried on with hardly any disruption.

On the last day of 1460, at Wakefield Green, Richard and his sixteen-year-old son, Edmund, were killed. Young Edmund was butchered while fleeing over Wakefield Bridge by Lord Clifford, who also cut off York's head to show it to the queen, who immediately ordered it to be placed on the walls of York with a paper crown on its head.

The new Duke of York, eighteen-year-old Edward, vowed vengeance. Two months later at Mortimer's Cross, every Lancastrian captured was executed, including Owen Tudor, who was beheaded at Hereford market cross, his head placed on its highest step. A mad woman set candles around it, combed his hair and washed his face.

A month later the citizens of London, supporters of York, cheered Edward and acclaimed him king. He left his coronation celebrations to go and fight the bloodiest battle of all at Towton, in thick falling snow. So many men were slain that the countryside for miles around was stained with blood. The

Lancastrians fled. In sporadic fighting during the next few years, Henry VI was again captured and imprisoned in the Tower. Calm followed.

But Margaret had not given up. She mustered an army and invaded England in July 1470, forcing Edward to flee for his life, leaving behind his pregnant wife, Elizabeth Wydville. Henry VI was delivered from the Tower, a bewildered man tied on to his horse wearing a moth-eaten gown. His 'second reign' lasted eight months. The Lancastrian forces were overwhelmingly defeated at the Battle of Tewkesbury. Seventeen-year-old Prince Edward was slain, his mother was captured and Henry was returned to the Tower. Two days later, he was dead. Many believed he had been murdered.

Edward's first, public move back in London, to popular acclaim and cheers, was to kiss his wife and newborn son and heir, Edward.

Over the next few months, even peaceful Lancastrians were hunted down and executed. Jasper Tudor, and his brother's fifteen-year-old son, Henry, Earl of Richmond, barely escaped as they were chased almost to the ends of the kingdom. They sailed from Tenby, expecting never to see England again.

Edward settled back into luxury and indolence.

England at this time was a rich country with flourishing trade. In necessities or luxuries, apart from wine, it was self-sufficient. People, in town or country, lived on what they grew in fields and gardens. Craftsmen made every product that could be desired and any excess was sold at the fairs held up and down the country. Livestock was pastured on common land. The rest of the land was heavily forested, with wild boar and red deer roaming among the trees, interspersed with chases, parks and heaths. Wood was the mainstay material for houses, bridges, ships and carts. It was used for fires to warm the houses or to forge household necessities.

Meat was abundant for most in the form of pigs, cattle and rabbits. Nobles ate herons, peacocks, partridges and fish such as pike and carp, matured in their own fishponds. There were even swans. An Italian diplomat wrote that it was a 'truly beautiful thing to behold one or two thousand tame swans upon the river Thames ... eaten by the English like ducks and geese'. Kites kept the streets clean and 'so tame' that they will take 'bread smeared with butter' from the hands of little children.

Englishmen and women were deemed well dressed, handsome and courteous, keen to share meals with visitors. Dinner, the main meal of the day, was served between ten in the morning and noon; supper was between five and seven in the early evening, dependent upon season and occupation.

London, with a thriving population nearing 75,000, was the busy and wealthy hub for merchants from all over Europe.

This season of tranquillity and thriving trade was abruptly disrupted when forty-year-old Edward IV died suddenly in 1483, leaving his younger brother, Richard, to rule on behalf of his twelve-year-old heir.

Richard certainly began preparations to crown his nephew. Elizabeth, who had fled into sanctuary at Westminster, was persuaded to allow nine-year-old Richard to join his brother in the Tower. The two boys disappeared. Historians still argue over whether they were murdered or spirited away; contemporary rumours provide both scenarios.

What is certain is that, on 26 June, Richard III was crowned. Dynastic warfare for the throne resumed, and two years later Henry Tudor landed at Milford Haven and marched to Bosworth Field where, on 22 August 1485, his army met Richard's.

Richard III was killed, aged just thirty-two. Some say he died because of treachery; others through his own impetuousness when, on White Surrey, his warhorse, he charged to within striking distance of twenty-eight-year-old Henry before he was struck down and slain.

KING HENRY VII
1485–1509

Henry Tudor, Earl of Richmond was crowned two months after the Battle of Bosworth, and it was a further three months before he married Edward IV's daughter and heiress, Elysabeth of York. Nor was she crowned until after their first son and heir, Arthur, was born. The years 1489 to 1503 saw the birth of four daughters and two more sons.

For the first few years, small pockets of dissension and dissatisfaction rippled throughout the country. Throughout his reign, Henry would be harassed by Yorkist risings and pretenders to the throne. Two in particular were dangerous: Lambert Simnel in 1486, when Henry threatened that if any of his subjects were disposed to hear false tales and rumours and repeat them as true to others they would be pilloried; and Perkin Warbeck, who caused trouble for five years between 1492 and 1497.

Henry had been kind to Richard III's presumptive heir, the twenty-three-year-old John de la Pole, Earl of Lincoln, son of Richard's sister Elizabeth and the Duke of Suffolk; however, the ten-year-old Edward, Earl of Warwick was imprisoned in the Tower. He was the son of Richard III's brother George, Duke of Clarence, executed for treason on Edward IV's orders by drowning, supposedly at his request, in a butt of malmsey wine. Young Edward's was an attainted line, but an obvious dynastic threat. His sister, Margaret, joined Elysabeth's household.

The early years saw Henry undertaking long progresses, imprinting his presence and authority throughout his realm and keeping an eye on trouble through an effective spy network.

Henry favoured adventure. In 1489, Bartholomew Columbus, brother to Christopher, presented the king with a map of the world. Henry agreed to provide finance to help Christopher discover the West Indies. Unfortunately, Bartholomew was captured by pirates and suffered so many mishaps that by the time he returned home, his brother had received finance from Ferdinand and Isabella, the joint sovereigns of Spain, and had not only already sailed but had returned after finding Cuba and Jamaica. The following year, the Spanish monarchs financed his second voyage.

In March 1497, Henry commissioned John Cabot to sail from Bristol in search of 'new islands'. Five months later he returned with a map of the world and a solid sphere crafted to show the king where he had travelled. Henry commissioned Cabot again in May 1498 for a second expedition. In 1501 and 1502 he issued licences to sailors wanting to make their own 'voyage of discovery'.

In 1488 the king began overtures for a marriage between his son Arthur and Katherine, daughter of Ferdinand and Isabella. Ten years later, the Spanish ambassador wrote that Henry's crown 'is undisputed, his government strong, the queen is beloved' and that 'the king looked old for his years but young for the sorrowful life he has led'.

Henry had brought stability to the realm, the monarchy and the government; the latter by selecting ministers with talent, initiative and efficiency. He found humble birth no bar so long as he received intelligent and loyal service. Grumbling and ambitious lords were kept in check with fines and obligations – and, in extreme cases, with attainder and forfeiture.

Some historians have accused Henry of avarice and being niggardly with money, citing how every page of his account books was personally checked and signed. The queen did the same. But his privy accounts show no signs of miserliness. He gave generous alms and compensation, and gifted his wife jewels and money to pay her debts. He had a keen appreciation of music, playing lute and clavichord himself, purchased instruments for his children, and favoured those who played harp, fiddle and clavichord. Rewards of money were given to musicians and poets; for example, in 1495 a 'woman that sings with a fiddle' received 2s; May 1496 saw payment to an Italian poet of £20, and once, in August 1492, he paid children singing in a garden in Canterbury.

Financial records tell us that his other enjoyments included playing cards, tables (backgammon), dice and chess, and more physical pursuits such as tennis (he built a tennis court at his favourite castle, Kenilworth), hunting, hawking and shooting at the butts with his crossbow. There are also many entries for books being bought or perhaps copied. He patronised printers, painters and writers and derived much pleasure from watching fools, minstrels, tumblers, little dancing maidens and the revels, masques and jousts given throughout his reign.

Henry's financial acumen and fine eye for detail led, unusually, to the king paying his loans, wages and bills on time. He agreed payment terms in advance for his musters of soldiers. Nor was he eager to make war if peace served better. And his commercial trade agreements show he was supportive of his merchants.

It was a joyous occasion when Princess Katherine of Spain landed in England in October 1501 to marry Prince Arthur. It showed Henry had gained European recognition of both his monarchy and the peace and stability of his kingdom. Gaiety was foreshortened, however, by the death of fifteen-year-old Arthur a few months later at Ludlow Castle. His parents were heartbroken. Their second son, ten-year-old Henry, became heir to the throne.

Less than a year later, Queen Elysabeth died and Henry shut himself away in sorrow, never to be the same again. His health began to deteriorate.

A few months later he sent thirteen-year-old Princess Margaret to Scotland to marry King James IV, reducing his household even further.

After a while, Henry gave thought to remarrying. He first considered Arthur's widow. Isabella said no. Ferdinand offered his niece, the widowed Queen of Naples. In 1505, Henry toyed with marrying Margaret of Angouleme, sister to Francis, heir to the French king Louis XII. Late in 1506, he entertained thoughts of marrying Margaret of Savoy, sister to Philip and daughter of Emperor Maximilian, while at the same time marrying his son, Henry, to Philip's daughter, Eleanor. With Queen Isabella of Castile dying in November 1505, leaving Ferdinand merely King of Aragon, matching Henry with Katherine was not as important a match as it had once been. In 1507 he reached agreement for his eleven-year-old daughter, Mary, to marry Charles of Castile, Philip's son, now Archduke of Austria, who was being brought up by his aunt Margaret of Savoy.

Less than two years later, in April, fifty-two-year-old Henry died. In his will, dated a few weeks before his death, he wished for his wife to be moved to his chapel so they could lie together. He left £2,000 with the Abbot of Westminster for alms to be distributed to 'lame, blind, bedridden and most needy' poor folk, and to debtors in prison for less than £4 or those who remained 'in prison only for lack of payment of their fees in the city and suburbs'. He also bequeathed funds for the building of his hospital 'beside Charingcrosse' for one hundred needy poor people to be 'lodged, visited in their sicknesses, refreshed with meat and drink, and if need be with cloth, and also buried if their fortune is to die'.

3 September 1485: Henry VII's State Entry into London

Henry VII, after a leisurely journey from Leicestershire, made his state entry into the City of London, warmly greeted at Shoreditch by the Mayor of London, the aldermen in robes of scarlet and other city officials dressed in violet.

The king rode through cheering crowds to St Paul's Cathedral. As he entered St Paul's, an 'angel' came out of the roof and 'censed' him. At the altar, the king offered his three standards: St George, the fiery red dragon of Cadwaladr sharp against a background of white and green, and the dun cow painted on yellow silk.

After prayers and singing of *Te Deum* (a hymn of thanksgiving), he departed to the Bishop's Palace while all around the city and palace the populace celebrated with 'plays, pastimes and pleasure'.

Dating the start of his reign from 21 August, the king attainted all those who had fought for Richard III, gaining much-needed funds for the coffers; since the battle, the king had spent over £336 on materials for new clothes: gold and purple cloth of gold with black satin for lining to make two short gowns, black and crimson satin to make doublets, Holland for shirts, and tawny velvet for a long gown to be lined with violet satin.

Today, John English delivered to the king six black satin doublets, a black velvet demi-gown and a black-velvet-lined black camlet cloak. He is also having made a long black velvet gown and crimson velvet harness for his horse and hobby.

At the same time, in readiness for the coronation at the king's command, Sir Robert Willoughby has scoured the city to buy up all the scarlet cloth, crimson satin, purple velvet, cloth of gold, silk fringe for banners and powdered ermine.

30 October 1485: Margaret Beaufort Cries as Her Son Is Crowned

Cutting a noble figure at Westminster Abbey's high altar dressed in robes of purple velvet, Henry bared his chest as he was anointed with holy oil. Crowned with St Edward's crown and mantled with his cape, the king changed into robes of cloth of gold.

'My Lady the King's mother', Margaret Beaufort, cried as the crown descended on her son's head.

At six feet, Henry is of above average height, strong but of slender build, blue-eyed with hair of burnished gold. Though not fashionably handsome, he appears so when he smiles either with happiness or when enjoying good conversation.

After the ceremony Henry VII left the cathedral to go the great feast in Westminster Hall, now wearing his own crown and holding the cross and ball in his right hand and his sceptre in his left.

The king's mother, Countess of Richmond and Derby, was born in 1441. When she was three years old her father died and she was made a ward of William de la Pole, Duke of Suffolk. When she was nine years old, the duke wished her to marry his son, John de la Pole, but King Henry VI wished her to marry his half-brother, Edmund Tudor. Asked to choose, she told Bishop Fisher that she fervently prayed to St Nicholas and that, around four o'clock in the morning, the saint appeared to her and 'bade her take' Edmund. She married Edmund in late 1455 when he was twenty-six years old and she half his age.

In under a year, Margaret was a widow after her husband had been captured during the war and died either of his wounds or starvation on the third day of November. On 28 January 1457, nearly three months after her husband's death, she gave birth to her only child, Henry, at Pembroke Castle.

The king's mother has since remarried twice. Her current husband, Sir Thomas Stanley, was created Earl of Derby by her son in the same ceremony in which he granted his uncle Jasper the office of Duke of Bedford.

18 January 1486: Elysabeth Plantagenet Finally Marries Her Prince

Today, at Westminster Abbey, Henry VII married the beautiful nineteen-year-old Elysabeth Plantagenet, daughter and eldest child of Edward IV and Elizabeth Wydville.

The bridegroom stood tall, slim and handsome in cloth of gold, making a wonderful contrast to the princess with her blue eyes, fair skin and silver-blonde tresses twined with gems, dressed, as John Gigli says in his poem of the event, in robes that glowed 'with gold and purple dye'. Her gold wedding ring cost 23s 4d.

Their marriage unites the houses of Lancaster and York, as shown by the red and white Tudor rose.

It has been a long road to marry her prince for Elysabeth. In 1469, aged three years old, she was betrothed to George Neville, nephew of the Earl of Warwick, and in 1475 she was promised to Charles, the Dauphin of France, heir and son of Louis XI. But at Christmas 1483, while still in Brittany, Henry went to Rennes Cathedral, accompanied by Elysabeth's half-brother Thomas Grey, Marquis of Dorset, and gave oath he would marry Elysabeth immediately after he ascended the throne.

Like her husband, our queen has had many ups and downs during the recent Wars of the Cousins, culminating in the unknown fate of her two brothers, Edward V and Richard, Duke of York, believed to have been murdered by their uncle and known as the Princes in the Tower. Elysabeth and her siblings were declared illegitimate by an Act of Parliament, the *Titulus Regius*, in 1484. The king has since repealed the Act, thereby legitimising all the children of Edward IV, acknowledging Edward V as one of his predecessors – but King Henry wisely added a clause providing that nothing could prejudice his 'establishing the crown to the King and the heirs of his body'.

After producing the necessary papal dispensation, Cardinal Bourchier, Archbishop of Canterbury, officiated at the wedding 'in due conformity with ancient custom'. The wedding was followed by a banquet in Westminster Hall and later by a 'great jousting'.

20–26 September 1486: Birth and Christening of Henry's Heir

As Henry VII shrewdly planned, his first son, 'a fair prince and large of bones', was born at Winchester, named Arthur after their reputed ancestor king of Camelot. His grandmother, Margaret Beaufort, recorded in her Book of Hours that he was born at one o'clock in the morning this St Eustace's Day. Church bells pealed and bonfires were lit in towns all over the country, the news travelling despite the particularly stormy weather and muddy trackways, in some places knee-deep.

Margaret devised a comfortable birthing chamber for her daughter-in-law. Tapestries were hung on walls and windows, apart from one window that was curtained to admit light and air when required. A featherbed and bolster was placed on top of a wool-stuffed mattress on the bed, and for her further ease there were pillows of down and four plump crimson-damask cushions. The floor was carpeted to aid the atmosphere of peacefulness. For extra warmth, Margaret had thoughtfully provided Elysabeth with an ermine-furred crimson mantle.

Keen for the Earl of Oxford to be one of Arthur's godfathers, the king delayed the christening for six days to give the earl time to travel from his house in Lavenham in Suffolk.

The day came. In the cathedral, a red-carpeted square stage had been built, bordered by rails to contain the press of people and with seven steps leading up to it. On its top, brought from

Canterbury, was a silver font lined with fine linen cloth, a canopy of estate over it. All around tapestries were hung, for warmth as much as bright decoration.

Tidings came: the Earl of Oxford was 'within a mile'.

The procession began from the stair foot of Elysabeth's great chamber: henchmen, squires, gentlemen, heralds and pursuivants walked in pairs with unlit torches. Following them were lords carrying basins, an unlit taper and a gold salt cellar. Lady Anne, sister to the queen, had a rich chrisom pinned on her right breast. Another sister, Lady Cecily, proudly carried the prince in his furred crimson mantle. Elizabeth Wydville, appointed his godmother, was already in the church waiting to hold the infant prince.

Everyone waited in the chilly cathedral for the Earl of Oxford to appear. Two hours and more they waited until the king signalled for the ceremony to proceed. The prince was put into the font. All the torches were lit. The prince was christened by the Bishop of Worcester and... in came the Earl of Oxford, too late.

Arthur's christening gifts comprised a rich cup of gold set with stones from his grandmother Elizabeth, a pair of gilt basins from the Earl of Oxford and a gold salt cellar from the Earl of Derby, while Lord Maltravers (Elysabeth's brother-in-law) gave him a coffer of gold.

Back in the nursery, the king's trumpets announced Arthur's return and the couple gave him their blessing.

16 June 1487: Victory at Stoke Field

This day King Henry gave 'humble thanks for his triumphant victory and overthrow of his enemies' at the Battle of Stoke Field earlier in the morning, with celebrations and prayers of thanksgiving to continue for three days, while the king intends to take his leisure with his wife and mother at his favourite castle of Kenilworth.

The conflict started because of two pieces of fake news: first, that the sons of Edward IV were alive and had escaped from the Tower; and secondly, that Edward, Earl of Warwick was to be immediately executed.

An Oxford tutor and priest, Sir Richard Symond, had instructed a ten-year-old boy named Lambert Simnel in 'princely behaviour', convincing him he was really Prince Edward, and took the boy to Ireland, where he persuaded the Irish peers to nobly entertain 'their royal son of York'. Messages were sent to England to those who had been 'true and faithful friends to King Richard'. Messengers travelled to Flanders to treat with Richard's sister Margaret, Duchess of Burgundy.

King Henry, foreseeing the result of the 'deceit and fraud of such a dunghill knave' as Symond, issued a general pardon to try to forestall 'bloody and mortal war' in its tracks. 'But to brainless men this medicine nothing availed', and John de la Pole, Earl of Lincoln, sailed to Flanders to his aunt Margaret's court where she helped him raise an army, paying for 2,000 German mercenaries captained by the doughty fighter Martin Schwartz. Lord Lovell and Sir Thomas Broughton, partisans of Richard III, were already at her court and they all sailed to Ireland on 5 May.

On May Day, the king moved to the centre of his realm, making Kenilworth Castle his headquarters. On 13 May he sent Thomas Butler, Earl of Ormond, to bring his 'dearest wife and mother' to the castle. They arrived in time to celebrate Whitsunday Mass together on 24 May, and there awaited news of the coming invasion.

That same day, young Lambert was crowned as Edward VI of England at the Cathedral of the Holy Trinity in Dublin.

Henry didn't have to wait long. Lincoln, Lovell, Broughton, Schwartz and his men, with Thomas FitzGerald, captain of the Irish forces, landed near Furness in Lancashire on 4 June. The king responded by marching to Nottingham, where he 'pitched his field' and awaited his three captains – his uncle Jasper, Edward Courtenay, Earl of Devon, and John de Vere, Earl of Oxford – coming with men already alerted to be ready at an 'hour's warning'.

His soldiers mustered, the king issued strict orders that they would spoil no churches, ravish no women, nor quarrel with any man except in the coming battle. Food or drink was to be paid for and not stolen. He told them at the first trumpet blast, horses should be saddled; at the second, bridled; and at the third they should be ready to ride.

In the meantime, Lincoln, marching through Yorkshire, was disheartened to find no man ventured to join his army. Nevertheless, he was 'determined to try the fortune of battle', knowing that King Henry 'with a small power of men vanquished King Richard and all his mighty army' not two years before. Lincoln marched to Newark, believing the king did not know his whereabouts, but the king 'was in his bosom and knew every hour what the Earl did'.

The earl made camp at East Stoke. The king lodged near the village of Radcliffe close by.

Rising early, the king heard two Masses. Before nine o'clock he and his army were a mile outside of East Stoke and battle commenced shortly after.

The fighting was fierce. The Irish were easily slain, being almost naked and without armour. The armies fought so ferociously that 'no man could well judge to whom the victory was like to incline'. It was the last and bloodiest battle of the Wars of the Roses. Lincoln and his captains were killed, and his soldiers fled, but near 4,000 dead lay on the battlefield.

And Lambert 'the youngling', who was the start of it all? Being but a child, he will serve in the king's kitchen and scullery; Symond, for his part, will be committed to perpetual imprisonment.

23–25 November 1487: Queen Elysabeth at Last Crowned

Sailing from Greenwich to Tower Wharf on Friday 23 November to lodge that night at the Tower in preparation for her entry to London, Elysabeth's craft was surrounded by every elegant barge on the Thames, their ribbons and streamers of silk flying and shining in the wind, with music and pageants to gladden her eyes and ears. The Bachelors' Barge caught everyone's eyes with a great red dragon spouting 'flames of fire'.

The next day, when she left the Tower, her kirtle of white damask cloth of gold gleamed beneath a white-ermined mantle, fastened with knots of gold and silk. Her hair hung loose, a silver-blonde stream down her back, kept in place by a simple gold diadem.

The streets had been swept, both sides hung with tapestries and banners, for her easy carriage to Westminster in a litter, its timberwork covered in gold damask, packed with down pillows for her comfort. As she passed, children sang sweet songs and the people cheered from house windows and doorways, and lined the streets shouting greetings to her.

On Sunday, St Katharine's Day, Elysabeth entered Westminster Abbey, dressed in a kirtle and mantle of purple velvet, furred with ermine. On her head was a circlet of gold covered with pearls and jewels. Lords carried her crown, sceptre and rod. She walked slowly towards the high altar where the Archbishop of Canterbury awaited her, before whom she knelt. He parted her gown and anointed her breast twice with holy oil. After blessing the regalia, he slid her coronation ring onto the fourth finger of her right hand, placed the crown upon her head, the sceptre in her right hand, and the rod in her left.

A banquet in Westminster Hall followed the ceremony. First-course dishes included perch in jelly, shields of brawn, venison with frumenty, swan, capons, lamprey in galantine, crane, pike in sauce, mutton, custard royal and a 'subtlety' which had celebratory ballads written all over it. For the second course there were quails, larks, peacock, pheasant, egrets, partridge, sturgeon with fennel, plovers, honey-baked quince, marchpane and castles of jelly. Lastly, fruit and wafers were served.

Two ladies-in-waiting sat under the table at the queen's feet throughout the proceedings, while two lady countesses knelt either side of her holding napkins for her use.

With the dinner over, William Whorne, Mayor of London, served the queen spices and Hippocras wine, after which she departed to her chambers with, as all men said, 'God's blessing and the rejoicing of many a true Englishman's heart'.

7 July 1488: Will Prince Arthur Marry Katherine of Spain?

Negotiations have begun with the ambassadors of King Ferdinand and Queen Isabella for the marriage of their thirty-month-old daughter, Katherine, to Prince Arthur. The ambassadors were invited to see the prince naked, and afterwards to look at him asleep. They said he was 'well-formed and admirable'.

27 July 1488: Slaying of Lord Scales

Sir Edward Woodville, Lord Scales, uncle to the queen, was killed at the Breton town of St Aubin fighting for the Bretons alongside Louis, Duke of Orleans, and the Prince of Orange against the French. In the melee, Lord Scales was slain, fighting on foot like a common soldier to prove mounted nobles did not flee at the first glimpse of fighting. Because of the fearsome reputation of English archers, the Breton captains had dressed 1,700 of their soldiers in English colours. The French fought more ferociously than ever, nearly annihilating all the soldiers dressed in red coats with white crosses.

The trouble began when Henry offered himself as peacemaker between Charles, King of France, and Francis, Duke of Brittany, both of whom had earned his gratitude for their help when he was in exile. To help Henry out of his dilemma, and knowing he really favoured the duke, Lord Scales, a valiant captain and a bold champion who had been in exile with Henry and fought for him at Bosworth, secretly stole over to Brittany from the Isle of Wight, without licence or passport, with a troop of 400 men. After the battle and Scales' exposure, the French ambassadors accused Henry of a ruse.

Henry now intends to send an army to Brittany, albeit for defensive purposes only, not to invade or make war in the French king's realm. The French king said he regarded this 'as little as the biting of a flea'.

28 April 1489: Earl of Northumberland Cruelly Murdered

Henry Percy, 4th Earl of Northumberland, was 'furiously and shamefully murdered' by rebels from Durham and Yorkshire. The earl had met them at Thirsk in his attempts to persuade them to pay their taxes towards the war against the French. Angrily, they said they had already paid for the defences against the Scots. It is known that they have borne a grudge against the earl since he had refused to fight at Bosworth for Richard III, whom they loved.

The unarmed earl had entreated the rebels with 'fair words to come to reason', but the rebels were egged on by a vociferous spokesman, one John Chamber. The men have since armed themselves and declared they will battle the king in defence of their 'common liberty and freedom' if necessary.

21 May–3 June 1489: Thomas, Earl of Surrey marches north

Thomas, Earl of Surrey, ten weeks released from the Tower and appreciated by the king for his 'wit', has been given the opportunity to show his fidelity by being sent northward; what is more, he succeeded. By the time the king marched into Yorkshire, the Earl of Surrey had efficiently restored order and apprehended John Chamber and other rebels – although many, after the first hot rashness, had melted away, their hearts 'in their heels'.

The king was inclined to mercy and gave pardon to his subjects, executing only the 'inventors of the mischief', who were hanged at York.

The Earl of Surrey, son of John Howard, 1st Duke of Norfolk, who was killed at Bosworth fighting for Richard III, has been appointed Lieutenant General from Trent Northward and Warden of the East and Middle Marches of England against Scotland. Although his attainder is reversed, the king has not allowed him to inherit his father's dukedom.

29–30 November 1489: Westminster Ceremonies

Today, a princess was born at Westminster at nine o'clock in the evening.

Queen Elysabeth had retired to her inner chamber on All Hallows' Eve with her mother, the king's mother, the Duchess of Norfolk and other ladies; with men not permitted to enter, many acted as household officers. Walls and windows were hung with plain blue arras decorated with golden *fleur-de-lys*, tapestries unused in case their pictures induced nightmares. The birthing pallet had a canopy of estate decorated with red roses. To guarantee the queen a safe and easy delivery, relics had been set up on an altar.

While the queen was in labour, three-year-old Prince Arthur's 'bath was set up in the king's closet prior to his being made a Knight of the Bath'. The prince had enjoyed an exciting day. After an early breakfast he had boarded the king's state barge at Sheen to sail to Westminster. Between Mortlake and Chelsea, the barges of high-born nobles glided into formation behind him, with music and singing, joined by the barges of the

Mayor of London and the craft guilds at Chelsea, with pennons and banners fluttering in the wind. As the procession came to Lambeth, ambassadors and merchants in longboats on the river shot guns and pretended to fight, throwing apples at each other. Once docked at Westminster, the prince was led to his father in the Great Chamber.

Next day, early in the morning, while the prince was being prepared for his ceremony, the newborn princess was carried from the queen's chamber into the White Hall by the Lady Marquis of Berkeley. She was christened by the Bishop of Ely in the silver font brought from Canterbury and given the name Margaret, after the king's mother, who was godmother along with the Duchess of Norfolk. Her godfather was the Archbishop of Canterbury.

As the princess was returned to her mother, taper and torches now lit, Prince Arthur was mounting his horse. The Earl of Essex bore the prince's sword and spurs, followed by the nineteen men being dubbed Knights of the Bath in his honour. Dismounting, they entered the White Hall. The Marquis of Berkeley and the Earl of Arundel led the little prince into his proud father's presence in the Parliament Chamber. His spurs were attached to his heels; he was girded with his sword, and the king dubbed him knight, then when he was dressed in his robes of estate the king formally invested him Prince of Wales.

The king departed while his son seated himself beneath the cloth of estate and gave permission for the new knights to dine with him.

21 December 1489–6 January 1490: A Royal Christmas

On St Thomas' Day, the king and queen, with the king's mother and the rest of the court, sailed from Westminster to Greenwich. Christmas was kept quietly because of the epidemic of measles which had killed so many of the queen's ladies. A few plays were performed, but no pageants. An Abbot of Misrule was elected to provide amusement. All Christmastide the king wore no robes of estate, relaxing in rich sable-furred cloth of gold gowns wrought by the queen's ladies.

Awaiting the king at Westminster when he returns are officers of arms and ambassadors from France, Brittany and Scotland and a legate from the Pope.

28 June 1491: Spare to the Heir

Today, at Greenwich Palace, Queen Elysabeth gave birth to her second son, in the presence of her mother and the king's mother. No time of birth was announced. He was christened Henry at the Church of the Observant Friars at Greenwich by Richard Fox, Bishop of Durham. His main residence will be with his sister at Eltham Palace.

8–10 June 1492: Funeral of Elizabeth Wydville

The queen's mother, Elizabeth Wydville, died at Bermondsey Abbey on 8 June. Born on 3 February 1437, she was fifty-five years old and had lived in retirement at the abbey for just over five years, although was present at various state occasions.

The king had thought at one time to marry her to James III of Scotland.

At her request, she was buried next to her second husband, Edward IV, in St George's Chapel at Windsor in a simple ceremony 'without pomp'. Conveyed, unremarked upon, on the evening of 10 June by river in a wooden coffin, she was buried that night, with only four candlesticks around her, by a single priest and clerk. Her son Thomas Grey, Marquis of Dorset, eldest son from her first marriage to Sir John Grey, paid for the funeral.

In her will, dated 10 April, she declared that she had no worldly goods to give to her 'dearest daughter', nor to reward any of her children according to her 'heart and mind'; instead, she gave them and 'her grace my blessing'.

October–November 1492: *Victory without a Stroke*

In October 1492, Holy Roman Emperor Maximilian, in a great rage with French king Charles VIII, asked King Henry to join him in invading France with 'fire, sword and blood'. He wished to inflict upon the French king 'a thousand deaths'.

The reason for the emperor's outrage was that Duke Francis of Brittany had, with the help of Englishmen, just repelled the French from his duchy when he died, leaving his daughter, Anne, as sole heiress. She was crowned duchess at Rennes Cathedral, and Charles, thinking it easier to annex Brittany to his kingdom than to conquer it, decided to marry the duchess. The problem was that she was already married by proxy to Maximilian, and Charles was already betrothed to Maximilian's daughter Margaret. Anne had agreed when Charles told her that her marriage was not valid; that lying naked in a bed while a deputy put a naked leg under the sheets to the knee was not a true consummation of marriage. At the same time, Charles despatched Margaret, who had been brought up at the French court, back to her father.

King Henry summoned Parliament and asked them for their benevolence, commending them for their true and loving hearts and assuring them that by their open gifts he would measure their loving minds towards him; that he who gave the most would be judged to be most loving. The people still gave only grudgingly.

Men were mustered and armed, and the king had the navy rigged, manned and provisioned, ready to set forth at any hour. He then sent his uncle Jasper and John de Vere, Earl of Oxford, to tell Maximilian all was ready. By return, they informed him that Maximilian could not be more 'unprovided or more destitute of men and armour', that he 'lay lurking in a corner, sore sick of the flux of the purse', and that the king should neither trust his aid nor puissance.

A declaration of war having been made, Henry prudently studied his options.

He gathered more soldiers and went to war.

Henry sailed to Calais from Sandwich on 6 October 1492 and camped long enough to ensure all his men were harnessed and armoured, lacking neither weapon nor engine of war. Then he removed to the town of Boulogne, pitched his tents and ordered a daily bombardment of the walls.

While Maximilian lay still 'like a dormouse', Henry, deciding against the needless shedding of blood, sent commissioners to meet with the chief French captain, Lord Cordes. They discussed the terms the English king would accept for peace, one of which was that Charles was to desist from aiding Henry's rebels or enemies. Charles considered. Immediately, he ordered a lad who had come to his court in May, one Perkin Warbeck, to leave France. He then agreed peace terms.

Rumours of peace were pleasant to the French but bitter and sour to the English, who were hoping for rich gains. The soldiers said the king had robbed them of a great victory. He pacified them by saying that he preferred to safeguard their lives in front of his own 'wealth, health and advantage', and led them back to Calais.

Returning to England, 'he began to smell certain secret smoke which was like to turn to a great flame': a new pretender in Flanders calling himself Richard Plantagenet, Duke of York, second son to Edward IV, as though he had been 'resuscitated from death to life' with a story of escape credible enough for many to believe it. Henry's spies told him he was in truth a boy from Tournai. His name was Perkin Warbeck.

29 October–13 November 1494: Prince Henry created Duke of York

Three-year-old Prince Henry, astride a courser, rode through cheering crowds thronging the London streets as he arrived around three o'clock in the afternoon. The following day, during supper, the prince served towels to his father when he washed and dried his hands before and after eating. Afterwards, in the king's closet, the prince got into the bath prepared for him. His father dipped his fingers into the water, made a cross on his son's shoulder and kissed it. In the afternoon of the next day, the prince was dubbed knight by his father, who stood him upon a table while he dubbed the twenty-two men made Knights of the Bath with him.

On Saturday, All Hallows' Day, the king, wearing his crown and robes of estate, stood under his canopy in the Parliament Chamber, attended by the nobles and prelates. A great press of people gathered, including the aldermen and mayor. Into the chamber came Edmund, Duke of Suffolk bearing the sword, pommel upward, while the Earl of Northumberland entered bearing the gold rod. Thomas, Earl of Derby carried the cape of estate furred with ermine and a rich coronal, followed by the Earl of Shrewsbury carrying the young prince. Set on his feet, the prince was led by the Marquis of Dorset and the Earl of Arundel to the king, who created him Duke of York, bestowing with the dukedom a gift of £1,000 per annum.

In honour of his son, and for the pleasure of his 'fairest young princess' Margaret, the king arranged a joust royal in the tilt yard. A canopied spectator stand, covered with blue arras adorned with gold *fleur-de-lys*, had been built for the nobles, with cushioned seats for Henry and Elysabeth. There was a carnival air as citizens flocked in, smiling and staring around at all the spectacle, enjoying the display of dressage given by Lord Bergavenny on a small black horse. The four challengers – the earls of Suffolk and Essex, Sir Robert Curzon and John Peche – entered in the king's colours of green and white, and bearing a badge of the queen's blue and purple. With jangling chains of gold, bells on their horses tinkling, trappings glistening with spangles, they ran six courses each against the 'answerers'.

The Earl of Essex ran against Roland de Veilleville, rumoured to be the king's illegitimate son born in Brittany in 1474. That night at the dancing, five-year-old Princess Margaret awarded John

Peche a gold ring set with a ruby, the prize for his 'valiant jousting'. On the second day of jousting, the challengers entered in blue and tawny cloaks, Prince Henry's colours. They came in under crested pavilions: the Duke of Suffolk's red with a golden lion's head; Sir John's light tawny also with a lion's head; the Earl of Essex's dark tawny with a silver flying falcon; Sir Robert's black with a red dragon's head. All jousted furiously.

On the third and last day, two knights rode in, their horses trapped in paper, one in torn fragments and the other with a drawing of two men playing dice. The heralds proclaimed: 'One lance and then to swords.'

The two ran at each other. And missed.

To 'cause the king to laugh' as they took up their swords, one knight gave 'great strokes' and lost his sword. His opponent returned it to him and was immediately struck on the helm, while the other mimed the great sting he had received. Their slapstick turn over, they left the field as challengers-turned-answerers were led on reins of blue and white silk, the king's mother's colours, into the field by four golden-belted, white-gowned ladies on white palfreys. Normal jousting resumed.

4 February 1495: Lord Thomas Howard Marries Lady Anne, the Queen's Sister

Today, Anne, the queen's nineteen-year-old sister and First Lady of the Bedchamber, married Thomas, Lord Howard, the twenty-two-year-old son and heir of the Earl of Surrey, at Westminster Abbey. His grace gave an offering of *6s 8d*.

16 February 1495: Sir William Stanley Executed for Treason

At eleven o'clock this morning, the traitor Sir William Stanley was drawn to Tower Hill. In mercy, the king allowed him to be beheaded upon the scaffold. He was buried at St Dunstan's Church.

Despite the king's grief and disbelief that his friend was conspiring against him, he had appointed the Privy Council to examine Stanley. At that examination, a bewildered Sir William had confessed that all he had said was that if Perkin Warbeck was undoubtedly Richard, son of Edward IV, then he would not take up arms against him. He swore he did not believe his words to be treasonous.

His peers disagreed. Sir William was arraigned on 6 February and found guilty of treason.

14 March 1495: Assassination Plot Revealed

Bernard de Vignolles, sick for more than six months, decided to confess his sins. Giving a deposition in Rouen, he said that on a recent journey to England he had been given a little box of ointment to deliver to the Prior of St John. With it were instructions that the ointment should be spread along some passage or door through which the king often passed. He said that before he set off, he opened the box. It smelt so vile he threw it and its contents down the toilet.

Afraid that his companions might notice the absence of the concoction, he purchased a similar box and some quicksilver. Returning to his room he took dry earth, soot from the chimney and water and mixed them with the quicksilver to make an ointment of a similar colour. He took the box to the prior but was told to go away and to get rid of the box. He did this, and a few weeks later, though by then he was ill, the prior pressed him to leave England, giving him money and horse to do so.

31 May 1495: Death of Cecily, Duchess of York

The queen's grandmother, Lady Cecily Neville, Duchess of York, died peacefully at her castle of Berkhamsted, just attaining eighty years of age. She will be buried alongside her husband, Richard, and their son, Edmund, at Fotheringhay Castle.

Her will, begun on 1 April and finished on the day of her death, had the following bequests: to the queen a cross with crosslet of diamonds, a psalter with silver clasps and a small box or pyx with the flesh of St Christopher; to the queen's mother a portable breviary with gold clasps; to Prince Arthur a bed with arras and tester of the wheel of fortune; and to Prince Henry three tapestries showing the lives of St John the Baptist, Mary Magdalene and St George. To her daughter, Elizabeth, Duchess of Suffolk, she left 'the chariot with its covering, cushions, horses and harness and all my palfreys'.

3 July 1495: A Landing in Kent

While Henry VII was on his summer progress in the north, making his way to Worcester, Perkin Warbeck, aided with ships and men by Maximilian, Archduke Philip and Margaret of Burgundy, landed some 500 to 600 of his troops at Deal in Kent, though he himself did not land. The king's subjects fought them, capturing five captains and 160 other persons. Two men were slain. Many others drowned trying to get back to the ships. Those who survived were fortunate the ships had stayed near, otherwise 'not a single man of them would have escaped alive'. They drew up their sails and were seen to sail westwards, most likely back to Flanders.

The Sheriff of Kent, John Peche, brought the prisoners roped together in lines to London Bridge, handing them over to the sheriffs of London who conveyed them either into the Tower of London or to Newgate, depending on nationality, to await execution.

14–17 September 1495: Death of Princess Elizabeth

Princess Elizabeth died suddenly at Eltham Palace. There was no warning of any illness and her parents were at Sheen when it happened. She was aged three years and two months.

The princess's body was conveyed to Westminster Abbey in a black chariot with six horses trapped in black, her coffin covered with a black cloth fringed with red and white roses. An inscription at the foot of her effigy – 'Death snatched her away' – reflects the feelings of her grief-stricken parents. Her chest tomb, on the left-hand side of St Edward's Altar, is of grey marble, topped with a slab of black marble costing just over £371.

The queen is in the fourth month of her pregnancy and it is hoped grief will not lead her to lose the child.

18 March 1496: Birth of Princess Mary

Today, Princess Mary was born at the Palace of Sheen. When she is old enough, she will join Prince Henry and Princess Margaret at Eltham.

17–18 September 1496: The Scottish Invasion

The King of Scots and his army, his banner openly displayed, together with Perkin Warbeck and his multinational company of 1,400 men, entered 4 miles into England on 17 September, believing they could not fail to succeed as Perkin had announced 'after his own fantasy' that he would be aided by friends in England.

The soldiers, making 'great boast and brag' of the spoil and riches they would be taking home, burnt and destroyed houses. Men, women and children, whether sick or well, were cruelly slain. Englishmen refused to fight in Warbeck's cause, even when threatened, and to the king's anger, Perkin bewailed the deaths, fires and havoc.

When the news reached James IV that Lord Neville was on his way with 4,000 men, with more joining him, he decided to retreat. The dash over the Tweed started at midnight. Though he and his army were two days in their coming, they were only eight hours in the going.

Such was his belief in Warbeck, the 'Prince of England' – many had commented on his royal bearing and close resemblance to Edward IV – that James had received him at Stirling Castle with great honour the previous November. Two months later, he had allowed his cousin, Lady Catherine Gordon, daughter of Alexander, Earl of Huntley, to marry the young man in Edinburgh and provided him with 'a spousing gown of white damask'. At the celebratory tournament the king arranged, Perkin wore armour covered with purple brocade.

17 June 1497: The Battle of Blackheath

Tax collectors sent out to gather funds for the Scottish war had no trouble until they reached Cornwall, where the people said they could not 'bear its weight'. Hot words were spoken, the king's name was insulted and many of the commons armed themselves and headed for London, believing that people would soon flock to their cause.

At the news of the uprising, many noblemen and brave knights came to London from all sides, bringing companies of soldiers. The Cornishmen went to Salisbury, then Winchester, and finally to Kent. Finding nobody joined them, but believing the king must be panic-stricken at their coming, they continued until they reached a hill near London called Blackheath. Here they camped and readied themselves to either fight the king or attack the city.

Citizens of London panicked at first until they heard that the king was lying that night at Lambeth. At daybreak, the king directed the earls of Essex and Suffolk to surround the hill to the left and right, so blocking all roads. At six o'clock in the morning he attacked.

By two o'clock the king was riding over London Bridge to St Magnus Church where the mayor, with his brethren in scarlet, received him. He gave them 'cheerful thanks' for their good diligence in the keeping of order in the City and the victuals they had sent. He then rode to St Paul's to give his own thanks to God. From there he went to join his wife and Prince Henry at the Tower, where he had sent them for safety.

July 1497: Peace with Scotland

Richard Fox, Bishop of Durham, was instructed by the king to treat with James IV for peace, and to negotiate compensation for damages and the delivery of Perkin Warbeck.

To ensure his safety, James IV urged Warbeck to depart the realm and make his abode more 'surely and more quietly until such time as fortune would provide a more prosperous wind' for he could no longer provide refuge, especially as all his striving was in vain and 'all his words were but wind'.

King James concluded a league and concord with King Henry, agreeing to marry Princess Margaret.

7 September–28 November 1497: Perkin Warbeck Returns

With Cornish rebels sending messages to Warbeck that they wanted to fight against the king, he resolved to make one more attempt to gain the throne and landed with men from four small ships at Whitesand Bay on 7 September.

Leaving his wife, Catherine, at St Michael's Mount, Warbeck marched to Bodmin, proclaimed himself Richard IV, and stirred the common people to take up his cause. They swore they would 'follow him to death'. His small band of six-score men swelled to 3,000.

He marched on Exeter, arriving an hour after midday on 17 September. Taking two hours to array themselves in battle, the men assaulted the east and north gates, which withstood their attempts. Next day, ladders were used in attempts to climb over the walls. The citizens put up a spirited defence and slew about 200 of the pretender's soldiers. On top of that he had already lost 300 to 400 men.

When Warbeck had landed, the king was already at his manor of Woodstock, busy mustering an army. He sent a group of light horsemen towards Glastonbury for messengers and to 'certify men of his coming' while he sent ships out to sea to prevent any escape overseas. Once prepared, the king advanced on Exeter.

Meanwhile, giving up on Exeter, Warbeck marched on Taunton. He mustered his men as though ready to fight, but he could not ignore how his force had been diminished. He still commanded thousands, but many were poor and without armour, and he knew the king was close by.

Perkin lost his courage.

At midnight on 21 September, he fled secretly to sanctuary at Beaulieu where he sent to beg for the king's mercy. The commons he deserted were left 'amazed and disconsolate'. When the king came across them, they cast away what armour they had, held up their hands and asked for mercy. Except for the ringleaders, the king granted it to them.

The king had twenty-three-year-old Warbeck taken prisoner and brought to him at Taunton on 5 October. He was examined and pardoned on the condition that he served the king.

Two weeks later, the king caused Perkin's wife to be removed from St Michael's Mount and brought before her husband to hear his confession. Before he did so, he first gave her words of sympathy, 'called forth no less by her beauty and youth, than by her tears'. She was sent to join the queen's ladies.

Yet again the king showed mercy to a pretender to his throne. He was brought to court on 18 November, although not allowed to sleep with his wife, and has had certain keepers appointed to attend on him 'which should not (the breadth of a nail) go from his person'.

On 28 November, King Henry ordered the lad to ride through Cheap and Cornhill to the Tower of London and then back through Candlewick Street, through Cheapside and to Westminster.

Londoners heaped curses upon his head throughout the whole journey.

24 February 1499: A Third Prince
The king and queen's third son was christened at the Friars Church of Greenwich in the silver font brought from Canterbury, lined with 24 yards of linen. He was named Edmund.

23 November 1499: Execution of Perkin Warbeck
Perkin Warbeck, having been incarcerated since June, attempted an escape from the Tower. On 16 November he was arraigned for high treason and today, St Clement's Day, was drawn to Tyburn. Standing on a little scaffold, he read aloud his confession, affirmed it to be true 'on his death' and asked the king's forgiveness.

His head was cut off and set upon London Bridge; his body was buried at Austin Friars.

28 November 1499: Edward, Earl of Warwick Executed
Today, Edward, Earl of Warwick was brought to Tower Hill, led to the scaffold and beheaded. His body and head were laid in a coffin, taken back into the Tower and on the next tide, between two and three in the afternoon, conveyed to Bisham Abbey beside Windsor for burial near his ancestors at the king's expense.

A prisoner in the Tower for over fourteen years, Warbeck had enticed Warwick into trying to escape with him. The Earl of Oxford, as chief judge, accused the earl of treason. Warwick admitted his guilt, asked for the king's grace and mercy, and was found guilty.

19 June 1500: The Sad Death of Prince Edmund
Prince Edmund died today at Hatfield aged sixteen months. His funeral, held at Westminster Abbey, cost £242 11s 8d. Edward Stafford, Duke of Buckingham, was chief mourner.

12 *November 1501: The Entry of Princess Katherine into the City of London*

Princess Katherine left Lambeth Palace to meet with her English entourage of lords and nobles at St George's Field near Southwark. They crossed London Bridge and pageants were set up for her delight all along the route: at Gracechurch Street a castle of timber and canvas painted to look like stone, decorated with the king's arms, greyhounds, peacocks and sunbeams and in every battlement alternating red and white roses, and at the very top a red dragon holding a staff with a crown of gold; at Cornhill a pageant of the moon where the angel Raphael, surrounded by planets and stars, blessed her and her marriage in verse; at Cheapside men were dressed as bears, lions, horses, fishes, and bulls in the Pageant of the Sun; and at the Standard in Cheap lions, dragons and greyhounds were around God sitting on a throne. All the conduits ran with wine.

On railed platforms from Gracechurch to St Paul's, Londoners packed the streets to see the princess go by, others hanging out of every upper window. Her parents-in-law and Prince Arthur, with favoured nobles, watched from a merchant's house near the Standard as she rode by on her mule in the manner of Spain; Arthur's brother, Henry, riding by her side, escorted her to St Paul's and from there to the Bishop of London's Palace.

A young law student, Thomas More, declared the princess 'most beautiful' with her fresh complexion and grey eyes. She wore a charming little hat, like a cardinal's hat, with lace of gold to keep it on, her fair auburn hair hanging about her shoulders.

14 *November 1501: Marriage of Princess Katherine and Prince Arthur*

Today, St Erkenwald's Day, saw excited crowds of people gather in the streets of London waiting to see the fifteen-year-old Prince Arthur pass by on his way to St Paul's Cathedral to marry his pretty, sixteen-year-old Spanish princess.

Inside the church a long, red-carpeted 'timber bridge', railed on both sides and six feet high, extended from the west door, where the bride was to enter, to the first step of the choir. From there steps on it rose to a dais large enough for eight standing persons, enabling the ceremony to be seen by everyone present. Henry and Elysabeth watched from a latticed closet built near so that their presence did not detract from the betrothed pair. All the walls of the church were hung with tapestries depicting noble and valiant acts of all 'reason and imagination'.

Between nine and ten in the morning the prince rode to the south door of St Paul's. Dismounting, he took a private way into the Bishop's Palace where he changed into his white satin wedding garments. Then came the princess, led by Prince Henry to the choir. Dressed all in white satin, Katherine wore a gown with a tight pleated bodice and sleeves, somewhat like a man's. Under her skirt to shape the gown was a Spanish farthingale, a fashion not seen in England before. On her head, concealing her auburn hair, was a veil of white silk that covered part of her face and a large quantity of her body with an inch-and-a-half-wide gold border set with pearls and precious stones. Lady Cecily bore her white satin train.

Arthur and Katherine, hand-in-hand, he on her right side, moved towards the high altar, and before they entered through the choir door they turned to the south and to the north, with the intent that everybody present might see them, before ascending to the altar for the Mass of the Trinity.

After the Benediction, three to four hours after they had entered the cathedral, the young couple left by the west door amid minstrels singing and trumpets, shawms (medieval oboes) and sackbuts (medieval trombones) playing in joyful harmony.

Outside a pageant awaited them, running with wine throughout the wedding. It was designed as a green mountain covered with herbs, trees, rocks and precious metals; on its top were three great green trees. The first bore gold flowers and red roses, and sprouting out of one of the roses was a white greyhound; the second tree had red roses, from one of which sprang a red dragon, showing a picture of the armoured King of England inside a ship, sword in hand; the third tree bore apples and oranges and out of an orange sprang a red lion.

A royal feast went on until five o'clock in the afternoon, with 'delicate dainties and curious meats', wines from many countries, and 'spices, pleasures and subtleties'. The 'cunning preparation of the cooks' was not to be missed. Afterwards, there was dancing.

15 November 1501: Prince Arthur Says He Has Been in the Midst of Spain

Last night the young couple were put together in one bed. The princess was led first to the chamber and was already sitting in bed before Arthur entered and got into bed beside her. The couple were blessed and left alone to consummate the marriage.

This morning, unusually, Arthur called for his servitors to bring him a drink. One of his servants asked why he was so thirsty, and the prince answered merrily that he had been last night 'in the midst of Spain, which is a hot region, that journey makes me so dry, and if you had been under that hot climate, you would have been drier than I'.

18–28 November 1501: Marriage Celebrations

On Thursday 18 November, a tilt was set up from the Water Gate almost to the entrance of the King's Street Gate. Excitement blossomed, with an artificial green-leaved tree with flower blossoms set up for hanging the shields of knights wanting to compete. Viewing platforms were erected and the tilt area railed to stop the public wandering among lances, coursers and troubling those taking part.

The atmosphere was electric. On the walls, in the battlements and at the windows of buildings all that could be seen were faces, so crowded together no bodies could be seen.

The trumpets blew. The challenger, a fully armed Duke of Buckingham, entered in a pavilion of white and green silk, covered with turrets festooned with red roses. On his helm was a mighty 'bush of ostrich feathers'. His horse was trapped in blue velvet covered in gold castles. The Marquis of Dorset was chief defender, his pavilion of cloth of gold. Lord William Devonshire rode into the tilt in a red dragon led by a giant with a great tree in his hand. The Earl of Essex entered in a green mountain with trees, rocks, herbs and marvellous beasts below a young lady 'in her hair'.

After the jousting had finished the court made their way into Westminster Hall for the disguising, which came in three pageants. First, a castle was drawn with chains of gold by four great beasts, the first two a silver lion and a gold lion. At the rear were a hart and ibex. Looking out of the windows were eight ladies. In each turret a chapel boy dressed as a maiden sang sweetly. A ship on wheels, with realistic masts and sails, followed in which sailed a lady made to look like the princess of Spain. Sailors cast anchors to bring it to the side of the castle and dropped a rope ladder. Two ambassadors, Hope and Desire, went to the castle saying they were on embassy from the Knights of the Mount of Love. The ladies ignored them. The ambassadors left in high dudgeon. Then the Mount of Love was wheeled in. Eight knights left it to assault the castle until the ladies yielded and danced.

'Exhibition' dances followed. Arthur and Lady Cecily danced two dances before returning to the royal dais, while Princess Katherine descended and danced with her ladies in Spanish fashion. Lastly, Prince Henry came down to dance with his sister, Princess Margaret, and danced two rounds. To his parents' amusement, he, 'feeling encumbered by his clothes', threw off his gown and danced in his jacket.

Between rest days there were costly banquets, masques and dances that lasted until midnight, with jousts held in between.

After the last tourney, two mountains chained together were wheeled into the lower end of the hall. One was green and covered in olive, orange, laurel and juniper trees as well as herbs and flowers; The second was bare, scorched and burnt, covered with precious metals and stones: gold, silver, lead, copper, crystal, coral and amber. Halting in front of the king, steps were placed at the entrance of the green mountain and lords and knights, strangely dressed, descended playing tabors, lutes, harps and recorders. Out of the rocky mountain came ladies in Spanish dress making music on harpsichord and dulcimer to dance new and traditional round dances. The void was brought in (a kind of after-dinner course to conclude the meal), and with it the gifts and rewards for the jousters.

Taking their barges at Westminster Bridge with timber posts set with lions and dragons and other beasts on their tops, the court rowed to Mortlake, and then rode to Richmond. The king allowed the company to wander through his beautiful gardens. For their pleasure, he had sanctioned tables, dice and cards, plus the butts for archers and the bowling alleys to be set up for play. In another area, a Spaniard amused crowds with somersaults and tumbles on a cloth made taut by rigging and posts.

At supper there was a new disguising drawn by three seahorses. On one side were mermaids, on the other mermen – all children of the chapel singing sweetly. Then men of honour came forth and let loose rabbits all around the hall, then danced; not to be outdone, the ladies entered and let fly white doves that flew about the hall making all the guests laugh. This last joyful day was ended with a void.

Celebrations over, Prince Arthur and Katherine are removing to Ludlow from Westminster to get to know one another away from the distractions of the court, while the king and queen will celebrate Christmas at Westminster and then spend the New Year at Richmond.

2 April 1502: *Death of Prince Arthur*

Prince Arthur died at the castle of Ludlow on 2 April after a short, unknown illness. The king's confessor was sent to break the news to the king at Greenwich, which he did, knocking on the door early in the morning long before his grace would usually rise.

When his grace understood the news, he sent for the queen, so they could be together. Elysabeth, coming into the chamber and seeing his terrible grief, comforted him, saying he should remember God, the wealth of his own person and realm, how his mother had no more children but he, how they still had a fair prince and two princesses and that they were still young enough to have more children.

After the first rush of grief the king thanked her. She left him then to return to her own chamber where she gave full vent to her own grief, as 'remembrance of that great loss smote her so sorrowful to the heart' that her ladies feared for her. Greatly concerned, Henry came to comfort her in turn.

23–27 April 1502: *Funeral of Prince Arthur*

Prince Arthur's body, which had laid in state in his chamber, was on 23 April removed by yeomen for its journey through the town to Ludlow parish church. The Earl of Surrey was principal mourner and on every side eighty poor men, wearing black mourning, held lit torches along the way. The coffin was covered with black cloth of gold with a white cross. The corpse had been wrapped tightly in strips of waxed cloth and dressed so well with sweet spices, it did not need 'chesting in lead'.

The coffin was placed in a hearse in the choir of the church for two days of Masses, while wax tapers burned continually. For its journey to Bewdley Chapel on the 'foulest, coldest, windy and rainy day', the coffin, with a further waxed black cloth laid over it for protection, was placed into a black cloth-covered chariot, drawn by six black-trapped horses. In some places on the journey the horses had to be replaced with oxen.

Wednesday 26 April dawned fair, to everyone's relief, and the horses pulled the chariot all the way to Worcester Cathedral. Once again, the coffin was placed in a hearse, this one with eighteen lights, surrounded by two great standards and many banners of arms: Arthur's own, his father's and mother's, and those of Spain, Wales and one of Cadwaladr.

Next morning the funeral began at eight o'clock. At the offerings of his armour, crested helm and coat of arms, it was said, 'To have seen the weeping when the offering was done, he had a hard heart that wept not.' The rich palls of cloth of gold laid on the coffin were removed and the body laid in the grave at the south end of the high altar. A weeping Bishop of Lincoln recited the prayers, sprinkling the coffin with holy water and earth. The prince's officer of arms took off his coat of arms and cast it into the grave, while the tearful officers of the household broke their staffs of office over their heads and threw them into the grave.

11–23 February 1503: Death and Funeral of Queen Elysabeth

Queen Elysabeth, the 'most gracious and best beloved princess', died at the Tower on her birthday, Saturday morning, 11 February. At the news all the bells of London rang, and all the churches were draped in black.

On the night of 2 February, the queen unexpectedly went into labour and was delivered prematurely of a daughter. The queen's health had been poor throughout her pregnancy and she did not recover from the birth. The baby, christened within the parish church in the Tower, was named Katheryn. She was still thriving when the king ordered a wool mattress and down pillows for her cradle for his 'right dear daughter', but she died a few days later.

After ordering the queen's burial with the Earl of Surrey and Sir Richard Guildford and 636 Masses to be said in London, the king removed himself, no one knew where, to grieve privately and undisturbed.

At noon on 22 February, the queen's corpse, baby Katheryn laid beside her, was removed from the chapel of St Peter ad Vincula for its journey to Westminster. Her coffin, covered with white and black velvet with a cross of white damask, was placed in a chariot lined with black velvet and blue cloth of gold, drawn by seven coursers, trapped in black velvet. With her hair flowing to her shoulders, her crowned effigy, placed on top, was clothed in robes of estate, with her sceptre in her right hand and gold jewelled rings on her fingers.

Ahead of the funeral chariot went the lords, knights, aldermen and mayor. Her sister, Katherine, was chief mourner. Six chariots, covered in black cloth, followed the corpse and between them her ladies and gentlewomen riding upon palfreys. After them were one hundred citizens of London in long black gowns.

Lining one side of the streets all the way from Whitechapel to Temple Bar were burning torches, above 2,000 at the king's cost, while the citizens carried a further 5,000, with torchbearers from France, Spain, Venice and Portugal. At Fenchurch Street thirty-seven virgins, one for each year of Elysabeth's life, were dressed in white linen, white and green wreaths on their heads, each holding a burning wax taper of wax; the lady mayoress arranged the same at Cheapside.

At Westminster, the queen was placed on a hearse, hung with black cloth of gold and the words of her motto, 'humble and reverent', written in gold letters. With 1,100 lights, an all-night vigil was kept by her ladies and gentlewomen.

The funeral the next morning began at seven o'clock with Our Lady Mass. Masses done, the queen's image, crown and rich robes were hidden in a secret place in the Shrine of St Edward. The grave, a vault specially made for her, was opened, the coffin placed inside, blessed by the Bishop of London, while her weeping officers broke their staffs of office and threw them inside. The whole funeral cost £3,000.

25 June 1503: Prince Henry and Princess Katherine Betrothed

Prince Henry, three days short of his twelfth birthday, was formally betrothed to Katherine of Aragon at the Bishop of Salisbury's house. The wedding will not take place until the prince has attained fifteen years of age. Katherine had to give up her dower rights as Arthur's widow.

3–8 August 1503: Union of the Thistle and the Rose

Much of the court removed with Margaret to witness her state arrival in Scotland and marriage to thirty-year-old King James IV, whom she met for the first time on 3 August, but ever since he has attempted to put her at ease, dancing and one evening playing the clavichord and lute for her pleasure.

The state entry into Edinburgh was on 7 August. The king, on his bay horse, rode near Margaret travelling in a litter. He wore a jacket of cloth of gold bordered with purple velvet, a doublet of violet satin and a shirt covered with pearls, over scarlet hose. She was dressed in a rich gown of cloth of gold with black velvet, decorated with a necklace of pearls. Nearing Edinburgh, the king dismounted, kissed her and contrived for the two of them to ride together into the capital, she riding pillion behind him to the delight of the crowds lining the streets and the lords and ladies watching from doorways and windows.

Next day, the thirteen-year-old bride wore a crimson velvet robe and on her head a gold crown inset with jewels and pearls on top of a rich coif falling down the whole length of her body, covering her long hair. Around her neck was a gold collar decorated with jewels and pearls. The Archbishop of York took her right hand; the Earl of Surrey, in a long gown of cloth of gold and wearing his Garter collar, took her left hand as they led her to Holyrood Chapel. His wife bore her train. King James, wearing his sword, entered the church and made reverence to Margaret standing at the font. He wore a gold-embroidered white damask gown over a jacket with sleeves of crimson satin, crimson doublet and scarlet hose. His bonnet was black, enlivened with a large ruby.

The ceremony was performed by the Archbishop of Glasgow. Trumpets blew as the king, bareheaded, took the queen-to-be by her right hand to lead her to the high altar where cushions were placed for them to kneel upon while she was anointed. The king himself gave her the sceptre and, leaving the church, his arm was around her waist.

At dinner, Margaret was served before James, and the dishes were varied and many, including a gilt wild boar's head and roast swan. All of Edinburgh was alight with bonfires that night while the nobles danced and supped.

21 December 1507: Betrothal of Princess Mary to Prince Charles of Castile

The king sat under his cloth of estate to watch as Lord Burgo, on behalf of the Prince of Castile, took Princess Mary's hand and spoke the words of matrimony. Mary, now styled Princess of Castile, in her turn took his hand and, with no prompting though the speech was long, spoke her words 'perfectly and distinctly in the French tongue'. Lord Burgo, slipping the gold wedding ring on her finger, kissed her.

The emperor gifted Mary an 'orient' ruby and a fair diamond with pearls. From her betrothed she received a diamond-encrusted 'K' for *Karolus* (Charles) garnished with pearls.

21 April 1509: King Henry VII Dies

Henry VII, 'consumed by disease', departed this life on 21 April at his manor of Richmond, aged fifty-two years. He reigned for twenty-three years and seven months. He said he would be called 'a king who chose to rule rather than be ruled'.

KING HENRY VIII
1509–1547

Henry was seventeen when he ascended the throne. Exuberant and impetuous, his first act was to chivalrously marry his brother's widow, Katherine, rescuing his 'damsel in distress' from years of neglect.

The first ten years of his reign veered between a foreground of gaiety and a background of war. In among the amusements of jousting, revelry and music, Henry dreamt of emulating his warrior ancestors and invading France. All his life Henry was interested in warfare. He collected weapons including guns, he had ships built and increased the navy, he bred horses, and he bought the best armour, as can be seen in his purchase of 'Almain rivets' for his armoury at Eltham.

He was also the scholar who sat up late with Thomas More discussing geometry, divinity and astronomy, observing the motions of stars and planets from palace roofs. From his prescription book we see Henry devised his own healing plasters, herbal lotions and ointments to ease inflammation and pain, and founded the Royal College of Physicians. An interest in theology led to his writing a book against Martin Luther, for which the Pope awarded him the title of 'Defender of the Faith'.

One of Henry's dreams was realised in the summer of 1513 when he led an army into France to fight with the Holy Roman Emperor, Maximilian, in a league concluded by his ambassador in Brussels, Sir Thomas Boleyn. It amounted to a few skirmishes and feasting; there was even a joust. Meanwhile, the real war was near Scotland where the Earl of Surrey killed Henry's brother-in-law, the invading James IV, at Flodden Field.

Owing to promises broken by both Katherine's father Ferdinand and Emperor Maximilian, Henry made peace with France in the summer of 1514. He cemented the truce by marrying his younger sister, Mary, to Louis XII, who was thirty-four years her senior. Mary only agreed after her brother promised that after Louis' death she would be free to marry after her own heart. It happened sooner than anyone expected, and Henry made her pay for that promise in money and jewels after she secretly married his closest friend, Charles Brandon, Duke of Suffolk.

The new King of France, Francis I, married to Louis' daughter Claude, was twenty years old, and in looks, personality, culture and warfare was in many ways in competition with Henry. Among Claude's household was Sir Thomas Boleyn's daughter Anne, newly arrived from Brussels.

In 1519, Maximilian died, succeeded by his grandson, Katherine's nephew Charles V, son of her sister Juana. Giustinian, a Venetian diplomat, wrote that Katherine, who was six years older than her husband, was 'not handsome, but has a very beautiful complexion. She is religious and virtuous as words can express.' The same man described Henry as 'very accomplished, a good musician, composes well, a most capital horseman, a fine jouster ... extremely fond of tennis'.

Hall wrote in his chronicle that when Henry was not jousting, shooting, hunting or hawking he exercised daily, indulged in dancing and singing, played the recorder, flute and virginal, and liked to set songs and write ballads. He composed two Masses in five parts, sung often in his chapel and elsewhere.

Henry's chief minister was Thomas Wolsey, who started the reign as Henry's almoner and became a cardinal, Archbishop of York and Lord Chancellor of England. When Guistinian first knew him, he wrote that the cardinal would say, 'His majesty will do so and so.' After a while it became, 'We shall do so and so.' Later still, it became, 'I shall do so and so.'

In 1520, a meeting known as the Field of the Cloth of Gold was arranged between Henry and Francis. It was a magnificent, costly display, already undermined by secret negotiations between Henry and Emperor Charles. War soon superseded peace, and all the English were called home from France.

9–10 May 1509: *Funeral of Henry VII*

Henry VII's funeral procession of nobles, knights, henchmen and heralds, bearing his swords, spear, shield and helmet with its gold lion, left St Paul's for Westminster Abbey at one o'clock, through streets set with long torches and lined with children holding tapers. Hundreds of commoners in black joined the procession.

Sir Edward Howard, second son of the Earl of Surrey, in armour but face uncovered, bore the king's battle axe, its head resting on his right foot, followed by a knight carrying his armour. The coffin, with the king's crowned effigy dressed in his robes of estate on top, was conveyed by chariot with rich cushions of gold drawn by seven black-trapped great coursers, and then borne into the abbey by twelve guardsmen, watched all night by knights and heralds.

Next morning, before six o'clock, all were present for the three solemn Masses and offering of the King's Great Banner and his standard. The king was laid with great reverence into the vault by the side of his wife. The archbishop cast in earth and the chief officers threw in their staves. The vault was closed. The funeral expenses came to just above £8,474.

11 *June 1509: Henry Marries Katherine*

Seventeen days short of his eighteenth birthday, King Henry was married privately to twenty-four-year-old Katherine of Aragon in the oratory of the Church of Observant Friars outside Greenwich Palace. The bride wore a white satin dress, with her reddish-gold hair hanging loose down her back.

23–24 *June 1509: Double Coronation*

Henry and Katherine came through London to Westminster at four o'clock in the afternoon. The crowds lining the streets, hung with tapestries and cloth of gold, had been waiting for hours to see and cheer them.

Riding a horse trapped in gold damask, Henry wore an ermine-furred robe of crimson velvet. His jacket of raised gold was embroidered with diamonds, rubies, emeralds and great pearls. His knights and esquires of the body were dressed in crimson velvet, and the gentlemen of the chapel, his officers and servants of his household wore scarlet livery. After him rode Edward, Duke of Buckingham in a long gown of needlework with a great chain of rubies about his neck. Following Henry's retinue, Katherine, with a circlet of silk, gold and pearls on her head, sat in a canopied litter carried by two white palfreys trapped in white cloth of gold. Her gown was of white embroidered satin. Her ladies, following, were all dressed in cloth of gold. A little past the Cardinal's Hat inn in Cornhill, the queen was drenched by a sudden rain and forced to take shelter under the drapers' stalls, continuing on her way when it passed.

On Midsummer's Day the king and queen walked from the Palace of Westminster to the abbey upon cloth of ray, the common people cutting it for souvenirs as soon as they had passed. At the high altar the king and queen were anointed and crowned by the Archbishop of Canterbury.

There followed a banquet that ended with the customary spices and Hippocras, the latter made of a mix of red wine, sugar and spices such as cinnamon, ginger, spikenard, pepper, cloves and mace. Celebratory jousts and tourneys were arranged, and a castle with battlements covered in roses and pomegranates was built for a viewing place for the king and queen to watch together. Made of wood, its walls were painted with white and green diamonds, in each one a decoration: a rose, a sheaf of arrows, a pomegranate or 'H&K' in gold. A gold leafy vine with clusters of grapes coiled around the whole. Inside stood a fountain out of which red, white and claret wine ran from the mouths of gargoyles.

In the midst of rejoicing, some sorrow – during the celebrations, Margaret Beaufort, the king's grandmother, died.

1 November 1509: *The Queen with Child*
The king and his people rejoiced at the blessed news that the queen is pregnant. For her comfort the king ordered eight fine pillows to be made and delivered to Greenwich.

12 January 1510: *The King's Secret Joust*
When Henry discovered some of his gentlemen had devised a Twelfth Day joust, he conspired with his friend William Compton to attend secretly. Dressing in armour in the little park of Richmond, they entered as unknowns. The two ran well and broke so many staves that great praise was heaped upon them.

At the last, Sir Edward Neville ran and his opponent was badly hurt and nearly killed. Someone cried out, 'God save the king!' His subterfuge revealed, the king removed his visor so everyone could see it was not he who had been injured.

18 January 1510: *A Gladness for the Queen*
The king, with the earls of Essex and Wiltshire, Lords Hastings, Sir Edward Howard, Sir Thomas Boleyn and others to the number of twelve, suddenly appeared in the morning in the queen's chamber, disconcerting the queen and her ladies by the strange

entrance. All were disguised as Robin Hood's men in the hoods, short green coats and hose of Kentish Kendal, along with one dressed as Maid Marian. Each had longbow and arrows, sword and buckler, and after certain pastimes and dancing they departed.

26 February 1510: *The Nursery*

The cradle of estate ordered by the king was delivered into the nursery today. It is covered with crimson cloth of gold and a blue buckram-lined sarcenet canopy with double valances and three large curtains. For the nurse and two rockers, pillows, sheets and bearing sheets, swaddle bands and beds were also ordered.

Shrove Sunday 1510: *Strangers' Banquet*

On Shrove Sunday, the king invited all the resident ambassadors to a banquet in the Parliament Chamber at Westminster. While Queen Katherine sat under estate, King Henry restlessly walked around, talking first to one person, then to another, before disappearing for a while. He then returned with the Earl of Essex. Both were dressed in Turkish robes, girded with scimitars, and on their heads were crimson velvet hats with great rolls of gold. Following them were two fellows in long gowns of yellow satin cross-striped with white and a line of crimson, and Russian-style grey-furred hats, while Lord Admiral Edward Howard and Sir Thomas Parr, like Prussians, entered in doublets of crimson velvet. They danced after supper.

The king slipped away again. In his place came players of drum and fife, in green bonnets and hose underneath white damask, heralding gentlemen in blue damask holding torches. Their light showed the king and five gentlemen following, wearing short garments of blue velvet and crimson but with long sleeves, cut to show gold glimmering beneath. Six ladies came in also: two in gold-embroidered crimson and purple satin, two in crimson and purple covered with a gold tabard to the knee, and two in the same colours but embroidered with gold pomegranates. All the dresses were half-sleeved, revealing arms as black as their necks, hands and faces as if they were Moors. The leading lady was Princess Mary, but one lady remained a mystery; the king danced with her.

1 May 1510: A-maying

To go a-maying the king dressed all his knights, squires and gentlemen in white satin and all his guard and yeomen in white sarcenet and led them into the woods to fetch green boughs and shoot arrows with their longbows.

Every man, including the richly attired king, returned with a green bough in his bonnet. Crowds awaiting the king's return asked to see him shoot, for it was well known that Henry, above six feet in height, could shoot as strong and as great a length as any of his guard, and he was happy to oblige.

22–23 May 1510: Feats of Arms

On the lawn of Greenwich Park, a green tree was set up with a white shield for challengers to write their names for a feat of arms, two challengers meeting all comers on foot at barriers with lance and sword the following day.

The first challengers were the king and Sir Thomas Boleyn, wearing breast plates and helmet, with lances fourteen hands long with blunt iron points, which they followed by twelve strokes with two-handed swords at the waist-high barrier.

27 May 1510: Court Intrigues

Queen Katherine wrote to her father, telling him that by the will of God she had some days ago given birth to a stillborn daughter. Rumour says she also bore a stillborn daughter on 31 January, with her doctors saying there was still a child in her womb. When in labour the queen vowed to present her richest headdress to St Peter the Martyr and has sent it off with one of her ladies who intends to become a nun.

The queen 'stormed' at Henry. While pregnant, the king had been carrying on an intrigue with twenty-six-year-old Anne, a sister of the Duke of Buckingham. After an argument the duke stormed out of the place, while the lady's husband, George Hastings, sent her to a convent 60 miles distant. The king also removed the queen's favourite lady with her husband out of the palace to punish the lady's tittle-tattling.

17 August 1510: Appeasement

Former loyal officers of Henry VII, Sir Edmund Dudley and Sir Richard Empson, arrested on the king's accession, were executed on Tower Hill. They had been found guilty of treason. They were buried at Whitefriars. Many men believe they paid with their lives to mollify those aggrieved by the unpopular tax-collecting methods of the late king, which have made his son the rich man he is today.

1–5 January 1511: Birth of Prince Henry

On New Year's Day, between two and three hours after midnight, Prince Henry was born at Richmond. As the news reached London, bonfires were lit in the streets with many a toast given in wine. The christening took place on Sunday 5 January. Ambassadors from the Pope, France, Spain and Venice were present.

The godfathers were Louis XII, with the Lord of Winchester acting as his deputy, and Archbishop Warham of Canterbury; his godmother was Emperor's Maxmilian's daughter, Margaret, Duchess of Savoy, represented by the Countess of Surrey.

12–13 February 1511: Joust at Westminster

To honour Queen Katherine, the king devised a solemn joust: four knights of the Savage Forest were to run at the tilt against all comers.

On the first day, drawn in by wild men with ladies riding on a lion of gold damask and an antelope of silver, a forest pageant was brought into the tilt yard and set before the queen. With leafy oaks, maples, hazels, birches, fern and broom, with deer and birds sited among the trees. Six foresters in green velvet stood near a gold castle. Before its gate a gentleman sat making a garland of roses for the prize.

The foresters blew their horns. The pageant was parted to reveal four knights wearing blue coats decorated with gold portcullises over their armour: King Henry played Sir Loyal Heart, who broke more lances than Valiant Desire, Joyous Hope and Good Wish. A thousand onlookers watched the king joust against eight opponents, marvelling at his prowess, the sound of their cheering and clapping resounding around the tilt yard.

Courses finished, the king came out of his pavilion riding a grey courser. Becoming him 'wondrously well', he wore a figure-hugging coat of cloth of gold, sleeves cut and fastened with ribbons. In silence, the king, unmoving on his horse, gave a masterly display of dressage. At the end of the leaps and turns, he signalled the horse to put its hooves against the tilt and beat the boards, which echoed like a shot of guns.

On the second day, imprisoned within a tower entered Edmund Howard with a grey-bearded old man in prisoners' russet. The gaoler, holding a great key, took a note to the queen. On her answer the old man, divesting himself of clothes and beard, was revealed as Charles Brandon in bright armour. Next to enter were two pilgrims wearing black velvet tabards of black velvet and 'palmers hats' on top of their helmets, with horses trapped in black velvet edged with gold scallop shells. They revealed themselves to be the Marquis of Dorset and Sir Thomas Boleyn. Then in came the king, under a pavilion of cloth of gold and purple velvet, his three aides in crimson and purple, all decorated with the letters 'H&K' and on the top of every pavilion a great gold 'K'.

After that night's supper, a pageant, 'The Golden Arbour in the Orchard of Pleasure', was drawn in. Inside, among roses, lilies, marigolds and primroses, in an orchard of orange, pomegranate, apple, pear and olive trees, sat twelve lords – the king among them – and twelve ladies. They danced.

After the dancing, all those who participated in the jousting wore garments decorated with gold letters and jewels which were torn off their bodies, 'taken by any who could', so that all, even the king, had nothing on but their doublets.

22–27 February 1511: Death of Prince Henry
Prince Henry died at Richmond Palace.

He was buried at Westminster to the mourning of the whole court and his household. The knight bearers of his coffin were Sir John Peche, Sir Maurice Berkeley, Sir Edward Darrell and Sir Thomas Boleyn.

Wax used for the hearse came to 974 lbs and 4,327 lbs in torches. An offering of 40s was made.

1–4 May 1511: Fame Laden with Renown
Returning into Westminster Hall after the Mayday joust, the company viewed a ship 'under sail'. The master mariner hailed them, saying he had come from 'many a strange port'. A herald asked the name of the ship and the answer came, 'She is called Fame and is laden with good Renown'. The ship shot a peal of guns and sallied forth into the tilt yard, where it oversaw three days of jousting in which many 'a sore stripe was given and many a staff broken'.

At the final banquet, the heralds cried to the departing company, 'My lords, for your noble feat in arms, God send you the love of your ladies that you most desire.'

1–6 January 1512: Greenwich Revelry
On New Year's night, a castle entitled 'Le Fortress Dangereus', complete with artillery, weaponry, gates, towers and a dungeon,

was brought into the hall and settled before Queen Katherine. Visible inside were six ladies in russet satin gowns covered with leaves of gold, wearing gold caps and coifs. King Henry and five courtiers entered. Wearing caps of russet satin and coats, one half gold-spangled russet satin and the other rich cloth of gold, they proceeded to assault the castle until the ladies yielded and came out to dance.

On Twelfth Night the king and his men entered, disguised in the manner of Italy, in visors and caps of gold and long, broad garments, and invited the ladies to dance after the banquet. It being an uncommon thing, however, few consented as it was not thought meet.

Behind the revelry, King Henry had completed a league with Spain to defend the Holy Church and the Pope by uniting to invade France while the French king fights against the Pope in Italy.

1 June 1512: Dolorous Castle

Wearing white and crimson surcoats, four ladies rode into the tilt yard preceding a fountain, with eight gargoyles spouting water. Though made of iron, it was covered with russet satin decorated with small serpents. Sitting inside it was an unknown knight in full armour.

Behind the fountain rode in a lady dressed in black, her dress decorated with fine silver drops, pulling a horse litter with another unidentified knight sitting inside. Trumpets sounded, heralding the arrival of the coal-black Dolorous Castle, which opened to reveal knights coming to fight the unknowns, who, to cheering crowds, were revealed as King Henry and Sir Charles Brandon.

6 January 1513: The Rich Mount

Before the banquet on Twelfth Night, a mount with a lit beacon on its top among green satin branches and gold silk flowers was brought into the hall before Queen Katherine. Around the beacon sat King Henry with five men, all dressed in coats and caps of gold-spangled crimson velvet. They descended and danced before her.

The mount opened, and six ladies in crimson satin embroidered with gold and pearls, in French hoods, came into the hall to dance alone. The two groups danced together until the ladies re-entered the mount, which closed and was removed from the hall.

The king and queen sat together to eat.

30 June–23 August 1513: Invasion of France

King Henry, leaving his wife as regent, arrived at Calais with his fleet on 30 June and was saluted with such a peal of cannon it sounded like 'the world was coming to an end'.

For a few weeks, as the 10,000-strong army and 8,000 German mercenaries were mustered by his lieutenants, the king practised archery with his guard, every time hitting the mark, surpassing them in prowess, grace and stature. Leaving Calais on 21 July, when the army pitched camp that night 3 miles away, the king stayed dressed and rode around in the early hours 'comforting the watch'. At Ardres, owing to dense fog, one of the Twelve Apostles, the king's great guns, fell into a pond. Engineers sent to free the gun were killed.

On 1 August, the king pitched camp near Therouanne, the town he meant to besiege. There was such a heavy rain and violent wind that soldiers struggled up to their knees in mud as they set up tents. The king, meanwhile, was snug in his timber house with its iron chimney, the walls inside painted with rising suns.

After ten days, King Henry and Emperor Maximilian met and dined together. The following day, Lyon Herald reached the camp, sent by King James IV of Scotland to declare war on England if Henry did not desist from warmongering in France. Henry responded that his brother-in-law would do much better to count the King of England as his ally.

The French surrendered to King Henry. On 23 August he allowed them to leave at noon under safe conduct and proceeded to occupy the town.

9–16 September 1513: Battle of Flodden

The English and Scottish armies faced each other.

Between four and five in the afternoon, in utter silence, the English advanced evenly down the hill on foot towards the Scots. Reaching within a spear length of the Earl of Surrey, who had borne the brunt of the battle, James IV was slain, dying alongside his banner.

No prisoners were taken and many Scottish nobles were killed. The English stripped king, bishops, lords and nobles, leaving them naked, so that many 'well fed and fat' bodies were left on the field. The king's body was taken to Berwick and laid out in the chapel. He leaves his seventeen-month-old son as King James V.

Queen Katherine, on 16 September, sent a messenger to King Henry informing him of Surrey's victory. She expressed her wish that she could have sent him a piece of the Scottish king's coat for a banner; better still she would have liked to have sent his body, 'but our Englishmen's hearts would not suffer it'.

2 February 1514: New Creations

At Lambeth Palace, the king created the Earl of Surrey second Duke of Norfolk with an augmentation of the arms of Scotland. His son Thomas, the Lord Admiral, became Earl of Surrey in his place. On the same day, Sir Charles Brandon was promoted from Viscount Lisle to Duke of Suffolk. The king's chamberlain, Sir Charles Somerset, Lord Herbert, was created Earl of Worcester. Master Thomas Wolsey, said by Hall to be a 'good philosopher, eloquent and full of wit', was consecrated Bishop of Lincoln.

13 August 1514: Peace and Alliance

At Greenwich on 13 August, in a token of peace between France and England, King Henry and a clearly pregnant Queen Katherine, the latter in a loose robe of grey satin, watched the Duke of Longueville take the right hand of eighteen-year-old Princess Mary in his and recite the marital oath on behalf of King Louis XII. The princess reciprocated, saying her marriage lines in fluent French. The duke then gave Mary a gold ring, which she placed on the fourth finger of her right hand. Both were clothed in robes of purple satin and cloth of gold; unlike the duke, however, the princess wore hers over a kirtle of ash-coloured satin.

After Mass, in the same chamber, there was dancing for two hours to the music of 'flute, harp and violetta'. The king and the Duke of Buckingham and other lords danced in their doublets, and though the Venetian ambassador felt the inclination 'to throw off his gown' he abstained because of his age.

That night, after the bride undressed and climbed into the marriage bed, the Marquis of Rothelin entered. In front of witnesses, he touched the princess with his bare leg, while still otherwise clothed. With that, the marriage was declared consummated.

The rumour mill says that had Katherine's nephew Charles of Castile not broken his betrothal to Mary, and the King of Spain and the Emperor kept their promises, King Henry would never have made peace with France.

1 September 1514: Marriage in Scotland

Margaret, Queen of Scotland married Archibald Douglas, Earl of Angus without the consent of the Scottish Council.

30 November 1514: *Death of a Prince*
Queen Katherine was delivered of a boy child of eight months. Sadly, it 'lived not long after'.

25 December 1514: *Goodly Pastime*
King Henry, with the Duke of Suffolk, Sir Nicholas Carew and Sir Harry Guildford, masked and dressed in cloth of silver lined with blue velvet, with cuts showing silver beneath, wearing great capes, hose, doublets and coats in Portuguese style, came into the queen's chamber. With them were four masked ladies in gowns, hooped after the fashion of Savoy, made of blue velvet with silver mantles and gold bonnets. They entered with four torchbearers in white and blue satin, one of them being young Master Boleyn. The company's strange apparel pleased everyone, especially the queen, and after they had danced and revealed themselves by taking off their neck and face visors, the queen heartily thanked the king for her 'goodly pastime' and kissed him.

1 January 1515: *Death of Louis XII*
At six in the morning, Louis XII was discovered dead in his bed. People are whispering what folly it was for a fifty-two-year-old man with varying chronic conditions to marry such a young, vibrant woman as Mary Tudor.

The throne passes to the twenty-year-old Duke of Valois as King Francis I, husband of Louis' fourteen-year-old daughter, Claude, who by French law is not allowed to ascend the throne.

1 May 1515: *Breakfast with Robin Hood*
King Henry, riding with Queen Katherine around Shooters Hill, espied a company of tall yeomen, clothed all in green. Robin Hood asked if the king would see his band of men shoot. When the king consented, Robin whistled and 200 archers shot and loosed their

arrows at once, then repeated at a second whistle, the noise of their passing 'strange and loud'.

Robin invited the company to come into the greenwood. They were led to a large arbour made of boughs covered with flowers and sweet herbs, wherein they sat down and the outlaws, including Maid Marian and Friar Tuck, served them with venison and wine for breakfast.

13 May 1515: Third Time Happy

Queen Mary publicly married the Duke of Suffolk at Greenwich.

The king's anger at their secret marriage on 12 March and the semi-private marriage on 30 March in Paris during Lent – allowed in France but not in England – has been alleviated, perhaps by the deed whereby, on 2 May, his sister gave up her whole dowry, plate and jewels to him and pledged to pay him £24,000 in yearly instalments of £1,000 to reimburse the expenses he incurred on her behalf.

18–21 February 1516: Princess Mary

Queen Katherine was delivered of a girl child on 18 February at four o'clock in the morning at Greenwich.

On the day of her christening, the path between the court gate and church door was railed and hung with arras, strewn with rushes over fresh gravel. A timber house, to keep the baby warm while she waited for entrance into the church, was built at the church door. Inside, the church was hung with needlework decorated with jewels and pearls.

Preceding the baby, the basin was carried by the Earl of Devonshire, the taper by the Earl of Surrey and the salt by the Marquis of Dorset. His wife bore the chrisom. The Countess of Surrey, assisted by the dukes of Norfolk and Suffolk, carried the princess to the font under a canopy borne by Sir David Owen, Sir Nicholas Vaux, Sir Thomas Parr and Sir Thomas Boleyn.

The godfather was the newly made cardinal and Chancellor of England, Thomas Wolsey; godmothers were Agnes, Duchess of Norfolk and the baby's great-aunt Lady Katherine Courtenay, Countess of Devon at the font and Margaret, Countess of Salisbury for the confirmation.

11 *March 1516: Son for Mary*

Mary Tudor, Duchess of Suffolk and erstwhile Queen of France, was delivered of a son, Henry, Earl of Lincoln, between ten and eleven o'clock at night at Bath Place. The christening on the following Thursday was attended by her brother, the king, who was godfather along with Cardinal Wolsey.

19–20 *May 1516: In Honour of Queen Margaret*

In honour of his sister, Queen Margaret, who is in London, King Henry prepared two solemn jousts. On the first day, he himself duelled with the Duke of Suffolk, while the Earl of Essex faced Nicholas Carew. Their apparel was of black velvet covered all over with 'branches of honeysuckle' in gold damask, in loose work with every leaf able to move. On the second day, the king and his company wore purple velvet with rose leaves of cloth of gold against defenders all in white satin and cloth of gold. King Henry and Sir William Kingston ran together, and though Sir William was a strong and tall knight, the king was stronger and threw him to the ground. The king said he would never joust again unless it be with as good a man as himself.

6 *January 1517: Garden of Esperance*

Seated in the hall at Greenwich, King Henry, Queen Katherine and Queen Margaret were presented with a pageant called the Garden of Esperance, towered at every corner, with banks of gold silk flowers and green satin leaves. In its middle was an antique foursquare pillar of gold set with pearls and jewels. On its top was a gold-crowned arch underneath of which were two bushes: one of red and white silk roses, the other of pomegranates. Within the garden six knights walked with six ladies who came into the hall and danced until the great banquet.

17 July 1517: A Stately Joust

For the entertainment of all resident ambassadors, King Henry prepared a stately joust: he and a band of twelve against the Duke of Suffolk and his band of twelve, six courses each.

The king entered on a tall white horse trapped in white and silver. Dressed in Turkish style with a jewelled scimitar, he was in white damask embroidered with roses made from rubies and diamonds. When the duke came in, he was in white velvet and crimson embroidered with gold letters 'C' and 'M' for Charles and Mary.

After the joust was a sumptuous supper lasting seven hours, with each meal served on a gold plate. Dishes were replaced incessantly, with every meat and fish dish imaginable, including prawn pasties. Everything placed before the king was served on designs after elephants, lions, panthers or other animals. The Marquis of Mantua's ambassador loved the jellies, some twenty sorts shaped like castles and animals, but he was most impressed by the 'very elegant manners and extreme decorum and politeness' shown throughout.

18 July 1517: Christening of Mary's Second Child

On 16 July, the 'French queen' and Duchess of Suffolk, Mary, was delivered of a daughter between two and three in the morning at Bishop's Hatfield.

The road to the church was strewn with rushes and the church porch hung with rich embroidered cloth of gold. Inside, the church was hung with the arras telling the story of Hercules. The altar was covered with rich cloth of tissue on which stood images, relics and jewels. The font had a crimson satin canopy decorated with roses, half red and half white, a sun shining and gold *fleur-de-lys*. Accompanied by sixty ladies and gentlemen, the baby was christened Frances. Deputising for the queen, who was asked to be godmother, was Lady Elizabeth Boleyn, wife of Sir Thomas.

12 April 1518: *Praying for a Prince*

The queen, at Woodstock with the king, is again with child, praying to God for a prince and to get through her 'dangerous time' around early summer.

16–18 June 1518: *The Venetian Galleys*

At Southampton, to view the Venetian galleys, King Henry was surprised to be greeted in Latin by the captain of the flag galley, not expecting a navigator-cum-merchant to be 'so able a rhetorician'. Prepared with a spacious platform decorated with every type of tapestry and silk, the galley had on either side rows of tables with every sort of confection to serve the 300 persons present. The king passed down the centre and up onto the poop where he tasted an impressive variety of dishes, sponge cakes and other confections washed down with glasses of wine. Sailors then performed feats for him on slack ropes suspended from the mast to immense applause.

Before his visit the king had sent the Earl of Surrey ahead to request no cannons to be fired and for the powder to be disembarked, but before he left the port, being curious, he asked to see the guns fired and their range marked. The king was impressed, praised everything and enjoyed the fireworks display in the evening.

10 November 1518: *The Queen Miscarries*

In the night, Queen Katherine was delivered of a daughter, stillborn at eight months, and the nation sorrowed with her.

15 June 1519: The King's Son

The king's bastard son was born today and named Henry FitzRoy. His mother, eighteen-year-old Elizabeth (Bessie) Blount, daughter of Sir John Blount, last appeared at court on 3 October. Bessie, according to Hall, captured the king's heart 'in his fresh youth' with 'chains of love' with her singing and dancing which 'exceeded all other'. She first came to court as maid of honour to Queen Katherine at the end of 1512, at a yearly wage of 200s.

27–29 May 1520: A Fashionable Whitsun

After meeting Charles V at Dover the night before, King Henry rode with him to Canterbury where they, with Queen Katherine, who met her nephew with tears, attended the Whitsunday Mass at the cathedral, preceded by ambassadors and 600 lords and knights.

Following Cardinal Wolsey up the steps to the high altar, Henry and Charles wore new-style 'simars', rich embroidered robes that are open at the front. The emperor's, of cloth of silver on the right and gold-and-silver striped on the left, was lined with sable. Henry's was entirely lynx-lined cloth of gold. Their pew was level with the fourth step, covered in gold brocade embroidered with roses and carpeted in crimson velvet. Four steps lower was the pew for Katherine and Mary. The queen's gold rose-embroidered gown over a silver kirtle was lined with violet velvet. Her pearl necklace had a sparkling bright diamond cross pendant. Her black jewel-decorated headdress had gold stripes. Her sister-in-law wore a dress made of plates of silver lama joined with gold cords with pearl aglets.

For the Whit-Monday Mass, the emperor wore a half-silver, half-gold striped doublet under a sable-lined robe of gold brocade while the king wore a half-gold, half-grey simar with slashes buttoned by rubies, sapphires and diamonds, held closed with a jewelled belt. His black velvet cap was plumed and edged with white feathers. The queen's gown was half-gold, half-violet velvet with gold embroidered flowers with pearls, over a kirtle of cloth of gold against black, slashed and laced with gold and black laces, jewels and pearls for aglets. Her Flemish-style headdress with its long veil gave her additional grace. Her five-stringed pearl necklace had a pendant St George slaying the dragon.

The state banquet after the Mass lasted four hours. Behind the ladies stood 'enamoured youths'. The Count of Capra 'made love so heartily' that he had a fainting fit and had to be carried out until he recovered. The elderly Duke of Alva with his 'sweetheart' opened the ball, all the dances being in the Spanish fashion. The king danced, but the emperor declined.

On Tuesday, the emperor and the king sat in council until about an hour after sunset, leaving Canterbury by torchlight. Some 5 miles outside of the town, they separated. Henry and his retinue proceeded to Dover; the emperor with his company to Sandwich.

4–25 June 1520: *Field of the Cloth of Gold*

On Monday 4 June, King Henry and Queen Katherine, with their trains of nobles, gentlemen and ladies, in readiness for the meeting with Francis I, moved from Calais to Guisnes. The king and queen were lodged in the castle while nobles lodged in a village made of sumptuous tents.

Between the castle and the village was built the most opulent royal banqueting house ever seen, with 50-foot-high battlements, made mostly of wood and canvas painted to look like brick. It stood on a foundation of stone and brick to support a planked floor, beneath which were the kitchens, offices and cellars. Near the top a range of double-glass windows let in light and air, divided by wooden pilasters. A round tower at each corner had statues of mythical figures. In front of the building, two beautiful fountains dispensed wine into silver cups from which anyone could drink. From the courtyard, a great door led into a large hall, with a white and yellow chequered floor and red roses at the intersections. From here, many doors led to large chambers, all with ceilings and walls covered with tapestries, those with foliage seeming alive as they moved in any breeze. Some walls were covered with cloth of gold or silver, interlaced with silk in the king's colours of green and white and adorned with red roses. For comfort, there were rich chairs or silk-covered Turkish cushions everywhere.

On the day appointed for the meeting, King Henry set off on a horse trapped in gold. His outfit was cloth of silver damask, ribbed with gold, sleeves and frontlet covered with diamonds, rubies, emeralds and large hanging pearls. His jewelled bonnet was topped with jaunty white feathers. At the stopping place, Henry faced Francis, a field between them. They began a steady approach and, at the same moment, spurred their horses, like two jousters about to engage. As suddenly, they stopped, about two casts of a bowl from each other.

There was silence.

Trumpets blew.

The kings took off their bonnets, moved forward and embraced. Dismounting, arm in arm, they entered a fine gold pavilion set up for them.

On Saturday, the two kings inspected the tilt yard created halfway between Ardres, where the French king's 'village' was pitched, and Guisnes. At the main entrance, a glazed and tapestry-hung chamber had been built for the queens' viewing pleasure. At each entrance to the park were twelve French and twelve English archers who allowed anyone well-dressed to enter and sup from wine dispensers.

When Henry admired Francis' Mantuan stud, 'Dappled Duke', the French king dismounted and exchanged his horse for Henry's Neapolitan courser.

Sunday was set up for the kings to dine with each other's queens. For his visit to Ardres, Henry wore a double mantle of gold, embroidered with jewels and gold frieze and gold bonnet. Francis' mother, Louise, presented Henry to Queen Claude. His knee to the ground, bonnet in hand, Henry gave her reverence. Rising, he kissed her and then all her ladies. One of the courtiers described Henry as 'handsome, in manner gentle and gracious, rather fat, with a red beard which is becoming'. Queen Claude's robe was embroidered cloth of gold over a skirt of beaten gold, its sleeves covered from shoulder to wrist with diamonds. Against her neck lay the diamond '*la pointe de Bretaigne*', and ornaments around her head held diamonds, rubies and emeralds.

After they had dined, king and queen moved into a tapestried room carpeted with crimson velvet where they talked at leisure. When taking his leave, Henry could not resist making his horse bound and curvet in a fine display until the artillery sounded, signalling the departure of Francis from Guisnes.

The following day, the jousts began, but without lances as the wind was too strong for them to be safely wielded. The queens came to the lists: Queen Claude, dressed in silver over a kirtle of gold, was carried in a silver litter decorated with gold knots; Queen Katherine's litter was covered in gold-embroidered crimson satin; Mary in a gold litter decorated with lilies, porcupines interspersed with 'L' and 'M', for Louis and Mary. Viewing the ladies escorting their mistresses, the Mantuan ambassador thought English ladies neither handsome, graceful nor richly clad, and disapproved of one of the ladies drinking freely from a large flask of wine before passing it to her companions. He was also censorious of their drinking large cups of wine while watching the jousting, exclaiming, 'More than twenty times!'

Both kings, fully armed and well mounted, jousted. Francis ran first and broke spears like they were reeds. Henry ran second, with such vigour that the spears broke in his hand.

The two days following, strong winds and violent rain stopped all tilting, though while the queens stayed away the kings went to the field to witness archery contests and wrestling by Breton and English wrestlers. According to the French, the English only won in the wrestling because no *Bretagne* wrestlers were present. Although the weather abated enough for tilting on Friday and Saturday, very few spectators were present. On the latter day, Francis received an injury on his temple and eye and wore a black patch for the weekend.

So violent was wind and rain on Monday 18 June that there were murmurs they presaged trouble and hatred between princes to come. Then the weather brightened, and jousting resumed until the lists were closed on Saturday.

On Sunday 24 June, both kings mounted the platform to the open-air oratory set up the night before. Francis was on the right; Henry on the left. Claude and Katherine followed. Cardinal de Bourbon brought the *Pax* to the kings to kiss; each declined for the other. Suddenly, after both had kissed it, a great fiery dragon, over 20 feet long, flew over them, high as a bolt shot from a crossbow, as fast as a footman's walk, frightening many of the people as it vanished from sight. Cardinal de Bourbon, unfazed, presented the *Pax* to the two queens who, also declining to kiss it first, kissed each other instead.

Next day, the court returned to Calais.

10–14 July 1520: Sun and Moon Disappear

The king rode to Gravelines to meet with Charles V and conduct him back to Calais, where a banqueting hall had been constructed from sixteen masts 24 feet apart, spaces closed with board and canvas. In the middle, eight masts bound together with ropes and iron stood 134 feet high. The canvas roof stretched over it was painted with stars, a sun, a moon and clouds, and the walls painted with scenes of countries, ships and windmills.

Unfortunately, before the party came to Calais, a violent wind arose. Everything, including 1,000 torches and tapers for the hands of wickerwork figures, was blown away. The conference and banquets then took place in the king's residence.

17 May 1521: Execution of Duke of Buckingham

Edward, third Duke of Buckingham, aged forty-three years, was beheaded on Tower Hill at eleven o'clock. He was found guilty of high treason against the king. The hearsay evidence was that he listened to prophecies of the king's death and desired to kill him. The duke's daughter, Elizabeth, is married to the Earl of Surrey, whose father, the Duke of Norfolk, was made High Steward of England for the trial and wept when he gave the judgement. Edward was the son and heir of the second duke, Henry, executed by Richard III in 1483, nephew by marriage of Lady Margaret Beaufort and descended from a son of Edward III.

4 March 1522: Masque of the Chateau Vert

Shrove Tuesday night, Cardinal Wolsey invited the king and the emperor's ambassadors to York House for supper, and once replete the company were brought into a great tapestry-hung chamber, brightly lit by several candelabra, each holding thirty-two wax candles. At the nether end was a two-tiered embattled castle. The main tower and two smaller towers either side held banners: three torn hearts, a lady's hand gripping a man's heart, and a lady's hand turning a man's heart.

The castle was held by eight masked ladies: Mary, the king's sister; the Countess of Devonshire; Anne Boleyn; her sister, Mary; their brother George's bride-to-be, Jane Parker; and three others. All were clothed in white satin Milanese gowns and gold bejewelled bonnets. They represented Beauty, Honour, Constancy,

Kindness, Perseverance, Bounty, Mercy and Pity. Beneath the ladies, boys of the chapel, dressed like women of India, played Ladies Scorn, Danger, Disdain, Jealousy, Unkindness, Malebouche and Strangeness.

Eight masked lords entered, led by Ardent Desire, dressed in crimson satin with burning flames of gold. The other lords – Amorous, Nobleness, Youth, Attendance, Loyalty, Pleasure, Gentleness and Liberty – wore great cloaks of blue satin and cloth of gold caps. The gentle ladies yielded, but Ladies Scorn and Disdain refused to a great shot of guns. The ladies threw rosewater and comfits, the boys defended with bows and balls, while the lords attacked with dates and oranges. Finally, the lords captured the ladies of honour and they danced until the banquet arrived.

10 *March 1522: A Happy Augury*

With negotiations completed regarding the loan by King Henry of 100,000 crowns to assist Charles V in his endeavours, the ambassadors took leave of the king and were conducted to the queen's chamber to bid her adieu. Queen Katherine asked six-year-old Princess Mary to dance for them. In a slow dance, she twirled prettily, then performed an athletic galliard. After, she played for them on the spinet. The ambassadors noted she wore a gold brooch, jewels spelling out 'Charles', whom she had taken for her valentine on St Valentine's Day, which they thought 'a happy augury'.

27 *May–30 June 1522: State Visit of Charles V*

At Dover, where the emperor landed, King Henry took him first to see his new ship, the *Henry Grace a Dieu*, and afterwards had them rowed around all the ships then in port.

At Greenwich, King Henry honoured the emperor with a two-day joust. On the second day, to the great joy of the spectators, Charles rode into the tilt leading the king, who was that day jousting.

On Friday 6 June, Charles V made his state entry into London in readiness to attend St Paul's for Whitsunday Mass, riding with the king through streets richly hung with gold and silver cloth, arras and coloured velvets. Well-dressed citizens pressed hard against the rails, stretching out their hands to touch them as they passed, the heralds attempting to keep them back. In nearly every house a minstrel sang. A pageant across the street at Leadenhall showed an image of John of Gaunt, branches springing from him, leaves dripping sweet water, showing images of kings and queens descended from him, with Charles, Henry and Katherine shown on the sixth degree.

The Cornhill gates had crenellated towers built above them housing players of trumpets, shawms and sackbuts, serenading King Arthur sat at a round table underneath. At the stocks, an arbour of roses, lilies, birds and beasts was surrounded by a moat full of fish. Around the whole moved planets and stars.

The day following the Whitsunday High Mass at St Paul's, king and emperor rode to Windsor, stopping at Richmond and Hampton Court, hunting all the way. The serious business of council followed the week after. Then the emperor leisurely hunted his way back across the country until his departure at the end of the month.

20 February 1523: Murder or Miscarriage of Justice

Today, the beautiful Lady Agnes Hungerford was hanged at Tyburn for conspiring to murder her first husband, John Cotell, steward of Edward Hungerford. Her stepson, Walter Hungerford, alleged that on 26 July 1518 when John and Agnes were at Farleigh Castle, residence of his father, John was strangled by two of Agnes' manservants who burnt his remains in the kitchen's great range. Agnes, and her servants,

William Mathewe and William Ignes, stayed on at Farleigh Castle and soon after Christmas of that year, Agnes and Edward Hungerford married.

On 22 January 1522, Edward Hungerford died. In his will, dated 14 December 1521, he left all his property absolutely to Agnes, leaving nothing to his nineteen-year-old son from his first marriage. Walter made the unsubstantiated allegation that his stepmother had killed her first husband and she and her servants were indicted for murder on 25 August.

Was it true she had murdered John Cotell five years previously, or was it a case of malice on Walter's part?

Agnes, Mathewe and William were tried on 27 November. William Ignes claimed benefit of clergy but then it was found he was a bigamist. The two men were hanged alongside Agnes, who had been found guilty of inciting them to murder. Lady Agnes was buried at Greyfriars in London while the Crown gave all her seized estates and possessions to her stepson, Walter.

16 June 1524: New Creations

Henry FitzRoy, the six-year-old bastard son of King Henry, was created Duke of Richmond and Somerset, and Earl of Nottingham, in the king's great chamber at Bridewell Palace. Lord Henry Courtenay, Earl of Devonshire was created Marquis of Exeter; Sir Thomas Manners was made Earl of Rutland and Sir Thomas Boleyn became Viscount Rochford.

24–26 June 1524: Funeral of the Duke of Norfolk

In Framlingham Castle chapel, a hearse, with lights burning day and night, had housed the body of Thomas, second Duke of Norfolk, since his death, in his eighty-fourth year, on 21 May. The coffin was at last laid in the chariot for its journey to Thetford Priory for burial. His son, Thomas, now the third duke, was chief mourner, supported by his brothers, Edmund and William, and his brother-in-law, Sir Thomas Boleyn. Garter, Clarencieux, Richmond, Carlisle and Windsor heralds attended.

After Mass and the offering, six gentlemen placed the coffin in the consecrated vault, and after household officers had thrown in their broken staffs of office, the Bishop of Ely sprinkled on holy water.

Penny alms, to the amount of £100, were given to the poor; 1,900 persons received liveries of black cloth for gowns and coats. The funeral cost £1,340. In his will, Norfolk left to his son and heir his great hanged bed with white damask and black velvet and his tapestries of the story of Hercules. To the king, for a poor remembrance, he left a pair of gilt pots called 'our Scottish pots'.

9 September 1524: *The Pope's Rose*
Pope Clement VII sent a rose of gold for a token to the king, delivered at a solemn Mass sung by the Cardinal of York at Windsor. Set in a gold pot, the rose was actually a gold tree standing about 20 inches high, with branches, leaves and roses. In the uppermost rose was a sapphire about the size of an acorn.

27 December 1524: *A Christmas Joust*
Windsor Herald, calling himself *Chasteau Blanche*, entered Queen Katherine's great chamber on Christmas Day to give a call to arms. His red silk coat bore a castle with four turrets in beaten silver, a lady in each turret.

Two days later, six fully armoured knights emerged from a castle built in the tilt yard to await challengers. Two ladies rode in on palfreys, leading two greybeards wearing purple damask robes. The two old men asked Queen Katherine if, 'although youth had left them and age was come', they could do feats of arms. At her assent, to cheers, they revealed they were King Henry and Charles, Duke of Suffolk. Jousting eight courses along with his friends Sir Nicholas Carew, Sir Francis Bryan and Henry Norris, the king broke seven spears. Everyone marvelled at his strength.

The Scottish ambassadors, at court to sue for peace, asked a courtier if the king had been so merry all wartime. They were told the English and their king gave not 'one bean' for Francis I.

24 February 1525: Taken Prisoner
Francis I was defeated and taken prisoner during fighting at the Italian city of Pavia by Charles V's imperial army.

13 February 1526: Is Henry VIII Pricked with the Dart of Love?
On Shrove Tuesday at Greenwich, King Henry, with a band of eleven, jousted. All wore cloth of gold or silver, embroidered with a man's heart in a press, with flames all around it. Encircling the flames were the words, 'Declare I dare not.' Twelve challengers, led by the Marquis of Exeter, were all dressed in green velvet and crimson satin, their outfits embroidered with 'hearts burning, and over every heart a lady's hand coming out of a cloud holding a garden water pot, which dropped silver drops on the heart'. In a past Shrovetide joust, King Henry had embroidered on his outfit a picture of a heart, with the words 'she hath wounded my heart', his horse embroidered with gold 'Ls' under the words 'heart of man wounded'. The devices always cause speculation.

Many lances were broken by all the combatants. Sir Francis Bryan lost an eye to a 'chance shivering of a spear'. One of Henry's closest companions, thirty-year-old Sir Francis is an accomplished jouster, poet, gambler and tennis player.

At the banquet afterwards, the king served the queen and ladies himself.

The King's Great Matter: 1526–1536

Francis I, after a year of imprisonment, sent Henry VIII a message of thanks for not invading his realm. In Italy, meanwhile, the imperial army was starving for want of payment. But Henry's thoughts were no longer on France. He was in love.

Henry's conscience and earnest scouring of scripture had led him to conclude that God had not given him a son because he was living in mortal sin having married his brother's widow. He grew determined, to the point of obsession, that his marriage to Katherine must be annulled. Then he could marry his love, Anne Boleyn, 'fresh and young, passing sweet and cheerful', and God would grant him an heir while he would have a virtuous wife 'skilled in music and poetry', 'excellent in gesture and behaviour'.

When Hall wrote in his chronicle that there was nothing worth writing of in the summer of 1526, it was likely Henry was courting Anne, sending her bucks and love letters. Those letters, now kept in the Vatican, reveal him writing: 'I have put myself into great agony, not knowing how you intend them, whether to my disadvantage as you show in some places, or to my advantage as I understand them in some others, beseeching you with my whole heart to expressly certify to me your whole mind as to the love between us two ... having been for above a whole year struck with the dart of love, and not sure whether I shall fail or find a place in your heart.'

Finally, Anne surrendered. In his letter, Henry thanked her 'not only for the fine diamond and the ship in which the solitary damsel is tossed about, but principally for the beautiful interpretation and the too humble submission which your kindness has used towards me ... The demonstrations of your affection are such, the beautiful words of the letter so cordially couched, that I am obliged always forever to truly honour, love and serve you...'

Anne, daughter of Sir Thomas Boleyn (now Lord Rochford) and Elizabeth Howard, sister to the third Duke of Norfolk, was born in 1507 according to Camden and died 'not twenty-nine years of age' according to Jane Dormer, Duchess of Feria. Anne was exotic, educated in Brussels and France, with cultural and religious beliefs shaped by women like Margaret of Savoy, Queen Claude and Marguerite of Navarre. Anne, fully of the Catholic faith, had reformist beliefs that the Bible should be available for anyone to read in the vernacular and that all priests should be well educated. Like Erasmus, she favoured reform of abuses and superstitions.

The king's Great Matter, as the annulment saga was euphemistically entitled, was supposed to remain a private matter, yet by 13 July 1527 the Spanish ambassador was writing to Emperor Charles V that the king was trying to 'dissolve the marriage between the queen and himself, alleging ... there had been between them no marriage at all'. On 16 August the ambassador told Charles it was openly believed if the king's marriage was annulled he would immediately marry Anne, Lord Rochford's daughter.

Henry expected the annulment of his marriage to go through easily and quickly, but an event in early summer of that year was to have a bearing on events which ultimately culminated in the English church breaking with Rome.

6 May 1527: *The Sack of Rome*

The imperial army, with banners displayed, came before the city of Rome. Despite a valiant defence by the Romans with handguns, pikes and stones they were, on the third assault, overrun by the emperor's starved and destitute soldiers as they poured over the walls and rampaged through the streets. They vandalised churches, killing any citizen in their way and raping any girl or woman they found. Many women drowned themselves in the Tiber rather than being dragged from hiding. The Pope fled by a secret way into the

Castel Sant'Angelo, 300 of his Swiss Guard giving their lives for him to effect his escape.

7 May 1527: *The Joust of Loyalty*

In honour of the French ambassadors, King Henry arranged a solemn joust at Greenwich. The challenge device was 'Loyalty', the symbol a right hand holding a sword surrounded by pennies. Though it rained, the challengers still ran against defenders covered with gold-edged clouds and mountains full of gold olive branches.

A two-chambered banquet house with clear windows was built. The roof, made of purple cloth, was decorated with roses and pomegranates. The chamber was well lit by hundreds of small white wax candles on amber candlesticks in the corbels. The entrance to the first chamber was through broad arches adorned with gargoyles and serpents. Three long tables had been set up and supper was served on gold plates. When the king took the ambassadors through the arches, they saw a Holbein painting of the Siege of Therouanne.

After supper, they were led into the second chamber. The bottom part of the roof was painted to look like land encircled by sea, with the zodiac and seven planets painted in the apex. Spectators were seated in three tiers, each row with a beam placed in front for the audience to lean upon; no tier interfered with another. The ambassadors were surprised at the 'order, regularity and silence' with which entertainments were conducted in England. Praising peace between England and France were songs and a Latin oration, followed by a dialogue between Cupid and Plutus arguing whether it was better to have wealth or love, with the conclusion that princes needed both.

At the end of the hall, a curtain was whisked away to reveal eight lords sitting upon a towered mount of rocks of crystal and ruby dotted with trees of roses and pomegranates. Beneath them a cave opened. Princess Mary issued forth with seven ladies, all dressed in gowns and bonnets of gold and crimson tinsel with sleeves almost to the ground. The princess was so bedecked with jewels that she dazzled the eyes as she moved. Lords and ladies danced. Six gentlemen entered, in silver and black, all of them wearing black slippers in solidarity as the king had hurt his left foot while playing tennis. They wore hoods in the fashion of Iceland, masks and silver beards, and each took a lady to dance, the king dancing with glee.

Afterwards another banquet was laid on. No one reached their beds until daybreak, with 'such sleepy eyes that the daylight could not keep them open'.

3 August 1527: Beaulieu House Party

King Henry, on his summer progress, lodged at Beaulieu with an unusually large party of nobles including the dukes of Norfolk and Suffolk, Marquis of Exeter and the earls of Oxford, Essex and Rutland and their wives. Also staying was Lord Rochford, who had sold Beaulieu to Henry after he inherited it from his grandfather the Earl of Ormond. With him were his wife, Elizabeth, and daughter, Anne, to whom the king has given the gift of an emerald ring.

1 January 1528: New Year Gifts

For New Year, King Henry gave Mistress Anne two bracelets set with ten diamonds and eight pearls. He has also commissioned trueloves of crown gold with nineteen diamonds, two borders of gold with diamonds and pearls for her sleeves, and two diamonds on two hearts for her head.

25 February–16 March 1528: King Henry at Windsor

In the lodge of the Little Park at Windsor, King Henry gave an intimate dinner. Dishes served included beef, veal, capons, kids, lambs, plovers, herons, larks, rabbits and fresh cheeses with puddings and pastries. Among the party were Mistress Anne with her mother. On all the days of fair weather, they have walked or hawked with the king in the park, not returning until late evening.

Mistress Anne had been shown much favour for the king sends her dishes from his table at other times. Once, Mr Heneage was given the errand and she kindly asked him to dine with her. While together, she asked him whether he thought Wolsey might kindly send her some carps or shrimps and her mother a 'morsel of tunny'. The king recently gave Mistress Anne twenty-one hearts with diamonds and twenty-one roses set with rubies, perhaps a token for the number of her years.

20 June 1528: The 'Sweat'

Owing to 'the Sweat', King Henry moved to Hunsdon while sending Anne and her parents to Hever Castle after one of Anne's ladies became infected. During the day, the king wrote to reassure Anne that though her brother, George, had been ill, he was now recovered. Wishing she was in his arms, he asked her not be too uneasy at their parting. In the middle of the night, an alarmed King Henry received dire tidings that Mistress Anne had been stricken down. Distraught, he sent Dr Butts with a letter of love, hoping to see her well, which would be to him 'a greater comfort than all the precious jewels in the world'.

The illness known as the Sweat made its appearance six days ago. It is a terrifying disease, highly contagious, and starts with a little pain in the head. Suddenly, a sweat begins and in four hours, sometimes less, you can be dead.

23 June 1528: Death and Recovery

King Henry received news that Anne and her father had recovered and were past danger. Her sister's husband, William Carey, was not so fortunate. He had left his wife merrily that morning to go riding and hunting. By evening time, Anne's sister was a widow.

22–24 October 1528: *The King's Great Matter*

After six months of waiting for the legate, Cardinal Campeggio, to travel from Rome to hear his cause, King Henry impatiently insisted both legates should come to court, despite Campeggio being unable to ride, walk or sit without pain, having been bedbound with gout since his arrival on 7 October. A strange sight: the two cardinals abreast, Cardinal Wolsey on his mule, Cardinal Campeggio carried in a chair, both drenched by the torrential rain, while people pressed about them so thickly some of the company lost their shoes.

In respect of the king's conscience, Campeggio offered a new dispensation from the Pope which Henry refused. The legate then proposed that Queen Katherine should enter a convent, for which there were past precedents. The king said if she could be persuaded, he would settle the succession on Princess Mary if he had no male heirs.

The following day, Campeggio and Wolsey visited Queen Katherine. No matter what they said – that she would lose nothing she had not already lost; that she was nearing fifty; that she would preserve her dower, her rank, her daughter's rank – she was unmoved, saying only she knew the 'sincerity of her own conscience'.

Queen Katherine visited Campeggio on the next day to make a free confession. She told him that from the day she married Arthur until 2 April when he died, that they had not slept together more than seven nights, and that she was virgin still when she married Henry. She intends to live and die as Henry's wife, as God has called her to be.

28 May–31 July 1529: *The Blackfriars Court*

At Blackfriars in London, the great hall was turned into a court. Two chairs covered with cloth of gold and cushions with a table and a rail made it a solemn place for the two legates to sit. On the right side of the court was a chair of estate for the king and on the left a chair of estate for the queen; both were asked to appear on 28 May, when the legates declared that King Henry believed his marriage unlawful, damnable and directly against the Law of God and that they had been appointed by the Court of Rome to hear and judge his cause.

The king was called and answered he was present.

The queen was called, bringing with her four bishops, counsel and a great company of her ladies and gentlewomen. Making personal obeisance directly before the legates she said, with great gravity, that she protested against their jurisdiction and would make her appeal to the Pope for the cause to be heard at Rome.

The king countered it was unreasonable for the removal of the cause to Rome because of the emperor's power there with regard to the Pope, and that she had the choice of prelates and lawyers. The queen fell on her knees and begged him to consider her honour, her daughter's and his, saying it was reasonable the affair should be determined at Rome because the cause was already there.

Since that appearance the queen refused to appear further. Over the following weeks, evidence was presented and sifted when, suddenly, Cardinal Campeggio declared they could no longer be in session after 31 July until October as it was vacation in the Court of Rome, and they would duly have to stop sitting. King Henry took the ruling patiently until he was informed Cardinal Campeggio had been recalled by the Pope to return to Italy with all speed and realised he had been gulled by Rome. This caused Wolsey to lose the king's favour as an agent of the Pope.

Once the court had convened, the king rode out on progress.

17–26 October 1529: The Great Seal

Cardinal Wolsey surrendered the Great Seal to the dukes of Norfolk and Suffolk in the gallery of his house at Westminster. It was delivered to the king at Windsor on 20 October and then, five days later, delivered by the king at East Greenwich to Sir Thomas More, who took his oath as Lord Chancellor in Westminster Great Hall the following day.

30 November 1529: Reproaches

Dining with Queen Katherine, King Henry was berated by her, saying she was suffering the pains of Purgatory on earth, being badly treated by his refusals to dine with her as before or visit her apartments. He told her 'she was mistress in her own household where she could do what she pleased' but as to his visiting her and partaking of her bed, he could not for he was not her legitimate husband. She contradicted that he, without the help of doctors, knew well the principal cause alleged did not exist and she cared not a straw for any judge other than the Pope.

Later that day, at supper, Lady Anne noticed his downcast mood and when she heard of his dispute with the queen, she too reproached him: 'Did I not tell you that whenever you dispute with the queen she is sure to have the upper hand? I see that some fine morning you will succumb to her reasoning and cast me off. I have been waiting long, and could have contracted an advantageous marriage, and had issue. Alas, farewell to my time and youth spent to no purpose at all.'

8 December 1529: New Creations

Robert Radcliffe, Viscount Fitzwater was created Earl of Sussex; Thomas Boleyn, Viscount Rochford was created Earl of Wiltshire and Ormond; George Boleyn, meanwhile, was allowed the courtesy title of Viscount Rochford. George, Lord Hastings was created Earl of Huntingdon.

8 May 1530: Anne Rides Pillion

King Henry has been hunting around Windsor where people have seen the unusual sight of Mistress Anne riding pillion behind the king.

4–30 November 1530: Death of the Cardinal

Although Cardinal Wolsey had been stripped of his offices and property, including his palace of Hampton Court, King Henry permitted him to remain Archbishop of York. At the beginning of November, the king gave him leave to journey north to his diocese of York, where he arranged for his grandiose installation as Archbishop of York.

While at dinner in his house of Cawood Hall in Yorkshire, the Earl of Northumberland arrived and 'in a faint and soft voice' told the cardinal he was to return to London to face charges of high treason. Though ill, the cardinal began the journey but had to do so in easy stages, stopping at Pontefract, Doncaster and Sheffield Park, where the Earl of Shrewsbury welcomed him, and where he was allowed to rest a few days while awaiting the arrival of the Constable of the Tower, Sir William Kingston, to convey him the rest of the way. When Sir William arrived, he gave the cardinal much reverence and comfortable words but the cardinal replied, kindly, 'All these comfortable words you have spoken be but for a purpose to bring me in a fool's paradise, I know what is provided for me.' By this time he was continually sick and having to use the stool all night.

The next day the company reached Hardwick Hall, then Nottingham, but he was getting sicker by the day. Arriving at night at Leicester Abbey, with the cardinal barely able to keep astride his mule, the party were met by the abbot with torches, to whom the cardinal said, 'Father Abbot, I am come hither to leave my bones among you.' On his second night at the abbey, he managed a few spoonfuls of chicken broth; however, upon realising it was the early hours of a fasting day, he refused to eat any more.

Around daybreak, Kingston came to ask the cardinal how he did, who replied that had he served God as diligently as he had the king, 'he would not have given me over in my grey hairs'. He asked to be commended to Henry, then recounted how he had often knelt for hours before the king in his privy chamber trying to persuade him from his will and appetite. 'Master Kingston … I warn you to be well advised and assured what matter you put in his head, for you shall never put it out again,' he warned before his words faltered and he took his last breath at eight o'clock.

13 January 1531: Pope Angers King Henry
King Henry, to his great anger, received letters from the Pope, who wrote to him by request of Queen Katherine. The first forbade him to remarry and warned that if he did, any issue would be deemed illegitimate and he would be excommunicated. The second told him his cause was revoked to Rome for Queen Katherine had sent letters of continual complaint that it was unfair for her to have 'to submit to judicial proceedings at the will of the king whose word was law'. King Henry said that he did not care 'three straws: and when the Pope had done what he liked on that side, he would do what he liked here'.

14 February 1531: Supreme Head
Perusing the oath clergy give to the Pope and the one sworn to him as king, King Henry told the clergy they were guilty of submitting to a foreign jurisdiction and perhaps were not wholly his subjects. Accepting that King Henry is Supreme Head of the English Church, he has been offered the sum of £100,000 to remit their offences. The king was as pleased with their submission as the present he had received from the King of Hungary: two camels, two Turkish horses and two slaves. In fine humour he awaits the

arrival of an ingenious clock from France showing the movements of the spheres and the courses of the planets.

28 February 1531: Poisoning

Ten days ago, Richard, the Bishop of Rochester's cook, prepared some soup that killed two household members and some beggars to whom it had been given in charity. Immediately arrested, Richard confessed to putting powder in the broth but only as a joke to make his fellow servants sick, not to kill them. Today, at Smithfield, Richard was boiled in hot water until he died, under an Act specifically made in Parliament to deter other poisoners.

31 May 1531: The Queen's Conscience

The lords of the council were sent by King Henry to Queen Katherine to inform her he is displeased and aggrieved at being cited to appear personally in Rome – not a thing suitable to a king's estate – and how he was unable to understand the cause, having always treated her 'well and honourably'. Given that the universities and learned men believed the marriage was contrary to God's law, they asked her to allow the cause to be judged in England by four prelates and four temporal lords. The queen replied she would pray to God to send the king a quiet conscience for she was his lawful wife and 'in that point I will abide' until the Pope makes judgement otherwise.

The Duke of Norfolk, in conference afterwards with the king, advised him that the queen was ready to obey him in all things but she owed obedience to two others first. The king asked who these persons were to which the duke replied, 'God was the first, her conscience the second.'

14 July 1531: Separation

Over the last few weeks, King Henry has been hunting around Windsor, taking his meals in the small hunting lodge in the middle of the forest with Anne, her mother, Dr Cranmer and Nicholas Carew, master of his horse. Before removing to Woodstock, the king ordered Queen Katherine to remove herself and her household to The More, a palace that once belonged to Cardinal Wolsey, who had recently built an outer court and long gallery there. She was no longer to follow in his wake.

27 September 1531: King's Warrant

Princess Mary had delivered to her, by order of King Henry, five gowns: one each of cloth of silver tissue, purple velvet and black tinsel, all three lined with silver; a gold-lined crimson satin; and a black velvet furred with ermine. She also received on order a black velvet rabbit-furred nightgown and a night-bonnet of ermine.

11 October 1531: Passion, Not Conscience

The council once again visited Queen Katherine to request, by order of the king, she allow their cause to be heard in England while the emperor unfairly influenced the actions of the Pope. The queen, a sweet expression on her face, replied she had no intention of giving her consent where everybody, either for fear or subornment, would say black was white', for she now realised her husband was moved not by 'scruples of conscience' but only 'by mere passion'.

As one, they knelt before her, and begged her to do as they asked. In response, she knelt before them and begged them to persuade the king to return to her, she being his true and lawful wife. Before leaving, they asked where she would prefer to live. She replied, 'It was not for her to choose. Wherever the king commanded her, were it even to the fire, she would go.'

1 January 1532: Almost a Family Affair

New Year gifts to the king were led by Mistress Anne giving King Henry a set of richly ornamented Biscayan darts. Her sister,

Mary, gave him a white shirt with blackwork on the collar, her sister-in-law, Jane, gave him two velvet caps and two satin ones with gold buttons, and her mother offered three gold and three silver shirt collars. Anne's father presented him with a black velvet box with a steel glass set in gold, her brother gave two gilt hangers with velvet girdles, and the Duke of Norfolk, Anne's uncle, presented him with a wood knife, a pair of tables, chessmen and a tablet of gold. From the king, Anne received rich hangings for a room and a bed covered with gold and silver cloth and crimson satin, all richly embroidered.

16–22 May 1532: *More Discharged*

Chancellor More asked his friend the Duke of Norfolk to make suit to the king to discharge him of the chancellorship because of 'infirmities of his body'. Sir Thomas Cromwell, once chief secretary and aide to Cardinal Wolsey and now high in the king's confidence, called on Sir Thomas More at his house in Chelsea, where More told him that he was 'now entered into the service of a most noble, wise and liberal prince; if you will follow my poor advice, you shall, in your counsel-giving to his grace, ever tell him what he ought to do but never what he is able to do ... for if a lion knew his own strength, hard were it for any man to rule him'.

1 September 1532: *Marchioness of Pembroke*

At Windsor Castle, Lady Anne, hair unbound, was created Marchioness of Pembroke by King Henry. He placed her ermine-furred crimson mantle on her shoulders and the coronet on her head, both carried by her cousin, Lady Mary, daughter of the Duke of Norfolk. With her patent of creation she was granted £1,000 a year. At the banquet held after the Mass, celebrated by Stephen Gardiner, Bishop of Winchester, the poet laureate, Robert Whittington, hailed Anne as a 'shining jewel, her beauty unrivalled'.

11 October–13 November 1532: Visit to Calais

Boarding *The Swallow* at Dover, King Henry and Lady Anne sailed with their respective retinues to Calais, where, while waiting to meet with King Francis, the king inspected the walls, towers and bulwarks, devising new fortifications for the town's defences.

For his meeting with King Francis on 21 October at Boulogne, the king wore a braided coat of gold laid loose over russet velvet with trefoils full of jewels and pearls. Anne, left behind at Calais, received a present of grapes and pears.

The kings met and embraced, as did their nobles, and all rode for a mile hand in hand. The two kings cast hawks to the kites until they neared Boulogne, where they were met by the Dauphin and his brothers, in black velvet embroidered with silver damask, with a retinue of other French nobles. Both kings were lodged in the abbey, its refectory being used as a banqueting hall, carpeted and hung with tapestry. The French king was served in the French way, King Henry was served by his people, bareheaded on their knees as was his custom.

The four days they were together were spent in music, singing, tennis and dice, the king losing to Norfolk and Cromwell.

On 25 October, the two kings rode to Calais, met just outside by Henry FitzRoy, Duke of Richmond, with a great company of noblemen. Again all the company embraced one another, the retinues comprising above a thousand men. At Calais, King Henry brought Francis to the Staple Inn where a chamber, all gold and damask with flowers of satin silk and silver, awaited him. His second chamber was all of tissue with a cloth of estate set with great pearls. His third chamber was all of velvet, purled green and crimson, embroidered with gold flowers and beasts set with pearl and jewels. King Henry's officers, to the wonder of those of the French king, served many dishes of wild fowl, venison and fish. As for wine, no one lacked.

Upon Sunday 27 October, both kings heard Mass in their lodgings and until supper were entertained by baiting of bears and bulls. After supper in a chamber hung with silver tissue and pearl, Anne entered with twelve ladies, all masked, wearing crimson tinsel satin, cloth of silver with gold laces, heralded by four damsels in crimson satin tabards. Anne partnered Francis, wearing a doublet overset with jewels and diamonds (valued by discreet men as at least £100,000), and the Countess of Derby the King of Navarre, and each lady took a lord and danced. After the last dance, Henry plucked away the ladies' masks and Francis and Anne talked for a while, she lamenting that Marguerite of Navarre, his sister and her close friend, was unable to be present.

On 30 October, King Henry accompanied Francis through the Pale of Calais, stopping at the place where wine, Hippocras and spice had been set up for a farewell. The two kings talked for a while before mounting their horses, embracing and parting ways, though not before granting one another so many gifts of plate, coin, raiment, horses, falcons and dogs.

As King Henry returned to Calais, a terrible wind and storm arose, so that he and Anne were unable to sail. They spent their time playing card games, such as Pope Julius and Primero. On Sunday, with the weather looking fair, the king's bed and gear were embarked. However, a mist rose up that was too thick to sail through, and it was midnight on Tuesday before they could sail. They landed at Dover at five o'clock in the morning.

12 April 1533: Queen Anne

The Marchioness of Pembroke was proclaimed queen today at Greenwich. Wearing cloth of gold and bejewelled, she attended High Mass with the king, and then dined in public.

In the meantime, the council visited Lady Katherine at Ampthill to tell her of the king's marriage to Queen Anne, which had taken place a few months previously, and that she had been awarded a yearly pension of £8,000 for her dowry in respect of her marriage to Prince Arthur. To every church door a proclamation was affixed that the king and Lady Katherine had not been lawfully married and she was henceforth to be known by the title princess dowager. This bastardises their daughter, Mary.

The marriage of Queen Anne and King Henry is rumoured to have occurred on 25 January in a small chapel in the Palace of Westminster. The ceremony is said to have been performed by Dr Rowland Lee.

29 May–2 June 1533: Coronation

Queen Anne, in cloth of gold, entered her barge, which had been painted outside in her colours, to sail from Greenwich to the Tower on Thursday 29 May. Hundreds of other barques and smaller boats sailed around her, including her father's barge, which stayed nearby.

The Thames was a river of banners and pennants attached to masts, of silk and beaten gold, shining and shimmering in the sun, their ropes dressed with little taffeta flags. All the way from Limehouse, a thousand and more guns were fired in salute, and tambourines, flutes, trumpets and oboes harmonised with minstrel song and tinkling bells. In front of the mayor's barge was a small foist with a great dragon breathing fire; to the left was another foist with the queen's crowned white falcon standing on a gold root on top of a mount covered in white and red roses.

At the Tower, a lane was made by the people for the pregnant queen to walk through to the King's Bridge, where the king awaited her at the postern by the waterside, and kissed her to the delight of those watching. Before entering, Anne turned back a moment to thank everyone, and the citizens hung around, continuing to make a great melody.

On Saturday, Queen Anne came out of the Tower for her journey to Westminster, dressed in a white surcoat and white ermine-furred mantle, long hair straight down her back, topped with a jewelled circlet. The chariot, covered in white satin, was drawn by two palfreys trapped in white damask. Her silver canopy, with silver bells tinkling at each corner, was held over her head by four knights.

Twelve ladies on hackneys, dressed in crimson velvet, came after her, followed by a chariot covered with cloth of gold, in which sat the queen's mother and grandmother, the Dowager Duchess of Norfolk. Leading the procession through the gravelled and tapestried streets were twelve French merchants in violet velvet, each one with a sleeve in the queen's colours, their horses caparisoned in violet taffeta with white crosses. All the fountains dispensed wine and at the crossways were pageants, plays and minstrels singing ballads of her beauty. The pageant at Leadenhall showed a falcon alighting upon a rose, crowned by an angel, while children sang Leland's ballad 'The White Falcon'; stopping at St Paul's Churchyard, Anne highly commended the children's singing. At last, Queen Anne came to Westminster. Helped from her litter, she was led to the high dais under her cloth of estate. Spices, Hippocras and wine she sent to her ladies and the mayor, giving hearty thanks to everyone.

On Sunday, the day of Queen Anne's coronation, she walked to the abbey dressed in an ermine-furred purple velvet robe over a crimson velvet kirtle. On her head was a rich coronet with a net of pearls. The old Duchess of Norfolk carried her train as she mounted the red-clothed dais that had been arranged for her in front of the high altar where she stood. Dr Cranmer, recently consecrated Archbishop of Canterbury, anointed and crowned her with St Edward's crown, exchanging it for her own, lighter crown when she sat in her chair of state during Mass. She left the abbey holding her father's hand.

25 June 1533: Death of Queen Mary

The king's sister, Mary, having had bouts of illness for many years, died suddenly at Westhorpe Hall in Suffolk. Her last visit to London had been in April, for the marriage of her eldest daughter, Frances, to Henry Grey, the young Marquis of Dorset and great-grandson of Elizabeth Wydville. The ceremony had been conducted at Suffolk Place. While she was in London, she wrote to her brother that she intended to consult Master Peter, the physician.

8 August 1533: Bull

Pope Clement VII issued a bull commanding Henry to restore Katherine or be excommunicated. In that event, he would call upon Charles V, all other Christian princes, and Henry's own subjects to make him obey by force of arms.

7–10 September 1533: Birth of a 'fair daughter'

At three o'clock on Sunday 7 September, at Greenwich, Queen Anne was brought to bed of a daughter, for which event a *Te Deum* was sung solemnly at Paul's the day after.

On 10 September, the walls between the palace and the chapel were hung with arras and the path covered with green rushes. The silver font from Canterbury stood in the middle of the church on a platform with three steps, above it a square canopy of gold-fringed crimson satin. The old Duchess of Norfolk bore the princess, with the dukes of Norfolk and Suffolk either side of her. The Countess of Kent bore the child's long train, while Anne's father and the Earl of Derby on either side supported the train in the middle. Over the child was a canopy, held by her uncle George, Lords William and Thomas Howard, and Lord Hussey. After her baptising, heralded by a trumpet blast, the king caused the child to be openly and publicly proclaimed Princess Elizabeth. Then the princess was borne to her mother's chamber door.

Her godfather was Archbishop Cranmer, who gave her a standing gold cup; godmothers were the old Duchess of Norfolk, who gave her a gold standing cup fretted with pearl, and the old Marchioness of Dorset, who gave three pounced gilt bowls with a cover.

13–23 December 1533: *Joint Household*

Princess Elizabeth was moved to her own household at Bishop's Hatfield, leaving London in full estate with a retinue of nobles led by her great-uncle the Duke of Norfolk.

Lady Mary had sent a presumptuous letter of defiance to the king in October, writing that the failure to use her title in a previous missive must have happened without the king knowing, for she doubted not she was 'his lawful daughter born in true matrimony. If I agreed to the contrary, I should offend God; in all other things you shall find me an obedient daughter.' In response, the king resolved to join Lady Mary's household with that of Princess Elizabeth.

The Earl of Oxford, taking the place of the Duke of Suffolk after he had hurt his leg playing tennis, was sent to conduct Lady Mary to her new residence. On arrival, Mary was asked if she wanted to pay court to the princess. She replied that 'she knew no other princess in England but herself', adding condescendingly that, as the king acknowledged her as his daughter, she could treat her as sister, but in nowise princess.

Rumour says that Queen Anne has told the king she is once more with child.

17–23 December 1533: *Lock-in at Buckden*

The Duke of Suffolk arrived at Lady Katherine's residence of Buckden on 17 December to oversee her move to Somersham Palace, the Bishop of Ely's moated brick-built palace, with large garden, deer park and extensive fishponds.

On the day of his arrival, the princess dowager assembled all her servants in her great chamber to announce to them, and the council members, that she was the king's queen and true wife and anyone who swore to serve her in any capacity other than queen was dismissed. Over the next few days her baggage was packed and litters made ready for the move. During the upheaval, Lady Katherine said to move her they would have to 'bind her with ropes and violently enforce her', and that she considered all the king's officers guards and she a prisoner.

On the day of removal, she locked herself in her chamber. Talking through a hole in the wall, she told them if they wished to take her they would have to break down the door, for she had been informed the bishop's palace was 'pestilential' and she refused to be 'guilty of voluntary suicide'.

1 January 1534: Queen's Gift

Queen Anne's New Year gift to the king was a diamond-encrusted fountain designed by Hans Holbein, with water flowing from the breasts of three naked nymphs, in a gilt bowl garnished with rubies and pearls.

30 March 1534: Act of Succession

Any man or woman who gives the title of queen or princess to any except to Queen Anne and her daughter will be guilty of the crime of *lèse-majesté*. Every man and woman must take an oath to this effect. Dr John Fisher, Bishop of Rochester and Sir Thomas More are among those who refused to swear. All have been sent to the Tower.

21 May 1534: Council Visits Princess Dowager

Bishops and members of the Privy Council were sent by the king to Lady Katherine, now residing at Kimbolton, to inform her that her obstinacy could lead her to the scaffold. She replied that she prayed it would be done publicly before the people and not secretly in her chamber. When Chapuys, the emperor's ambassador, heard of the deputation he requested an audience with the king, who sent him a message via the Duke of Norfolk that he acknowledged no superior in his kingdom and that all his subjects are bound to obey the laws and statutes of the realm.

Since her move, the princess dowager has refused to leave her room except to hear Mass, will not see the appointed household officers and only eats and drinks what is prepared in her own chamber.

24 September 1534: A New Love?

Rumour in court is that King Henry has 'renewed and increased the love which he formerly bore to a handsome young lady'. When Queen Anne tried to dismiss the lady, feeling that she was treated with no respect by her in words or deeds, the king angrily countermanded her order and sent the queen a message that she 'ought to be satisfied with what he had done for her, for were he to commence again he would certainly not do as much'.

19 October 1534: Queen's Sister's Secret Marriage

Mary Boleyn, Queen Anne's sister, was banished from court after admitting secretly marrying William Stafford. She told her sister that 'love overcame reason' and that she would rather beg bread with him than to be the greatest queen christened.

3 November–18 December 1534: Acts of Parliament

Parliament decreed the Pope was henceforth entitled Bishop of Rome, with no authority in England. King Henry, as Supreme Head of the Church, has authority to reform and redress all errors, heresies and abuses.

A new Treason Act was passed. Any person who does 'maliciously wish, will or desire by words or writing' to bodily harm the king, queen or heirs apparent, or to deprive them of 'their dignity, title or name of their royal estates, or slanderously and maliciously publish and pronounce, by express writing or words, that the king should be heretic, schismatic, tyrant, infidel or usurper of the crown', would be guilty of high treason.

14 January 1535: Marriage Negotiations

A banquet was given for the Admiral of France, Philippe de Chabot, to discuss the marriage of Princess Elizabeth to the Duc d'Angouleme, the third son of the French king. When the admiral was seated with the queen, she began to laugh suddenly for no apparent reason. Thinking for some reason the queen was mocking him, Chabot frowned at her. She apologised, saying that when the dancing started her husband had said he would fetch Francis' secretary, M. Gontier, to pay his respects to her. But, she said, the king had forgotten to look for Gontier for 'whilst he was looking out for him he happened to meet a lady, who was the cause of his forgetting everything'.

21 January 1535: Vicegerent in Spirituals

Sir Thomas Cromwell, King Henry's chief minister, was appointed Vicegerent in Spirituals, taking precedence above the archbishops of Canterbury and York. He was ordered to send 'visitations' to every church, monastery and convent throughout the realm to check for abuses and suppress those found guilty of such.

22 June 1535: Execution of John Fisher

John, Bishop of Rochester was beheaded at Tower Hill. At his arraignment on 17 June, he was found guilty of treason for maliciously refusing the king's title of Supreme Head. In a bid to save him, the Pope elected him a cardinal. The cardinal's hat reached Calais but the king determined he would have no head to wear it. His body was buried within Barking Churchyard at the north door and his head set on London Bridge.

6 July 1535: Execution of Sir Thomas More

Five days ago, Sir Thomas More was found guilty of high treason and was today beheaded at Tower Hill, his head set on London Bridge while his body was buried in the Tower chapel. Hall, who witnessed the execution, said he did not know whether More was 'a foolish wiseman or a wise foolishman'.

As he climbed the scaffold, Sir Thomas asked one of the sheriffs to help him up, saying, 'See me safe up, and as for my coming down, let me shift for myself as well as I can.' The hangman knelt to ask him forgiveness, as custom dictated, and More cheerfully told him, 'Pluck up thy spirits, man, and be not afraid to do thine office: my neck is very short, take heed, therefore, thou strike not awry.'

7 January 1536: Death of the Princess Dowager

Katherine of Aragon died at two o'clock in the afternoon at Kimbolton Castle, aged fifty years. Before Christmas she had suffered violent stomach pains after drinking some Welsh beer, but seemed recovered; however, on 26 December the pains returned, stopping her from sleeping. Since then she had been unable to eat or drink, becoming so weak she could neither stand nor sit up in her bed, and was only cheered by the arrival of a friend from her youth, Maria de Salinas. She had gained entrance by the subterfuge of saying she had fallen from her horse and needed aid. Helped in, she stole away from her rescuers into Katherine's chamber.

Chapuys, with licence from the king, arrived before dinner on 2 January. For four days, he talked with her for two hours every afternoon, easing her frets about her daughter, how little the Pope and emperor had done for her, and lastly whether her obstinacy had caused the break with Rome and the deaths of so many good men. Reassured she was recovering after she seemed more cheerful, and had even laughed two or three times and slept well, Chapuys left.

On Twelfth Night, Katherine had managed to comb and tie her hair without help, but about an hour after midnight she began again to be unwell. At daybreak, after Mass and the sacrament, she prayed to God to pardon the king the wrong he had done her. She refused to make a will, saying a wife could not do so legally while her husband was alive, but asked the physician to write a little billet requesting rewards for her servants, to be buried in a convent of St Francis – she was unaware that none remained in England – and asking Henry to allow Mary to have her furs and a collar with a cross she had brought with her from Spain.

29–30 *January 1536: Funeral of Katherine of Aragon*

The late queen's coffin, covered with gold frieze and a cross of crimson velvet, was placed in a chariot covered in black velvet with a silver cross, drawn by six black-trapped horses. Four banners were carried by the heralds and the four great standards by gentlemen. The chief mourner riding after the chariot as it was conveyed to Peterborough Abbey was Lady Eleanor, daughter of Mary, the king's sister. Seven other lady mourners followed on hackneys, followed by Katherine's ladies and gentlemen, her thirty-six maids and other servants. Met by four bishops and many abbots, the coffin was carried to the eight-pillared hearse with 1,000 candles for the vigil, her device, 'Humble and Loyal', in great gold letters.

Next day, after Mass and an offering of cloth of gold to be turned into 'accoutrements for the chapel', she was buried in a grave at the lowest step of the high altar. There was no hearse at St Paul's. Ralph Sadler had asked whether one should be built as the king's sister had one; the king replied that his sister had been a queen.

30 January 1536: Queen Anne Miscarries

To her sorrow, and the nation's, Queen Anne miscarried a male child, not quite four months. In her great and extreme grief, she consoled her weeping maids. King Henry entered her chamber, 'bewailing and complaining' about the loss of his boy. As she replied in tears, he turned and said that he 'would have no more boys by *her*'.

The court say the queen told the king the miscarriage has been brought on by her terrible fright, and her great love for him, when she was told he and the great horse he was riding at the lists on 25 January had both fallen so heavily that everyone thought it a miracle he had not been killed. Rumourmongers say it was because the king was unkind, dallying with Jane Seymour, to whom, they say, he has lately made great presents.

The queen fears Henry will treat her like Katherine, for many say that she has cried and lamented since hearing of Katherine's death, despite giving the messenger a goodly present at the news.

24 March 1536: Honour Greater than Riches

King Henry, on business in London, sent a letter and a purse full of sovereigns to Greenwich for Mistress Seymour. The young lady kissed the letter and returned it unopened to the messenger. Then, refusing to take the purse, she knelt before him and told him to entreat the king that being well born of honourable parents, she had no greater riches in the world than her honour, which she 'would not injure for a thousand deaths'. If he wished to make her a present of money she would rather it was a gift for when she made an honourable match.

Her actions have made the king love her even more.

The king commanded Thomas Cromwell to give up one of his rooms to the young lady's elder brother, Edward, and his wife to chaperone her. It is a room the king can access through galleries without being seen, but he said he would only converse with her in the presence of her relatives to prove the 'sincerity of his love and the honesty of his views towards her'.

28 April 1536: King Separating from the Queen?
The rumour mill is busy. It says the Bishop of London was asked by the king if he might separate from the queen. The bishop replied that he would be pleased to know the king's own inclination.

2 May 1536: Arrest of the Queen
At the Greenwich Mayday jousts, the king, with only six in his retinue, including Henry Norris, suddenly departed for Westminster. Queen Anne, out of favour with the king since her miscarriage, was subsequently arrested on 2 May and brought from Greenwich to the Tower of London at five o'clock in the evening.

The cannon thundered as she entered in at the court gate. Falling on her knees before the Duke of Norfolk and William Kingston, Constable of the Tower, she swore that she was not guilty of 'her accusement' before they led her to the lodgings she not long ago used during her coronation. She requested the sacrament in the closet by her chamber, saying to Kingston, 'I am as clear from the company of man as for sin, as I am clear from you.' She said her mother would die for sorrow and asked after her brother. Kingston did not reveal to her that George had been arrested earlier in the day.

Mr Henry Norris was also in the Tower, interrogated by the king on the journey to Westminster as to whether the queen had committed adultery with him. He affirmed his and her innocence. William Brereton and Sir Francis Weston, both of the king's privy chamber, and one Mark Smeaton, a musician, were also arrested and committed to the Tower.

Later that night, the queen asked Sir William whether she would die without justice. He told her, 'The poorest subject the King has had justice.'

At that she laughed.

9 May 1536: *The Calais Sword*
King Henry sent to St Omer for the 'Sword of Calais', who, as is the custom in France, uses a sword instead of an axe in beheadings. His arrival is expected on 18 May.

12 May 1536: *Four Found Guilty*
Today, at Westminster, Sir Frances Weston, Henry Norris, William Brereton and Mark Smeaton were arraigned and condemned for high treason against the king due to fornication with Queen Anne and conspiracy over the king's death. Judgement was that they be hanged, drawn and quartered, their members cut off and burnt before them, their heads cut off and bodies quartered.

15 May 1536: *Trial of Queen Anne*
A platform was made in the king's hall in the Tower with benches and seats brought in. Queen Anne, accused of treason against the king's own person, was brought in and seated opposite the Duke of Norfolk, sitting under the cloth of state as high steward representing the king.

To the indictment read out to her, Anne made so wise and discrete answers of her innocence to all the things laid against her, was so eloquent and quick of wit, that had the peers given their verdict according to that of the people assembled who heard her answers, she would have been acquitted.

Notwithstanding, each lord and earl found her guilty and condemned her to either being burnt or beheaded on Tower Green at the king's pleasure.

After her departure, George, her brother, was brought in and charged with incest with his sister against the law of God and nature, treason against the king and for conspiring the king's death. His answers too were so prudent and wise that spectators made wagers he would be found innocent, but all the lords found him guilty.

17 May 1536: 'These bloody days'

All the men accused with Queen Anne were beheaded on the scaffold at Tower Hill. Only Mark Smeaton said ambiguously that he 'deserved' to die. Their bodies and heads were buried within the Tower of London – George within the chapel, the others in the churchyard. The poet Thomas Wyatt, also imprisoned in the Tower, saw their executions and wrote, 'The axe is home, your heads be in the street, the trickling tears doth fall so from my eyes' and, in another work, 'these bloody days have broken my heart'.

That same day, Archbishop Cranmer annulled Henry and Anne's marriage. Now they had never been married, nor had she been queen, and their daughter was bastardised. The people were displeased, for 'it sounds badly in the ears of the public' that King Henry had meanwhile gone out to dine each day, returning one night by river to Greenwich with minstrels singing and musicians playing. A derisive ballad was written about Jane Seymour and the king, much to his anger. In the taverns people said it is no 'proof of adultery that the queen danced with her brother, or that she kissed him, for even the most coy kiss their brothers and it is the custom for young women to write to their relatives when they have become pregnant'.

18–19 May 1536: Execution of Anne

Told on 18 May that it would be another day before the executioner arrived, Queen Anne said she had heard the executioner was very good and she had but a little neck, putting a hand around it. Laughing, she joked that clever people would name her '*la royne Anne sans tete*', translated as Queen Anne Lackhead. Constable Kingston was perturbed at her levity, saying he had seen many men and women executed but that Anne showed 'much joy and pleasure in death'. She spent the night praying with her almoner. Before and after she received the sacrament, on damnation of her soul, she said she had 'never been unfaithful to the king'.

At eight o'clock in the morning, looking composed and beautiful, she was led to the scaffold, with its four or five steps, set up on Tower Green. She wore a crimson kirtle under a black damask robe with a cape, its outer side white. With her own hands she took the netted coif from her head and gave it to one of her ladies, putting on a little cap of linen to cover her hair. Gracefully, she knelt on both knees and prayed for a while. One of her ladies covered her eyes with a bandage. Then they withdrew away a little space while she prayed, 'To Jesu Christ, I commend my soul.'

The sword was hidden under a heap of straw. To distract Anne, the executioner called out, 'Bring me the sword' and as she turned towards his voice, he struck off her head. One of her ladies took up the head, the others the body, and both were covered with a sheet and put into a chest which stood ready and carried into St Peter ad Vincula.

The executioner received for his reward and apparel 100 crowns.

Many lamented her death, for she advanced many learned men and was a great almsgiver.

20 May 1536: Betrothal

Despite trying to keep it secret, King Henry was betrothed at nine o'clock to his sweetheart, Mistress Jane Seymour, who had been lodging in Sir Nicholas Carew's house on the river hardly a mile from Greenwich.

4 June 1536: Queen Jane

At Greenwich Jane was proclaimed queen, going to Whitsunday Mass in procession with a great train of ladies, and dined under a cloth of estate in her chamber of presence. King Henry married her on 30 May in the queen's closet at Whitehall.

The lady is not tall, considered no great beauty, so fair as to be considered pale, past twenty-five years of age with an inclination to be proud and haughty. King Henry, handsome and elegant, though soon to be forty-five years old, was 'graceful in his mien and in his walk'.

7–8 June 1536: Entry to the City

With trumpets blowing, drums and oboes playing, and ships shooting their guns, King Henry and Queen Jane travelled by water from Greenwich to Whitehall Palace. At Radcliffe, Chapuys, who had ardently hated Anne and had always refused to acknowledge her, stood and made an exaggerated reverence to the new queen as she passed. The walls quivered with great streamers and banners as the king and queen disembarked.

The next day, Queen Jane stood in the gatehouse to wave off her husband and his lords as they rode to Westminster in their parliamentary robes. The Earl of Sussex bore the sword before the king, while the king's son, Henry, Duke of Richmond bore his cap of maintenance.

22 July 1536: Death of Duke of Richmond

Henry FitzRoy, Duke of Somerset and Richmond, died at the king's palace of St James, leaving behind a wife, Mary Howard, the Duke of Norfolk's daughter. He was just barely seventeen years of age.

At their wedding, in the first week of December 1533, there had been 'great dancing' in which the late Queen Anne danced with FitzRoy, and Mary Howard with the king, but the pair had been too young to consummate their marriage, so Mary is maid, wife and widow. The Duke of Norfolk made plans to convey the duke's body for burial at Thetford Priory by command of the king.

Thorns of Matrimony: 1536–1547

Now that Anne Boleyn was dead, the king's daughter Mary believed her 'terrible sufferings' were over – although, had her father known that in October 1535 she had treasonously written to Charles V to apply 'a remedy to the affairs of the kingdom', she may have suffered much more. Mary waited for the king to welcome her to court, but the summons did not arrive. She had matched her will against her father's; it had not, after all, simply been 'that woman' she had resisted all those years. Henry now moved to impose his will upon his daughter. In tears, and signing the document without reading it, Mary capitulated, accepting the nullity of the marriage between her father and mother. By August she was in her own household, first lady after the queen, and according to her privy accounts enjoying dancing, coursing with greyhounds, riding and gambling.

The fourth month of Jane and Henry's marriage saw a rising in the north against 'southern heretics and Turks'. The Pilgrimage of Grace began in Lincolnshire and spread to Yorkshire, Durham, Northumberland, Westmorland and Lancashire, the rebels wanting to march to London to ask the king to restore dissolved monasteries and expel evil councillors, specifically Cranmer and Cromwell; so strong was their feeling that they threatened to wrap the latter in a fresh cowhide and set dogs on him. The onset of winter, broken royal promises and executions saw the rebellion abate. The dissolution of the abbeys continued, buildings were demolished, and monks and nuns given pensions. Anne had argued with Cromwell about the money so gathered, asserting that it should be used for schools and education. Cromwell and Henry, on the other hand, were more than happy for it to go into Henry's coffers.

When Queen Jane threw herself on her knees before Henry to beg him to restore the abbeys, he told her to get up and to not, like her predecessor, meddle with his affairs. That frightened her – especially as, just eight days into the marriage, while speaking with the Spanish ambassador, he had remarked of two beautiful young ladies that he wished he had met before he had married. Still, the king indulged Jane's fancy when she soon became pregnant, arranging for dozens of quails to be sent from Flanders and Calais, and it was Jane who gave him his 'most precious jewel', his son Edward, in October 1537. From the moment Edward was born, his household was given very strict instructions to 'avoid all infection, danger of pestilence and contagious disease'. All new clothes were to be washed before the prince wore them, and no one was to be allowed to visit the prince unless they had Henry's 'special token or command'.

Jane passed away twelve days after giving birth, ensuring her legacy as Henry's 'most beloved wife'. After months of mourning, though, court painters were busy painting eligible ladies. Cromwell encouraged Henry to ally himself with the Duke of Cleves, and Holbein painted his daughter, Lady Anne. Henry liked the portrait. They were soon betrothed. Unfortunately, when they met he did not like the woman, complaining all the while about putting his neck into the yoke of marriage. The marital alliance was quickly unpicked.

Seven months later, Anne wisely watched without protest as Henry married his fifth wife, Katheryne Howard, his rose without a thorn. Later, Henry was so enraged by what his council told him of her conduct that he had to be prevented from taking a sword to kill her himself; nonetheless, he had her beheaded, despite her naivety and youth. After her death, Marillac wrote that the king seemed 'very old and grey'. He began using a walking stick to assist his walking.

It was over a year before he took a sixth wife, the twice-widowed, thirty-one-year-old Kateryn Parr. Kind and well educated, she fostered a family atmosphere for Henry and his children. According to Foxe, despite this harmonious family life, Henry considered having his queen arrested for heresy in the summer of 1546. Fortunately, Kateryn explained she had only ventured her opinions against his to both learn from and entertain him to help move his thoughts away from the pain of his ulcerated leg. He decided they were once again 'perfect friends'. Like his first wife, Henry considered Kateryn Parr intelligent and competent enough to leave her as regent when he made a last-gasp attempt to invade France. He and Francis made peace just before he died.

In his will, he named his three children, one after the other, as successors to his crown.

12–14 October 1537: Birth of a Prince

At Hampton Court, on 12 October, St Edward's Eve, at two o'clock in the morning, Queen Jane gave birth to a prince. At the news, *Te Deums* were sung in Paul's and all the other churches of the city, with buffets and fires set up in every street and sounds of guns shooting day and night.

Two days later, the christening was held in Hampton Court chapel. First came the gentlemen, in pairs, bearing unlit touches; then came the children and ministers of the king's chapel, not singing. Then followed esquires, knights, abbots, bishops, and then the king's councillors and officers. A pair of covered basins were carried by the Earl of Sussex; the taper of virgin wax was carried by the Earl of Wiltshire, a towel about his neck. The Earl of Essex carried the gold salt. Lady Elizabeth, bearing the chrisom, was too young to walk and so was carried by Viscount Beauchamp.

The newborn prince, his long train carried by the Earl of Arundel, was carried under a canopy of estate by the Marchioness of Exeter. Lady Mary, being godmother, her train carried by Lady Kingston, joined the godfathers, the Duke of Norfolk and Archbishop Cranmer, at the font; the Duke of Suffolk would be the attendant godfather at the confirmation. As noon pealed, the prince was christened Edward and entitled Duke of Cornwall and Earl of Chester. The torches were lit.

Returning to the palace, Lady Elizabeth, with her sister Mary and Lady Herbert, bore the baby's train as he was taken to the king and queen for their blessing.

24 October–12 November 1537: Queen Jane Dies

After Edward's birth, Queen Jane fell ill of a fever, barely aware of anything going on around her. She died at midnight on 24 October. King Henry had stayed at Hampton Court while she was ill, but at news of her passing he moved to Westminster, leaving the Duke of Norfolk and Sir William Paulet to arrange her funeral.

After embalming, her entrails were interred in the chapel. Two days later, her body was placed in a hearse in her presence chamber. Her ladies and gentlemen kept vigil until All Saints Day, when she was conveyed to the chapel, the Marchioness of Exeter acting as chief mourner in place of Lady Mary, who was too grief-stricken to do so. Vigil was then kept by gentlemen during the night and her ladies during the day for the next ten days.

On 12 November, the coffin was put onto a chariot drawn by six horses for its journey to Windsor Castle, surrounded by banners borne on horseback by lords, themselves assisted by the earls of Sussex, Wiltshire and Surrey and the Duke of Suffolk. Chief mourner Lady Mary followed, her train carried by Lady Jane Rochford. All the way alms were distributed. At Windsor, the long procession of nobles, clergy and ambassadors with heralds was met at the bridge by the mayor and his brethren, their torches lit, and rode with them to the chapel, where a solemn watch was kept.

The next day, after the service and an offering of palls, Queen Jane was solemnly buried.

In response to Francis I's letter of congratulation, King Henry responded that divine providence 'has mingled my joy with the bitterness of death of her who brought me this happiness'.

18 March 1538: Portrait

Holbein, sent by the king to Flanders, has come back with the likeness of Anne of Cleves, with which he is 'singularly pleased'. Courtiers say Henry is in much better humour since he saw it. She is the second daughter of John III of Cleves and descended from the lines of both the kings of England and France. Cromwell was anxious to bring about the marriage as a bulwark against Catholic Francis I and Charles V ever combining forces against England.

3–7 May 1538: Elizabeth Boleyn Dies

After a long illness, Elizabeth, Countess of Wiltshire, sick with a cough that vexed her sorely even before her daughter's execution, died in London at the Abbot of Reading's house. She was conveyed by water to St Mary's Church at Lambeth and buried in the crypt beneath the floor of the Howard Chapel.

2–9 December 1538: *The Exeter Conspiracy*

Arraigned at Westminster Hall and attainted of high treason were some of the king's near kinsmen: his first cousin Lord Henry Courtenay, Marquis of Exeter and Earl of Devonshire, and his second cousins Henry Pole, Lord Montague and his brother Sir Geoffrey Pole. Sir Geoffrey was pardoned but Lords Montague and Courtenay were beheaded and their heads and bodies buried in the Tower's chapel.

Treason was said to be proved by letters between the marquis and Cardinal Reginald Pole in the handwriting of his wife, along with letters from the late Queen Katherine and her daughter. Cromwell said it was clear that the marquis intended to usurp the kingdom by marrying his son to Lady Mary and killing Prince Edward. They were also accused of encouraging Mary in her obstinacy against her father.

6 January 1539: 'naked without a penny'

Court rumour says that King Henry is much enamoured of Christina, Duchess of Milan. He so much likes the look and sound of her that he has said that he would willingly take her 'even if she were delivered to him naked without a penny'. The gossip is that the king has sent a gift of a diamond to her worth 16,000 ducats.

3 March 1539: *Nicholas Carew Executed*

King Henry, persuaded by Cromwell that Sir Nicholas Carew was involved in the Exeter plot the year before, had Carew arrested. He was found guilty of treason on 14 February and beheaded today on Tower Hill. With his last words he thanked the king for granting him time and opportunity to read the Bible in English, having before been staunchly Catholic.

Sir Nicholas had been in the king's household since 1502 when he was six years old and educated alongside him. He was well known for his jousting prowess and had been master of the horse since 1522. In 1514 he married the sister of Sir Francis Bryan, Elizabeth, who had also grown up at court, and they had five children. Elizabeth was also close to the king, who had given her beautiful diamonds and pearls and jewels that once belonged to Katherine of Aragon. Although related to Queen Anne, many believe Carew was behind a number of the rumours about her; after she died he actively championed Princess Mary, to the king's displeasure.

12 March 1539: Earl of Wiltshire Dies

Sir Thomas Boleyn, Earl of Wiltshire died at Hever Castle, aged sixty-two years, and is to be buried in the church of St Peter. In his will, he made provision for all the Ormond lands to go to Lady Elizabeth after his mother dies, and appointed Dr Cranmer as his executor.

28 April 1539: Parliamentary News

In Parliament, the elderly Countess of Salisbury, mother of Lord Montague, was attainted for treason without trial, as were Gertrude, wife of the Marquis of Exeter, and their children. All were committed to the Tower of London, with confiscation of all their goods and lands.

All the religious houses in England, 'suppressed or not suppressed', were granted to the king to the augmentation of his estate forever. Any disagreement by any person concerning the faith as agreed by the king in his Six Articles will offend, and they will be deemed a heretic and burnt without abjuration.

16 May 1539: King Henry's Devotions

Next morning in procession, it being Holy Thursday, Lord Cobham bore the sword of estate before the king as he entered the court at Westminster. The high altar in the chapel was 'garnished with all the apostles upon the altar' and Mass was conducted by 'note and organs playing'. On Good Friday last the king devoutly crept to the cross from the chapel door. His Grace receives holy bread and holy water every Sunday and daily uses all other laudable ceremonies. 'In all London no man dare speak against them on pain of death.'

17 June 1539: Thames Triumph

Before the king's palace at Westminster, two barges were set up with ordnance, guns and darts of reed for a fight to take place between the Bishop of Rome and his cardinals and the king and his men. A viewing platform, covered with canvas and set with green boughs and roses, released rosewater upon the spectators on the leads of his privy stairs and those in barges and boats. Three times, the barges rowed up and down between Westminster Bridge and King's Bridge, shouting defiance and shooting ordnance. On the fourth course they joined together to fight until the Pope and all his cardinals were overcome and thrown into the water.

1 January 1540: Too Impatient to Wait

The king, 'to nourish love', and impatient to see the twenty-four-year-old Anne of Cleves, who was now in England to marry him, decided to travel secretly to Rochester Abbey, with just eight men of his privy chamber. Without being announced, and to her astonishment, Henry strode into her presence. When she realised who he was, she with gracious and loving countenance fell on her knees to welcome him, but he gently raised her, kissed her and spent all afternoon with her. Later, the two supped together.

It was remarked that the dress of their country is so heavy and unbecoming, the ladies would be thought ugly even if they were beautiful. It is certain the king found her not at all to his liking, saying that she was not 'so fair as she has been reported'. Although not as beautiful as affirmed, she is tall and assured in her carriage and demeanour, showing that in her the 'turn and vivacity of wit, supplies the place of beauty'.

6–7 *January 1540: The Marriage*

A little before eight o'clock in the morning, King Henry came solemnly with his lords into the gallery at Greenwich. Dressed in a gold furred gown with great flowers of silver, his coat of embroidered crimson satin tied with great diamonds, the king waited while the lords went to fetch Lady Anne.

She was dressed in a silver gown decorated with large flowers of pearls, made round after the Dutch fashion. Her long, fair, yellow hair hung down her back. A jewelled gold coronal sat on her head set with sprigs of jewelled rosemary. As she came to the king, she made three low curtseys.

The Archbishop of Canterbury received them and they were married. Etched about her wedding ring were the words 'God send me well to keep'.

After the ceremony they went hand in hand to hear Mass and offered their tapers. They then had wine and spices, after which the king departed to his chamber and the queen, with her ladies, departed to hers. Next they dined together. The queen had not changed her attire, but the king now wore a rich tissue gown lined with crimson velvet.

That night at Evensong, the queen wore a sable-furred gown, like a man's, with long narrow sleeves and on her head a lawn cornet covered in pearls and jewels and judged to be of great value. After supper there were banquets and masques.

The next day, solemn jousts were kept and the queen came out, dressed in English fashion with a French hood which suited her face and showed off her beauty. But the king told Cromwell he 'misliked her even more' for after feeling her belly and breasts he was sure she was no maid and demanded a way out of the marriage, bemoaning that he would never have more children.

18 April 1540: New Creation

Thomas, Lord Cromwell was created Earl of Essex and made High Chamberlain of England at Westminster.

10 June 1540: Cromwell Arrested

In the council chamber at Westminster, as the captain of the guard entered to take him prisoner, Thomas Cromwell threw his bonnet to the ground in a temper and said to the king's councillors that 'this was the reward of his services' and appealed to their consciences to decide whether or not he was a traitor. They replied that he should be judged according to the laws he himself had made, when words spoken inadvertently with good intention had constituted high treason. The Duke of Norfolk particularly reproached him and tore the order of St George from around his neck, while the admiral untied his garter.

He was escorted to the Tower, while the king's archers went to his house to inventory his goods and remove those of value to the king's treasury. Several letters written to and from Lutheran lords were taken to the king. So exasperated was he by what he read, the king vowed to remove all the offices and titles of the 'greatest wretch ever born in England' and leave him only Thomas Cromwell, shearman, to be judged as an 'ignoble person'.

9 July 1540: Marriage of Anne and Henry Annulled

The marriage between King Henry and Lady Anne of Cleves was annulled in the chapter house of Westminster Abbey. The evidence from depositions and the confession of Thomas Cromwell led the convocation to agree the marriage was null owing to a precontract between Lady Anne and the Marquis of Lorraine when minors, and also because the king had been unwilling and the marriage remained unconsummated. Lady Anne confirmed 'the integrity of her body' and gave her consent to the judgement, well content to 'use her liberty'. She was given the title of 'king's sister', taking precedence over all ladies except for the king's wife and daughters.

For weeks Henry had complained 'before God he thought she was not his lawful wife'. Ominous words that, nonetheless, have not ended unhappily.

The rumour has been around for days that the king intends to marry one of Anne's maids, the sweet-natured and affectionate Katheryne Howard, daughter of Edmund Howard, a deceased brother of the Duke of Norfolk.

28 July 1540: *King Harry Marries Anew*

The king married petite seventeen-year-old Katheryne Howard privately in the chapel at Oatlands Palace. Situated beside the Thames, it is a pleasant place to marry on such a beautiful summer's day, with its formal walled garden and lovely views over the deer park from the gallery.

28 July 1540: *Thomas Cromwell Executed*

Thomas Cromwell was led from the Tower to be beheaded at Tower Hill. In his speech, he said that he died in the 'Catholic faith of the Holy Church', asked the onlookers to pray for the king and for his son, 'that goodly imp', Prince Edward, to long reign over them. He made his prayer, which was long, and, committing his soul into the hands of God, patiently suffered the ragged strokes of the axe by one who performed the office like a butcher.

Beheaded with Cromwell was forty-nine-year old Lord Walter Hungerford, attainted of sodomy, raping his own daughter and having practised magic to compute the day of the king's death.

4 March 1541: *The King Recovered*

The king has just recovered from a tertian fever and, to his alarm, the sudden closing-up of the ulcer on his leg which the doctors keep open to maintain his health; the last time it happened, he nearly died. His leg often pains him. No longer active as he once was, he still eats and drinks as he did when he was fit, and has grown very stout.

Brooding in his illness, the king lamented the death of Cromwell, saying that 'his councillors made him put to death the most faithful servant he ever had'; that the Privy Council pretended to serve him but only looked to their own profit; that 'he knew the good servants from the flatterers'. As for his subjects, they were 'an unhappy people to govern whom he would shortly make so poor that they would not have the boldness nor the power to oppose him'.

Courtiers say he sat doing nothing, not even enjoying music, and had veered from having one opinion at breakfast to an opposite view after dinner.

10 April 1541: *The Queen* Enceinte?

Queen Katheryne, to the joy of the king, may be with child. He is already saying he will crown her at Whitsuntide. All the embroiderers are employed making furniture and tapestry. The young lords and gentlemen of the court are practising daily for the jousts and tournaments to come.

27 May 1541: *Execution of Countess of Salisbury*

Margaret Pole, Countess of Salisbury, was at seven o'clock this morning executed at the Tower. When given the sentence of death, she asked of what crime she had been accused. She was told she had corresponded treasonably with her sons, including Cardinal Reginald Pole.

The sixty-seven-year-old daughter of the Duke of Clarence and niece of King Edward IV walked towards the space in front of the Tower to where the small block stood, no scaffold having been erected. Standing in prayer, she was told to make haste and place her neck on the block. Complying, she did. The usual headman had been sent north. The young lad appointed in his place, wretched and blundering, hacked her head and shoulders to pieces. Thus was killed the close friend of Katherine of Aragon and the godmother and governess of Lady Mary.

19 June 1541: *King of Ireland*

In Dublin, King Henry was proclaimed King of Ireland after a bill was put forward in the Irish Parliament and joyously accepted by both houses.

30 June–24 October 1541: *The Long Progress*

Instead of the normal summer progress, King Henry hoped to meet with his nephew the King of Scotland in York. He set off with between 4,000 and 5,000 horse and 2,000 tents, and had packed his richest tapestry, plate and dress for himself and his archers, pages and gentlemen. The king had also sent ahead artillery and munitions as he intended visiting areas where there had been uprisings.

The weather, which had been dry, turned dreadful with incessant rain, flooding all the roads north, bogging down carts and baggage in mud. That, and Queen Katheryne feeling unwell, delayed the progress by a month. Forced into a leisurely progress, on passing any town he had never visited, such as Stamford, the king would stop. Without any other solemnity than having the street to his lodging decorated, and with citizens allowed to greet him in ordinary clothes, he entered, mounted on a great horse, with all the noble lords in front, two by two, with sixty of his great archers behind. They were followed by the queen, his daughter Lady Mary and their ladies.

Reaching Lincoln on Tuesday 9 August, the king and queen, in a tent set up for them, changed their green and crimson velvet attire for cloth of gold for the king and cloth of silver for the queen. They remounted, and as the train came in sight, church bells all over the city rang as they made their way to the cathedral. There they kissed the crucifix and listened to the *Te Deum*. The following day the king rode to the castle to walk around it and from its ramparts viewed the city.

On Friday, the king and queen departed for Gainsborough Hall, staying for two or three days. On the way to Pontefract, one of the finest castles in England, they tarried for five or six days at Hatfield for sport on the ponds and marshes. With boats on the water, and guns and bows on land, two hundred stags and does were slain, a great quantity of swans, pikes and other fish and two boats' worth of river birds. At supper, the king pointed out from his tent the two or three hundred stags that were as near the company as if they were cattle. The deer were shared among the gentlemen of the country.

While Henry moved between the great houses around York, he sent 1,200 workmen to refurbish an old abbey for his lodging. Night and day they repaired, refurbished, painted, hung tapestries and erected tents and pavilions.

King Henry made his state entry into York on 18 September and stayed nine days, but after his nephew's failure to appear he returned south, reaching Hampton Court on 24 October.

1 November 1541: Queen Katheryne Accused

The queen, at Hampton Court, was put under house arrest and interrogated by Archbishop Cranmer who said her state was such 'it would have pitied any man's heart to see'. She was accused by him firstly of dissolute living before her marriage with one of her relatives, Francis Dereham, and of continuing with the association since her marriage to the king, having employed him as one of her secretaries and usher of her privy chamber. Secondly, she was accused of concurrently having an affair with Thomas Culpepper, one of the gentlemen of the king's privy chamber, and having given him a chain and a rich cap on Maundy Thursday.

A witness statement says Thomas was brought twice by Lady Rochford to her chamber at Lincoln in August, and on another night they were together from eleven o'clock at night until four o'clock in the morning, and that there had been assignations at other times, in Pontefract, York and Greenwich, contrived by the queen's lady-in-waiting, Lady Jane Rochford, wife of the attainted traitor George Boleyn.

13–14 November 1541: *The Queen Confesses*

Queen Katheryne's staff still at Hampton Court were discharged by Sir Thomas Wriothesley. He called all her ladies, gentlewomen and servants into the great chamber to tell them of 'certain offences that she had done in misusing her body'. The queen was conveyed to the late nunnery of Sion with Lady Baynton and two other gentlewomen and certain servants to wait on her until the king's further pleasure. Her jewels were removed, and she was allowed only dresses 'without stone or pearl'. Lady Rochford, meanwhile, was sent to the Tower.

In her confession, the queen admitted that when she was around fourteen years of age she had slept with Francis Dereham. However, she did not believe they were as husband and wife because what Dereham did was 'by force' and 'our company ended almost a year before' the marriage of the king to Anne of Cleves. She was sorry she had not grace to consider how 'great a fault it was' for she had 'intended ever during my life to be faithful and true' to the king. As for Thomas Culpepper, she spoke with him once at the stair head at Lincoln late at night, another time in her bedchamber at Pontefract and once in Lady Rochford's chamber in York. Nor had he touched 'any bare of her but her hand'. She had asked Lady Rochford to desist from encouraging him and was answered, 'You must give men leave to look for they will look upon you.'

10 December 1541: Culpepper and Dereham Executed

Thomas Culpepper and Francis Dereham, both arraigned at Guildhall ten days ago for high treason, were drawn from the Tower to Tyburn. Culpepper, standing on the ground by the gallows, asked the people to pray for him, then knelt and had his head stricken off. Dereham, less favoured by the king, was 'hanged, membered, bowelled, headed and quartered'. Both their heads were set on London Bridge.

22 December 1541: Howard Arraignments

In the King's Bench at Westminster, numerous members of the Howard family were condemned to lose their goods and their bodies to perpetual imprisonment. Among them were Lord William Howard, brother to the Duke of Norfolk; his wife, Lady Margaret; and Anne Howard, wife of Henry Howard, brother to the late queen.

25–29 January 1542: Parliamentary and Court News

The chancellor announced the queen's misdeeds to the Lords, who found her and Lady Rochford guilty of high treason, which was agreed by the Commons. To facilitate the execution of Lady Rochford, who has been periodically mad since her arrest, the king had a statute passed 'for proceeding against lunatics who before their insanity had confessed themselves guilty of high treason'. Agnes, the Dowager Duchess of Norfolk, and her daughter, Lady

Bridgewater, are sentenced to perpetual imprisonment and the loss of all their property.

Marillac, the French ambassador, said that people would like Anne of Cleves restored; she is said to be 'half as beautiful again since she left court'.

The king, showing himself merry on 29 January, gave a supper and banquet with twenty-six ladies at his table. The ladies for whom he showed the greatest regard were the Lord Cobham's pretty sister Elizabeth Brooke, whom Wyatt repudiated for adultery, and Anne Basset, daughter of Lady Lisle and niece of Anthony Browne.

10–13 February 1542: Execution of Katheryne Howard

During the afternoon of 10 February, Queen Katheryne was forced into a small, covered barge for her removal from Sion to the Tower. While she had been at Sion, the queen had neither eaten nor drank much, weeping and crying like a madwoman. Anything she could use to kill herself had been removed. On arrival at the Tower, the lords in their great barge landed first, then the Duke of Suffolk from his barge, then the queen in black velvet. They paid her reverence as they did when she reigned. In her lodging since she has wept, cried and tormented herself miserably without cease.

On Sunday evening, when told she had to prepare herself to die next morning, she asked for the block to be brought to her so she could see how best to place herself, permission for which was granted.

Just before nine o'clock, in front of lords and gentlemen, Katheryne was brought out of the Tower. She was so weak she could hardly speak but confessed she had merited a hundred deaths for offending the king who had so graciously treated her. She was beheaded with the axe. Her ladies covered her body with a black cloak and carried it into the Tower chapel. Lady Rochford, who had regained her wits, was beheaded immediately after.

A new law has now been passed that if any king should wish to marry a subject, the lady will be bound, on pain of death, to declare if any charges of misconduct can be brought against her.

1 October 1542: O'Neill Created Earl of Tyrone

Conn O'Neill was created Earl of Tyrone at Greenwich with remainder to his son, Matthew, and his heirs male. The bishops who came with him renounced the Pope and accepted their benefices from the king.

25 November–31 December 1542: Kindness for Unkindness

The 18,000 Scots who crossed the River Esk to enter England, intent on taking Carlisle, were instead beaten by Sir Thomas Wharton and others at the Battle of Solway Moss. Many were slain, the ordnance and artillery taken, and many fighters taken prisoner, among them Scottish lords who were sent under guard to be lodged richly in the Tower of London. Meanwhile, at Linlithgow Palace in Scotland, Queen Mary of Guise was delivered early of a baby girl on 3 December. The baby was christened Mary.

On 14 December, King James V died; some said wounds from the battlefield killed him, others the grief and sickness of defeat. A week later, the Scottish king's earls and lords in London were given new furred black damask gowns, coats of black velvet and satin doublets and shirts. They were taken to appear in the Star Chamber, where it was declared that though King Henry had cause of war against them for their 'traitorous invasions without defiance', he would show them kindness for unkindness, and right for wrong. They were then lodged with lords and gentlemen.

Afterwards, with news of the Scottish king's death, the Scottish earls and lords were brought to Greenwich on St John's Day, going with King Henry to the chapel, and lodged there until 30 December when they were allowed to depart and ride north.

17 June 1543: Treaty of Marriage

A treaty of marriage has been concluded between Prince Edward, now in his sixth year, and Mary, Queen of Scotland, now in her first year, as agreed with the Scottish Commissioners on 4 May.

12 July 1543: Queen Kateryn

Lady Kateryn, widow of Lord Latimer and sister of Lord Parr, was proclaimed queen after she married the king at Hampton Court in an upper oratory called the queen's privy closet. The ceremony was conducted by Stephen Gardiner, Bishop of Winchester in the presence of many of the king's council, his daughters Mary and Elizabeth, and his niece Margaret Douglas among others. The queen gave a gift to Mary on the day of a pair of gold bracelets set with rubies.

Courtiers already report that the new queen is wise, virtuous and gentle, and that King Henry could never have 'a wife more agreeable to his heart than she'. She is petite, with hazel eyes, gold-auburn hair and the fair complexion that goes with such colouring.

3 August 1543: Proclamation of War

Charles V and King Henry are joined in open war on the French king as a mortal enemy to them and all Christian princes for his alliance with the Great Turk.

12–17 February 1544: Visit of the Duke of Nagera

On Tuesday 12 February, hearing that the Spanish Duke of Nagera was in London, King Henry travelled a league away to view some ships being built. In his stead, he sent the Earl of Surrey with his compliments. On Sunday, Queen Kateryn's brother, Lord William, with Henry, Earl of Surrey dined with the duke and then accompanied him by water to the king's palace at Westminster.

They passed through three halls hung with tapestry, in the second of which, on either side, stood the king's bodyguard dressed in red and armed with halberds. The third led them through the nobles, knights and gentlemen to the chair of state, to which all present paid reverence.

The duke was, after quarter of an hour, called into the king's chamber. Two of his retinue were allowed to enter with him but no one else was allowed to even see the king. After a short audience the duke came out and was accompanied to the queen's chamber. With her were the king's daughter, Mary, and Margaret, daughter of the Queen of Scotland. The queen, dignified and commanding respect, wore a kirtle of brocade under an open robe of cloth of gold, its sleeves lined with crimson satin, trimmed with crimson velvet. Her train was more than two yards long. Her headdress was jewelled, and suspended from her neck she wore two crosses and a jewel of rich diamonds.

After kissing the queen's hand, the duke was conducted to a chamber for music and dancing. First the queen danced gracefully with her brother, followed by Mary and Margaret dancing together, and then afterwards with gentlemen. One gentleman of the king's household danced galliards with 'extraordinary agility'. After several hours, the queen offered gifts to the duke, who kissed her hand. He would have likewise kissed Mary's hand but she offered her lips which he kissed, and then those of all the other ladies present. Then all departed, the queen withdrawing into her own chamber.

3–7 May 1544: Oath-breaking Scots

Despite their promises, the Scots went marauding into England, laying waste to the country. In response, King Henry sent a great army by land and sea. Edward Seymour, Earl of Hertford was in charge of the army and Lord Admiral John Dudley, Viscount Lisle sailed with 200 ships to the Firth, landing on 3 May for the two forces to unite and march to Leith, the admiral at the front and the Earl of Shrewsbury with the rearward.

Between Leith and Edinburgh they were met by 6,000 Scots horse and foot along a brook, with ordnance laid in two straits that the army would have to pass through, effectively blocking their passage. The English fought 'so boldly' that the Scots suddenly fled, leaving their artillery behind them; the nobles were first to fly.

That night, the Provost of Edinburgh came to the English camp and offered the keys on condition they might leave with bag and baggage and for the town not to be fired. The earl replied that the army would not be there if the Scots had not kept breaking their promises and demanded the keys be yielded without condition and that every man, woman and child issue out into the fields. If not, he would put them all to the sword and fire the town. Spiritedly, the provost replied, 'It were better for them to stand to their defence'. Forthwith, the van was set forward and English gunners set on the gates. The English entered Edinburgh that same night.

Next day the town was fired and burnt for two days. Then every house in Leith was burnt. As the army returned to England, every fortress and village they passed was destroyed.

14 July–30 September 1544: *Siege of Boulogne*

Leaving his wife as regent, and she and his son at Hampton Court, King Henry left to invade France in a coordinated attempt with Charles V. The king landed at Calais from Dover at four o'clock in the afternoon of 14 July. With him was an army of 30,000 men. He split his force into two, with one part, led by the Duke of Norfolk and Lord Russell, sent to besiege the town of Muttrell; the other, led by the Duke of Suffolk and the Earl of Arundel, set up camp on a hill east of Boulogne.

Seven days later, King Henry encamped on the north side of the town and 'sore assaulted' it with great ordnance, ordering the undermining of the castle, tower and walls, until not one house was left whole. The town surrendered on 13 September and the king graciously allowed soldiers and townsfolk to pass to safety with bag and baggage. More than 4,000 took up the offer, leaving behind them a great number of elderly, sickly and wounded.

The king made a state entry into the town on 18 September, his sword borne before him by the Marquis of Dorset, with trumpeters on the walls heralding his arrival. Two days later he rode within the walls all around the town. He ordered the church of Our Lady of Boulogne pulled down and a mount built in its place for the greater strength of the town. Did he recall that day of 29 December 1527 when he had given Anne Boleyn a diamond brooch of our Lady of Boulogne as a play on her name?

In the meantime, Charles V, without warning the king, made peace with the King of France. On hearing of this, Henry promptly broke up his army and returned to England, arriving at midnight on 30 September.

6–28 July 1545: *The French Armada*

Spies sent out by King Henry alerted him to plans by Francis I to send his whole armada – 300 ships and twenty-four galleys – from Dieppe and Newhaven to disembark soldiers on the south coast and the Isle of Wight while a land army harasses Boulogne. By 14 July, the king had arrived at Portsmouth to oversee the defence of his realm. Four days later, twenty-two French galleys anchored at St Helen's Point off the Isle of Wight, facing Portsmouth Haven with over 100 sail in sight behind them, landed 2,000 men. The calm weather was advantageous to the galleys, which came abroad at every tide, complacently shooting their ordnance at the becalmed English fleet.

Without warning a gale arose. As the waves rose the galleys could 'not endure the rage of the seas'. English ships, at last under sail, set out towards them shooting. At shipmasters' directions, the English fleet was told to sail directly towards the French ships, forcing them to loose anchors so that, with the 'strainable wind' from the west, they would not be able to reach the Isle of Wight again. As the English ships manoeuvred, the *Mary Rose*, laden with much ordnance and with low ports left open, turned and the water entered her. She suddenly sank. All the men, save forty, were drowned including Captain Sir George Carew.

Despite the loss of the *Mary Rose*, so many Frenchmen were slain or driven back into the sea and drowned that by 24 July the coast was clear of Frenchmen. The French navy departed eastwards, but with the beacons fired the men of the counties came to the coast so thick that the French could not land anywhere; wherever they sailed they saw men ever ready to receive them. Eventually, they had to return to France.

1–7 August 1545: Recovery of the Mary Rose

Shipwrights have written to King Henry to tell him that they have looked at how to recover the *Mary Rose*. So far the sails and sailyards have been laid on land. Three cables with engines could be tied to her masts to weigh her up and on every side a hulk placed to try to set her upright. If this is done, and water and ordnance can be discharged, she will be gradually brought nearer the shore. Before it can take place, however, she must be emptied of all her victuals, ordnance and ballast, and using three of the greatest hulks of the fleet could weaken the navy.

22 *August 1545: Death of the Duke of Suffolk*

Charles Brandon, Duke of Suffolk and Lord Great Master of the king's household, a valiant captain in the king's wars in Scotland, France and Ireland, champion jouster and the king's closest friend, died at Guildford at four o'clock in the afternoon. His second wife, Katherine, and his daughters, Frances and Eleanor, were at his bedside.

Although in his will he asked to be buried in Tattershall Church in Lincolnshire, the king has decreed his friend is to be buried with full honours in Windsor Castle's St George's Chapel.

13 *June 1546: Peace with France*

On Whitsunday, universal peace with France was proclaimed. A *Te Deum* was sung in St Paul's. This was followed by a solemn procession of all the crosses and banners of the parish churches in London. The children of St Paul's led the procession out of the north door of the cathedral with two crosses, followed by choirs, heralds and the bishop, mayor and aldermen of London. They passed through Cheap, St Michael's, Cornhill and Leadenhall, eventually re-entering the cathedral by the west door. In the treaty, King Henry agreed to restore Boulogne to the French upon payment of 800,000 crowns within the next eight years.

23–28 *August 1546: First Public Appearance*

Prince Edward met the Lord Admiral of France, Claude d'Annebaut, 3 miles outside of Hampton Court to ride with him to the palace. With the prince was a retinue of lords and gentlemen in velvet coats and 1,000 yeomen in new liveries, all on horseback. They formed a path for the ambassador to ride through until he reached the prince.

The following day, the ambassador was brought to the king's presence and dined at his table. Every day there was banqueting and hunting, and every night rich masques with the queen and her ladies, with dancing in two new banqueting houses with rich cupboards of gold plate set with jewels and pearls that glowed richly in the light.

26 September 1546: Book Burning

A multitude of New Testaments by Tyndale and Coverdale, and other books by Frith, Wycliffe, Dr Barnes and Turner, were burnt at Paul's Cross by the king's command.

12 December 1546: Arrests

Arrested at the Lord Chancellor's place in Holborn, the Duke of Norfolk was conveyed by water to the Tower and committed to the Beauchamp Tower while his son Henry, the poet-earl, was escorted by the captain of the guard through the City of London, to the noisy sorrow of the citizens. At Kenninghall in Norfolk, the king's agents searched and seized all of the duke's goods, including the clothes of Bess Holland, who had lived openly with him as his mistress for the last twenty years. In her chamber they found girdles, rosaries, gold buttons and jewelled rings. They also seized her house in Suffolk. Furthermore, the agents confirmed they had searched the Duchess of Richmond's chamber, coffers and closet, which were bare, her jewels and clothes having been sold to pay her debts. The two women are being sent to London.

19 January 1547: Execution of the Earl of Surrey

After he and his father were arraigned at the Guildhall and found guilty of high treason four days previously, the Earl of Surrey was led out of the Tower today and beheaded on the scaffold at Tower Hill. He was buried at All Hallows Church on Tower Street.

Born in 1517, Surrey was close friends with the king's son Henry FitzRoy, having been brought up with him. They travelled and wrote poetry together. The earl had been found guilty of planning to usurp the crown from Prince Edward, treasonously quartering his arms (legitimately but perhaps not wisely) with the royal arms, and planning to entice the king to take his sister, Mary, as his mistress, even though she is his daughter-in-law. The duke was accused of turning a blind eye to his son's activities.

28 January 1547: Death of King Henry

Today, at two o'clock in the morning, the king yielded his spirit to God at his manor of Whitehall. To the question whether he wanted a 'learned man' to speak with, the king replied he would like Dr Cranmer but would sleep a little first. He died holding Cranmer's hand, having lost the power to speak.

KING EDWARD VI
1547–1553

In his will, Henry VIII tried to safeguard his nine-year-old son's minority by setting up a Privy Council of sixteen people of 'like and equal charge'. Yet before Henry was buried, Edward's uncle Edward Seymour, Earl of Hertford and later Duke of Somerset, was proclaimed Lord Protector and 'governor' of the king. John Dudley was meanwhile created Earl of Warwick and Thomas Seymour became Baron Seymour of Sudeley and Lord Admiral, but the latter, also being uncle to the king, was resentful at being granted so little.

While one brother schemed to his execution – attempting first to marry Lady Mary or Elizabeth before settling for sweeping Kateryn Parr off her feet and clandestinely marrying her with King Edward's consent, secured with treats and money – the other offended the Privy Council with his arrogance and 'snappish conduct', upsetting nobles and gentry for being 'desirous to please the most than the best' and made his nephew resent him for being too strict and treating him like a little boy. Neither brother heeded any advice.

King Edward was clever and well read. His schooling began when he was six years old with lessons in philosophy, logic and languages including Latin, Greek, Italian and French. He read Cicero and Aristotle, as well as Holy Scripture. Roman and Greek classics and poems alongside religious books abounded in his library, together with the voyages of a citizen of Venice, the chronicle of Edward Hall printed in 1548 and the *Book of Chronicles*, written in Hebrew, Greek and Latin. A visiting Italian said that Edward worked hard and had 'an amiable sweetness with a real eagerness to learn'. Edward wrote his own chronicle, adding notes of things that concerned him or decisions he had to make, and a treatise he referred to as 'his own arguments against the pope's supremacy', begun in December 1548 and finished the following March.

In the 'Loseley Manuscripts' we get a glimpse of his lighter side. He took part in the play *The Story of Orpheus* with his friends the young Duke of Suffolk and Lord Strange at his coronation celebrations; at Christmas 1551 at Greenwich he 'authored' a theatrical combat using mask heads, enacted with his father's fool, William Somer; and he also enjoyed exchanging letters with his 'sweet sister, Temperance', for he and Elizabeth shared interests and intellect.

In his diary, Edward followed his uncle's martial progress in Scotland in September 1547, known as the 'rough wooing', showing a fair understanding of events. He also recorded activities he thoroughly enjoyed: military events, ship launches, swordplay, shooting challenges and musters of a newly devised 'gendarmery' are all mentioned, and one sees the boy behind the king. He never revealed his deeper feelings, leading some people to conclude he was cold and unemotional. Yet in August 1551, an ambassador noted that the king had 'secluded himself because of his shock and surprise at the death of his friend the Duke of Suffolk, for the king loved him dearly'. No mention of his deep grief appears in his diary. Self-contained perhaps, but Edward was neither uncaring nor unfeeling. He wisely kept his emotions to himself.

Edward was England's first Protestant monarch. He believed God had put him on the throne to direct religious reform in his realm and eliminate superstition. Roods and images were removed from churches, the veneration of saints ended, and Holy Communion replaced the Mass, contributing to the unrest to come. The year of 1549 was one of general discontent. Rising prices and unemployment caused much hardship. In the West Country, during the summer the commons dismantled enclosures. The dissent spread to the counties around London, culminating in Kett's Rebellion in Norfolk and Suffolk, the latter being brutally put down by the Earl of Warwick. Using his popularity with the nobles, Warwick tried to clip the power of Lord Protector Somerset but his nephew defended him.

In August 1549, Edward wrote to his sister, Mary, requesting that she use the Book of Common Prayer. At the beginning of 1551, when Edward realised Mary was openly defying him, he wrote again to her, saying that if one of her servants openly disregarded her orders she would be angry, adding in his own hand that it was his duty to God to see the laws carried out without exception. His diary recorded their dispute in open court. The conflict between them continued unresolved and Mary carried on defying him because, she said, he was still a minor. The emperor's ambassador described Edward at the time as 'quick with a ready and well-developed mind, remarkably so for his age'. Mary ignored the fact that Edward was, by then, making decisions and signing documents in his own right.

That summer saw Edward's first true progress, visiting places other than his palaces. He wrote to his close friend Barnaby Fitzpatrick that while he in France had been 'occupied in killing of your enemies, in long marchings, in pained journeys, in extreme heat, in sore skirmishing and divers assaults, we have been occupied in killing of wild beasts in pleasant journeys, in good fare, in viewing of fair countries and rather have sought how to fortify our own than to spoil another man's'. In another letter about his visit to Portsmouth he wrote the bulwarks were well fortified but 'ill fashioned, ill flanked and set in unmeet places', leaving the town weaker than it ought to be; to make the town stronger, he had devised two strong castles on either side of the haven.

The antipathy between Somerset and Warwick, now Duke of Northumberland, had grown so great that October 1551 saw a second plot by Northumberland, which led to Somerset's execution in January 1552.

A year later, while at Whitehall, the young king fell sick. He never regained his health, and towards the end he prayed to die.

2–16 February 1547: *Funeral of King Henry VIII*

On 2 February, King Henry's lead-coffined corpse was moved to the six-pillared, railed hearse built in the chapel at Whitehall. Inside the rails were seats for twelve mourners to keep vigil day and night while a herald stood at the west end in the black-swathed chapel desiring people to pray for him.

At about ten in the morning on 14 February, the coffin was placed in a chariot for its journey to St George's Chapel at Windsor, with an overnight stop planned at Sion. The chief mourner was the Marquis of Dorset. The king's waxen effigy with imperial crown on a black satin nightcap was placed on top of the coffin, the gold collar of the Garter glowing against the ermined crimson velvet robe, under which was a gold-embroidered crimson doublet, scarlet hose and crimson velvet shoes. Jewelled gold bracelets encircled his wrists and his gloved hands had several diamond rings on the fingers. A sword was laid down the length of his side. In his right hand he held his sceptre, in his left the orb.

At the third sounding of trumpets, at six o'clock in the morning of 15 February, the chariot was drawn by eight great black-trapped horses and the 4-mile cortege set off on roads swept and widened. They arrived at the west door of St George's Chapel at one o'clock in the afternoon, received by the bishops of Winchester, London and Ely in full robes along with all the king's singing men. Sixteen yeomen carried the vast coffin into the thirteen-pillared hearse prepared in the middle of the choir, over the vault that held Queen Jane. There, in state, it remained all night.

The Communion of the Trinity began at four o'clock the next day, performed by the sub-deans of Windsor and the king's chapel, after which the chief mourner offered gold and the king's hatchments. Four gentlemen ushers removed the pall, while six knights removed the effigy into the vestry. Then the sixteen strong yeomen, using five strong linen cloths, lifted the coffin and lowered it gently into the vault next to his wife. The king's officers, after breaking their staves in three above their heads, cast them into the grave.

19–20 *February 1547: Coronation of King Edward VI*

King Edward, on Saturday 19 February, left the Tower to make his progress through the city of London to Westminster. He was a shimmering, shining figure in a rich cloth of silver gown with gold damask embroidery, with a sable-furred square cape over a white velvet jerkin flecked with rubies, diamonds and true lovers' knots of pearls and a silver-embroidered doublet covered with pearls. In stark contrast with his red hair, the grey-eyed king wore a white velvet cap ornate with jewels and pearls. On his feet were white velvet buskins. In comparison his horse was caparisoned in gold-embroidered crimson satin.

So the huge crowds could better see him, Edward stayed a little in front of his canopy. The streets had been newly gravelled and railed on one side for safety, and decorated with tapestry, arras, streamers and banners. Riding a little in front of him was his uncle the Duke of Somerset, followed by the Marquis of Dorset carrying Edward's sword of estate before him. Behind him was his master of horse, Anthony Browne, leading nine henchmen, all bareheaded and wearing cassocks parted in the middle, one half gold, one half silver. The men of arms, holding poleaxes, came after, then the guard, five in a rank, on foot bearing halberds. The conduits in Cornhill and Cheap were running with 'music, song and wine'; in the space of six hours, the latter had been 'with great diligence fetched away'.

At his first pageant in Cornhill, Edward received from four children the gifts of Grace, Nature, Fortune and Charity. The pageant, near Cheap, had an upper storey of suns, stars and clouds, and one hanging cloud of white sarcenet fringed with gold-rayed silk stars, from which a phoenix descended onto a mound of red and white roses among gillyflowers and hawthorn boughs next to an elderly crowned lion. Onto the stage bounded a juvenile lion, which was crowned by two angels, while both old lion and phoenix unobtrusively disappeared. At another pageant, a golden fleece was guarded by two bulls and a serpent, casting flames of fire from their mouths, but at the Standard in Cheap there were only trumpets blowing instead of the planned pageant.

At the Cross, the Mayor of London and his aldermen presented the king with a purse of 1,000 marks of gold, for which he thanked them. St George in full armour at the Little Conduit had barely time to give his speech in English before his grace moved on; the speech in Latin remained unsaid.

Then Edward's attention was snagged by a man laid face-down on a rope stretching from the battlements of St Paul's steeple to a ship's anchor by the dean's house. As Edward stopped, the man spread out his arms and legs and slid down the rope 'as swift as an arrow out of a bow'. Landing lightly, he crossed to the king, kissed his foot and walked back up the rope, tumbling and jumping from one leg to another. As he lingered to watch the man's acrobatics, hanging from one ankle and capering up and down the tightrope, the king held up his train 'a good space of time' before moving to Temple Bar and finally to Westminster.

Next morning, around nine o'clock, the king proceeded to the abbey, dressed in a crimson velvet robe, his long, powdered, ermine-furred train carried by the Earl of Warwick. He was preceded by nobles carrying his spurs, St Edward's Staff and three unsheathed swords. His uncle, Edward Seymour, carried the crown and his friend Henry, Duke of Suffolk carried his gold ball and cross, while Henry Grey, Marquis of Dorset carried the sceptre.

At the abbey he was first conducted to St Edward's Chair, and sat a while before moving to his own throne: a great chair covered in white damask, with two pillars topped with gold lions at the back. Two large cushions – one black, one gold – provided comfort. Once seated, Edward, so everyone could see him, was carried all around the abbey and up to the High Altar. While he lay on the black velvet cushion before the altar, prayers were said over him. Organs played, and pardon was given for all manner of offences as the king changed his attire. A lawn shirt went under a coat of squirrel-furred crimson satin, tied on either shoulder with ribbon, over crimson velvet breeches and hose. A gold coif with crimson satin cap of estate was placed on his head. Lying once again on the cushion, the Archbishop of Canterbury unlaced Edward's coat and shirt and anointed him with holy oil, after which he donned his third coronation outfit, a crimson satin hooded robe with a long train.

Back at the high altar, Edward offered the sword he was wearing while his regalia was blessed. Sat on the throne, trumpets blowing, the archbishop and his uncle crowned him with three crowns, one after the other: St Edward's Crown, the imperial crown of the realm, and his own. This last gold crown, made for him, was set with a sapphire worth £60, a diamond worth £200, an emerald worth £13, four rubies costing £43 and thirteen smaller diamonds and seventy pearls; the whole cost £429 11s. After the kiss of homage on the king's left cheek and completion of the Mass,

Edward again retired, reappearing in an ermine-furred purple velvet robe with a train.

Edward ate dinner in Westminster Hall, keeping his crown on his head. At the serving of the second course, Sir Edward Dymock rode into the hall in white and gilded armour on a richly trapped horse and 'cast his gauntlet' against any man that did not take Edward for 'right king of this realm'. The king drank to him and gave him a cup of gold. After dubbing forty Knights of the Bath, he finally left for his palace to rest before participating in the sumptuous banquet that night. Celebrations continued with jousts in Greenwich Park, banquets and the dubbing of fifty-five Knights of the Carpet.

2–29 *September 1547: The Rough Wooing*

To force the Scots to honour their agreement to send Queen Mary to the English court to grow up with her betrothed, King Edward, the Duke of Somerset went north with a 20,000-strong army – 6,000 of them cavalry – which arrived at Berwick on 2 September. On their arrival, Lord Admiral Edward Clinton was immediately ordered to take his fleet of thirty-five warships out to sea. They were trailed by thirty vessels carrying extra victuals and ordnance. The soldiers, having been allowed to rest for a day, crossed the Peaths, destroying castles on their route, camping on the 8th near Salt Preston. From there, the admiral was ordered to move his fleet to take station opposite Musselburgh, where the army camped on the 9th.

The Scots and English armies were now only 2 miles from each other. Both camps could see each other from the high ground. Both had the sea to the north, Fawside Brae to the south. As the Duke of Somerset, Earl of Warwick and captains viewed the Scottish camp, they perceived the strong position of Regent Arran's huge host: a great marsh to their right, their front defended by the steep-sided River Esk overlooked by field pieces and musketeers.

On 10 September, called by the Scots Black Saturday, Somerset had his army moving before eight in the morning. As they advanced, he was amazed to see that Arran, leaving his strong, defensible position, had crossed the river and was arrayed in front of them, obviously hoping to attack the English camp first. His force was soon stopped in its tracks by artillery from Lord Clinton's fleet.

The Scottish army moved towards Fawside Brae only to find the English, under cover of night, had already installed several field pieces on the summit, which they now brought to bear. In the end, they took up position in a ploughed field where a great ditch divided them from the English.

Undeterred by the sloughs and ridges, Lord Grey led the attack. Fighting fiercely, the Scots managed to grab hold of the English royal standard, severely wounding Lord Grey in the mouth. As the English foot began retreating in disorder, the cavalry made a stand and set upon the Scots afresh. The footmen turned and attacked with fresh courage and ferocity. The bewildered Scots took flight, throwing away weapons and their jackets. Many were overtaken, and very few spared, so that thousands of bodies littered the ground all the way up to the walls of Edinburgh.

That night, after bodies were stripped and plunder taken, the English pitched camp for the night on Pinkie Cleugh, beside Pinkie Slough. The following day the army moved towards Leith while the English fleet swept the sea of all Scottish vessels and stayed behind to assault various towns and set up a network of garrisons. On 17 September, word was given to the army for the tents to be struck. The march back to the borders began in the light of the red flames of Leith and its ships in the harbour. The army recrossed the Tweed on 29 September.

17 November 1547: *Images Forbidden*

In St Paul's Cathedral, and all the London churches, and soon throughout England, the rood and images of Mary and John, and all other images, were pulled down and broken. The walls were painted white with texts of scriptures against images written on them. By negligence of the labourers, some people were hurt and one killed when the great cross in the rood loft was pulled down. One of the papist priests said it was the will of God for breaking it.

5–7 September 1548: Death of Queen Kateryn

Queen Kateryn died at Sudeley Castle, six days after giving birth to a daughter, Mary, named after the Lady Mary. Both parents had thought the strong kicking in the womb presaged a son. She left everything she owned to her one true sweetheart, Sir Thomas Seymour, whom she had been 'fully bent' on marrying before any man she knew. She left everything she owned to her husband, wishing it could be a 'thousand times more in value'.

They married, with the consent of Edward, in a secret wedding at the end of April 1547, though it was not revealed until the end of the following month. She was buried in St Mary's Chapel in the grounds of the castle. Miles Coverdale preached the sermon. Lady Jane Grey, eldest daughter of the Marquis of Dorset and Frances, who was living in her household, was designated chief mourner and asked to be godmother to the baby.

26 October 1548: Dangerous Journey

Because of the incursion into Scotland, Mary of Guise decided to send her daughter, Queen Mary of Scotland, now nearly six years old, overseas to France for her safety. It was a dangerous crossing as England is still at war with Scotland's ally, and mother and daughter sailed within a band of galleys, clustered within the French fleet sent by King Henri II to harry English ships.

17 January 1549: Murder at the Palace

Alarm was raised by the gentleman who sleeps in the king's chamber crying out, 'Help! Murder!' when he was awakened by loud barking.

Attendants rushing into the chamber found Edward's favourite spaniel dying, much to the king's fright and distress. Suspicion fell immediately on the Lord Admiral, Sir Thomas Seymour, who had scattered the watch on several errands. He was arrested at eight o'clock and taken to the Tower. It is believed he entered the king's chamber to abduct him or to kill him and the Lord Protector.

Sir Thomas has been watched carefully for months because he had been making wild statements about killing or hurting his brother. A search of his house revealed over 200,000 crowns in silver, and plunder from seized ships.

21 January 1549: Act of Uniformity

Every church in the land from Whitsunday onwards must use the Book of Common Prayer for worship in place of the Latin missal. Any priest not using it will face imprisonment for six months for a first offence, a year for a second, and life imprisonment for a third.

1 March 1549: Shambles of a Murder

John Abram, a butcher from St Nicholas Shambles, was led through all the streets of London, tied astride a horse with his face to its tail. Left finally at the Standard in Cheapside, he was put in the pillory with a sizeable placard beside him, with large letters for everyone to read: 'For the keeping of another man's wife and hiring a man to kill her husband.'

Abram had tried to hire one Woodhawe, head of the King's Guard, offering to give him £40 to murder a fellow butcher in the shambles. The guard had 'no heart to do such a thing'. Abram, who is living in sin with the other man's wife, was made to stand there all night until eleven thirty, when he was taken down and returned to prison.

7 March 1549: Mistress Ashley Released

Kat Ashley, governess to Lady Elizabeth, was released from the Tower. She had been arrested on 21 January for possible involvement in the treasonous activities of Sir Thomas Seymour for a rumour had been circulated since Christmas that she had tried to assist him to marry her charge. To her manifest relief, she had been deemed foolish but not treasonous.

The truth behind the gossip is that Sir Thomas, after he married Queen Kateryn, moved into his wife's Chelsea home. As new master of the household he was given the master key. His wife, as stepmother, had also the care of the then thirteen-year-old Elizabeth, who lived with them. Not long after Seymour moved in, he began entering his stepdaughter's bedchamber before she arose and bade her good morrow. The governess confessed that sometimes he would open her bedcurtains and, if Elizabeth was up, would slap her buttocks familiarly as he passed through to his own lodgings.

When they stayed at Hanworth, both the queen and Lord Admiral came on two mornings and tickled the Lady Elizabeth while she was still abed. On one occasion, to the horror of the governess, the queen held her squirming stepdaughter while her husband cut a black gown she was wearing into a hundred pieces. At another time, Sir Thomas accused Elizabeth of having her arm around a man's neck, an accusation which, weeping, she strenuously denied, her ladies backing up her refutation. Her ladies also said that if Elizabeth heard the key in the privy lock of her door she would run from her bed to her maids, and once hid behind her bedcurtains with her maids concealing her. At Seymour Place, when he started to come in the mornings in his nightgown, barelegged in his slippers, Lady Elizabeth would, with her maids, arise early and be dressed reading her scripture.

Mrs Ashley, touching upon a marriage between Lady Elizabeth and Sir Thomas, said she thought there was some affection between them because her charge would often blush at the mention of his name when she teased her. Her mistress, though, had firmly said that no marriage could be considered with any person without the Privy Council's consent and as such was not to be spoken of. The last time she could recall Lady Elizabeth and Sir Thomas speaking together was when he accompanied her and her retinue to Cheshunt where they were staying for the summer at the home of Sir Anthony Denny, Kat's brother-in-law.

20 March 1549: Lord Admiral Executed

Sir Thomas Seymour, uncle to the king and the Lord Protector's brother, was executed today. It took two blows to sever his head. The Lady Elizabeth was heard to comment that this day died 'a man with much wit and very little judgement'. There was no trial. He was adjudged guilty of thirty-three charges of treason and other misdemeanours under an Act of Attainder put before Parliament on 25 February and consented to, after much debate, on 5 March.

The accusations were that, days after the death of Henry VIII, he plotted first to marry Lady Mary, then Lady Elizabeth (the council had found Elizabeth's letter of reproof discouraging his overtures); that he had married Queen Kateryn for her status when the two ladies had rebuffed him; that he had tried repeatedly to get a bill passed through Parliament for them to make him the king's governor in place of his brother, Edward; and that he had made bitter and wild threats against his brother, friction having arisen between them when the Lord Protector said that 'neither of them was born to be king, nor to marry king's daughters' and they 'ought to thank God their sister was given God's grace to marry a king'. Further accusations were that he had arranged for Lady Jane Grey to remain with his household, plotting to marry her to the king, and that he had encompassed the king's death and connived at piracy. At Christmas, furthermore, he had allowed rumours to circulate that he would marry Lady Elizabeth, who was pregnant by him. In not countering them he had infuriated Elizabeth, who had called him a 'false wretch' and had written to the council for a proclamation of denial to be issued.

He refused to answer any of the charges, merely requesting an open trial. Why he decided to break into his nephew's apartments at Hampton Court in January remains a mystery.

Born in around 1509, Sir Thomas had a varied career. He first served Sir Francis Bryan, promoted to a gentleman of Henry VIII's privy chamber when his sister, Jane, married the king in 1536. Henry thought about matching him with his daughter-in-law, the Duchess of Richmond, and gave him his first naval command in 1537. In 1539 he was in the entourage to meet Anne of Cleves at Calais and was a challenger at the joust held in her honour. As Lord Admiral and master of the munitions, he served in the 1540s Netherlands and Boulogne campaigns.

10 April 1549: *The Dance of Death Dances No More*

The cloister of St Paul's, with its cunningly wrought dance of death, together with the chapel in the middle of the churchyard, has been pulled down. The tombs and monuments of the dead in the charnel house and its chapel have also been demolished. The bones of the dead were buried in the surrounding fields.

The area around St Paul's is being converted for dwelling houses and shops. The newly built and beautiful church and steeple of St John of Jerusalem, near Smithfield, was undermined and blown up with gunpowder. The stone is being used in the building of the Lord Protector's house at the Strand.

July–August 1549: *Enclosures, Rising Prices and Starvation*

At the beginning of July, country folk assembled in various places, from the West Country to the Midlands, in unrest, tearing down hedges and fences around common lands enclosed by nobles and gentry, which has left them and their families starving. They insisted that they were only legally enforcing good Duke Somerset's proclamation issued in April that enclosed lands accustomed to lie open should be returned to their original state.

The enclosing of common lands for nobles to rear their cattle and sheep has not only given the poor nowhere to feed their animals but has resulted in fewer men being hired and the rich keeping produce and profit to themselves. In some places, to facilitate enclosure, villages have been demolished, tenants' houses pulled down and rents raised to force people out of their homes. This has resulted in rising prices, homelessness and unemployment, and a decline in wages. In effect, say the poor, the rich are robbing them. Their plea to the government is for victuals to be sold at reasonable prices, to be able to feed their animals, and guaranteed security of tenure. In the West Country they made further requests: for the Six Articles of Henry VIII be used until such time as Edward comes to his majority, and a restoration of the Mass, matins and confirmation.

The government's response was to send Sir William Herbert to put down the unrest in Wiltshire and Somerset; Lord Grey was sent to Oxfordshire and, fearing his terrifying reputation, many rebels 'fell away' while Lord John Russell was sent to Honiton and brought the king's forces upon the rebels 'rather as to a carnage than to a fight' and more than 2,000 slain. The sedition thus broken, Sir Anthony Kingston was deemed cruel and inhumane in his executions. At one point he ate with a member of the gentry while asking him to build a gallows to execute rebels; once finished, he told the man that the gallows was meant for him.

In Norfolk, the uprising that began on 8 July was considered more dangerous because the city of Norwich was behind the rebels. Men came from all around and the city, swelling their strength to 16,000 men, led by Robert Kett, a yeoman farmer who vehemently told them they were 'overtopped and trodden down' by the gentlemen who had 'rivers of riches' running into their coffers while 'they were pared to the quick' and were 'gnawed to the very bones'. On 1 August, Kett's host defeated an army led by William Parr, Marquis of Northampton, who barely escaped with his life after his soldiers fled. Dudley, Earl of Warwick, with 6,000 men and 1,500 horsemen, was next sent against them and he moved to a hill outside Norwich. Before he charged, the earl offered a general pardon. They replied they were resolved to live or die: 'what cared they for pardon who have nothing but a vile and servile life to lose?' Guerrilla warfare by the rebels took place for three days until they ran out of meat and victuals and were forced to flee on 27 August. Leaving his English footmen to overrun the town, Warwick 'chased them above three miles' with 1,000 of his German solders and horsemen. Overtaking them, they savagely killed 2,000 rebels, capturing Robert Kett and his brother, William, who were escorted to the Tower of London, and later conveyed back to Norwich for hanging in chains on the walls of Norwich Castle.

1–14 October 1549: Lord Protector Accused of Being a Traitor

On the afternoon of 1 October, the mayor, aldermen and citizens debated in court in the Guildhall their response to two letters received that day: one from the Lord Protector and his nephew at Hampton Court requesting them to send 1,000 armed men to defend the king; the other from the 'London Lords' asking for 2,000 men to defend the king.

At first the Recorder, friend of the Lord Chancellor, swayed them towards Warwick's cause. A prudent citizen thought otherwise, saying that aiding 'the designs of other men whose purposes we know not, we cast ourselves into the throat of danger' and that 'secret intentions' were 'commonly ambitions and only aim at private ends'. They prevaricated. They replied to the lords that they were ready to join with them in unarmed dutiful petition to the king; meanwhile, to the king they offered forces for his defence or his honour but asked that he hear the complaints against the Lord Protector before assembling forces in the field.

Somerset, aware that Warwick was leading a conspiracy against him, also sent out appeals to all the towns for men to aid the king against traitorous lords who were plotting his and the king's destruction. On the evening of 6 October, he told the people to depart, sent his wife away and then he and the king rode through the night to Windsor, arriving so early in the morning that no one was expecting them and no comfort was to be had for the king, who had contracted a chill from the night air and disliked Windsor Castle.

Letters crossed between Windsor and London. Somerset's letter lacked spirit. Warwick took the initiative and issued a proclamation that Somerset was a traitor; had cost the lives of thousands of the king's subjects; had built palatial residences while the realm was at war and soldiers went unpaid; incited inward sedition, dividing nobles, gentry and commons; unsettled the people by levying forces in a disordered uproar; and, worst of all, carried off the king to make himself sovereign lord.

Warwick won the propaganda war. Sir Anthony Wingfield, Captain of the Guard, was sent to Windsor on 11 October and immediately arrested the duke. Because his bedchamber adjoined the king's, Sir Anthony imprisoned him in the Beauchamp Tower while sending the duke's youngest brother and sons to his house at Bedington.

The duke was escorted to the Tower on 14 October. The Mayor, Recorder and sheriffs, flanked by halberdiers, lined the route from Soper Lane to Holborn Bridge. From there to the Tower, aldermen were mounted on horseback in every street with a number of householders standing with bills as he passed.

6 February 1550: Lord Protector Submits

The duke's second submission of all his offences, together with payment of his fine of £10,000, resulted in his release today from the Tower. He will be sworn back into the Privy Council after audience with the king at Greenwich.

Twenty-nine complaints were brought against him, among them that he, with his own authority, without the council's, wrote and sealed orders of arrests, prisoner releases, mustered armies and talked with ambassadors alone; that he had 'rebuked, checked and taunted privately and openly' councillors who held differing opinions to his own; that he had incited insurrections by making people rise because of enclosures and saying openly gentlemen were the cause of the dearth of products; and that he had written to nobles and gentlemen to 'speak fair to the rebels and handle them gently' while aiding the same rebels with money of his own. Lastly, it was asserted that on 1 October he wrote seditious bills which disturbed the realm and that he frightened the king, who, by being carried to Windsor, 'took such disease as was to his great peril'.

25–29 May 1550: Perpetual Peace

French ambassadors watched as King Edward took his oath consenting to the Treaty of Perpetual Peace made on 29 March. Boulogne has been ceded back to the French king for a price, leaving Calais the only English possession held in France. Afterwards, after dining with him, the king invited them to watch 'ten-versus-ten at the ring'. One band all in yellow was led by the Duke of Suffolk, the other by Lord Strange all in blue. Back at Durham Place, where the ambassadors were lodged, the city had customarily provided beer, wine, mutton, wildfowl, poultry, fish and wax.

During the following days the ambassadors were entertained with bear and bull baiting, and on 27 May were given licence to hunt in Hyde Park. When they supped with the king, he also gave them licence to visit Hampton Court. On their last day, supper was given to them by the Duke of Somerset, who afterwards took them to the Thames to watch a bear being hunted into the river while 'wildfire was cast out of boats'.

19 June 1550: Deptford Assault

Edward Clinton, Lord Admiral, invited the king to Deptford for supper, where a display was put on for his delight. First, men ran at each other on a barge wrestling each other into the Thames. While partaking of supper, a fort was erected on a great barge on the river. It had three walls and a watchtower in the middle, manned by forty or fifty soldiers dressed in yellow and black, captained by Mr Winter, the king's surveyor of ships. Moored to the fort was a yellow galley with other men and munitions awaiting to defend the castle. Men in white, in four pinnaces, attacked the yellow galley, driving it away. They then assaulted the fort with squibs, 'canes of fire' and bombards, finally breaking down the outer walls. The defenders fought back, pushing soldiers into the pinnaces and sinking one while men leapt from it into the Thames. Three more pinnaces came alongside. The fort was overrun, the yellow galley taken, and the admiral of the fleet captured the gallant captain.

13 July 1550: Escape Attempt by Lady Mary

Sir John Gates was sent into Essex to prevent Lady Mary from escaping to Antwerp, patrolling the Essex shoreline while the Duke of Somerset, Sir John Russell and Mr Seyntleger are patrolling other parts of the coast, also leaving men to watch each port and harbour in the neighbourhood of Lady Mary's house.

Lady Mary had moved from Beaulieu, ostensibly for cleaning and repairs to be carried out, to her house only 2 miles from the sea. The council were alerted by an informer that she had packed her property in great long hopsacks and bundled up her jewels and rings. Alarm bells rang even louder when they were informed that an enterprise was devised to take Lady Mary over the sea from Maldon on a vessel 'sent under colour of carrying corn to sell to her household as happens daily'. The sight of the emperor's ships hovering around Harwich did not help.

The plan was for Mary to leave on 2 July. She countered she wished to leave on another day and leave her house at four in the morning under the 'pretext of going to amuse herself and purge her stomach by the sea, as her ladies did daily'. No escape will be possible in the future as strict watch is being kept day and night on all roads, crossroads, harbours, creeks and other pathways, while no one is allowed to pass from one village to another without good reason.

14 *March 1551: The Murder of Mr Arden of Faversham*

Mistress Alys Arden was burnt at the stake in Canterbury today for the murder of her husband, Thomas, previously Mayor of Faversham. When Thomas and Alys were first married everyone said what a handsome couple they made, he being tall and comely, his wife young, pretty and shapely. So much in love with her was he that when she began an affair with a tailor, John Mosbye, he 'winked' at it.

But Alys began to hate Thomas. She tried to poison him one breakfast, which failed. She then entreated her lover to murder him so they could be together. John then asked a man named Greene if he would do the deed, knowing he bore a grudge against Arden over a land deal. Greene hired two ruffians, Black Will and Shakebag, who said they would do the job for £10. Thomas led a charmed life, for their three attempts failed. Then the conspirators decided a fool-proof plan would be to murder him in his own parlour.

One night, Thomas was met at his own door by Mosbye, who offered to play backgammon with him while Alys prepared supper. As they played, Black Will stealthily emerged from a cupboard behind Thomas and strangled him, while Mosbye hit him over the head with a pressing iron. They carried the stricken man into his counting house, where Alys stabbed him seven or eight times in the chest with a knife. Alys and her servant, Elizabeth, then cleaned up the blood and tidied the rushes that had been 'shuffled'. Alys threw the bloodied clothes and knife into a tub by the side of the well. Then she calmly supped with two London grocers, Prune and Cole, previously invited by Arden, wondering aloud where he was.

Meanwhile, it began to snow.

As soon as the grocers departed, the conspirators moved Arden's body into the field adjoining the garden, ten paces away from the garden gate. Having waited a while, Alys raised an outcry about her missing husband, and neighbours began a search of the surrounding area. Prune found the body. When the mayor came, he pointed to rushes sticking to the dead man's slippers and the footsteps in the snow. They followed them. At the house they soon found the bloodied items. Alys immediately confessed all.

John Mosbye was hanged in Smithfield and Elizabeth was burned at Faversham, crying that she would never forgive her mistress. Black Will, Greene and Shakebag eluded capture.

18 March 1551: Disputation between King Edward and Lady Mary

The Lady Mary, who came to London three days earlier with an entourage of ladies and gentlemen all wearing banned black rosaries, was called before king and council today. The council, for the king, declared to her that Edward had long suffered her to have Mass against his will in hopes she would eventually conform. She answered that her 'soul was God's, and her faith she would not change, nor dissemble her opinion with contrary doings'. The king told her that her faith was not constrained, but as a subject he expected her to obey him. Mary argued that 'riper age and experience would teach him much more'. Edward retorted that she 'might still have something to learn, for no one was too old for that'.

As he gave her permission to leave, Mary begged him to give no credence to any person who might desire to make him believe evil of her.

31 March 1551: Challenge by the King

King Edward, with sixteen of his chamber, ran at base, shot and ran at the ring. Though he lost when shooting at the butts, he won rovers, getting nearest to the agreed targets.

3 May 1551: Tourney with Swords

With trumpeters, ten horsemen and sixteen footmen, King Edward set a challenge running at the ring against his cousin, the Earl of Hertford. The king's troop were all in coats of black silk pulled with white taffeta, with cloaks of black and white. The earl's group were all in yellow taffeta, including their hats and banners. Though the king lost, he enjoyed every moment. He tried his skill five or six times at the tourney with the other young lords, watched by the French ambassador, who told Edward he 'had borne himself right well and shown great dexterity'. The king replied he made but a 'small beginning, and as time passed he hoped to do his duty better'.

Every day over the last few weeks, the king has showed himself to the people, riding 2 or 3 miles in full armour as well as charging at targets to exercise himself.

14–28 July 1551: New Betrothal for Edward

The Marechal de St Andre, chief French ambassador, had his first audience before dinner with the king at Hampton Court rather than Westminster owing to the latest, extremely virulent, outbreak of the Sweat. Talking privately later in an inner chamber, the ambassador said he trusted that the king neither listened to nor believed rumours that King Henri II was not his friend. The king replied that he well knew rumours were not always to be believed and although he sometimes provided for the worst, he 'never did any harm upon their hearing'.

On 16 July, the Marechal presented the French Order of St Michael to Edward, kissing him on his cheek as he looped the chain over his neck. Edward, newly betrothed to Elizabeth, the five-year-old daughter of Henri II, invited the Marechal on 20 July to be present while he dressed and to view his bedchamber. Later, after the Frenchman returned from hunting with hounds, he invited him to watch him shoot and at supper played the lute for him, knowing his proficiency would be reported to his betrothed.

Edward had built in Hyde Park for the ambassadors' last banquet a 'fair house', a temporary banqueting house 57 feet by 21 feet, with a turret and mouldings of antique heads, the whole decorated with boughs, ivy and flowers.

29 August 1551: Lady Mary 'would lay her head on the block'

Three of the Privy Council were sent by command of the king with his letter to Lady Mary, lodging at her house in Copthall, Essex. She received the letter upon her knees, and kissed it, saying she did so for the honour of his hand, not for its contents, being as she judged from the council rather than her brother. After reading the letter to herself, the councillors affirmed the king's command that she was no longer to hear private Mass, nor allow her chaplain to conduct Mass, nor her servants to hear it. They said that so far the king had treated her gently but, nonetheless, he wished her to use only the service set by his laws.

Mary informed the king, through his council, that though she was the king's most humble and obedient servant, if she cannot use the service as used at the time of the late king her father's death she would rather 'lay her head on a block and suffer death'. When the king had 'come to such years that he may be able to judge things himself' she would be ready to obey his 'orders in religion', but until then she declared she would not use the new service. As for her chaplains, the pain of the law was only imprisonment for a short time, so she left them to do as they thought most fit.

11 October 1551: New Creations
At Hampton Court, after the morning service, John Dudley, Earl of Warwick was created Duke of Northumberland, Lord President of the Council and Grand Master of the king's household. The Marquis of Dorset was created Duke of Suffolk, Sir William Herbert Earl of Pembroke and Sir William Paulet Marquis of Winchester.

16–18 October 1551: Duke of Somerset arrested
By command of the Duke of Northumberland, the Duke of Somerset was arrested by the Duke of Suffolk and the Marquis of Winchester and brought to the Tower, accused of plotting to take over the Tower and Isle of Wight to the destruction of London and 'substantial men'. Two days later, the duke's wife, Anne Stanhope, her brother, Sir Michael, and others were brought from Sion House to the Tower.

31 October–4 November 1551: Mary of Guise Meets King Edward
Driven by a storm to take refuge in Portsmouth Harbour, Mary of Guise, Queen Dowager of Scotland, requested a passport to land and travel to Scotland overland. Granted, Queen Mary arrived at Hampton Court on 31 October and was met by Lady Jane Grey, in her first public appearance, with sixty other ladies. Once rested, Lady Jane gave her a tour of the building and gardens,

and afterwards, as if it was a festival, the rest of the day and that following was given to dancing and deer coursing.

Early on 2 November, the queen returned to London to prepare for her formal audience with King Edward at Westminster. She was lodged at the bishop's palace, and the mayor and the city provided gifts of beef, mutton, veal, swine, swans, poultry, quails, sturgeon and salmons, bread, beer and wine, wax, torches, wood and coals.

On the day appointed, with a great entourage of knights, gentlemen and ladies, Queen Mary came in a chariot to Westminster. The king's guard stood on both sides from the outer gate up to the presence chamber. She was greeted by the Duke of Northumberland, who led her to the king. The Earl of Warwick, his son, held the sword of state. Queen Mary knelt in front of Edward who, bidding her rise, embraced and kissed her. Leading her by hand to her retiring chamber, he only retired to his own chamber after he had kissed all the Scottish ladies with her.

At dinner they dined under the same cloth of estate, she at the king's left hand, his and her service being brought together, richly served on gilt plate. With her were the king's cousins, Frances and Margaret. All the ladies of England and Scotland dined in the queen's great chamber and were served on silver.

After dinner, the king showed her his galleries and gardens. Around four o'clock in the afternoon he brought her by hand into the hall where he kissed her before she departed.

1 December 1551: *The Trial of the Duke of Somerset*

The Duke of Somerset was, at five o'clock in the morning, brought out of the Tower to Westminster Hall for his trial. The Marquis of Winchester sat as High Steward under the cloth of estate, with twenty-six peers of the realm. The duke denied the charges, of which there were five: that he intended to raise the north and London; that he intended to call the Earl of Warwick and others to a banquet to cut off their heads; that he with one hundred horse at the Muster Day would kill the new gendarmerie and their horses; and that he unlawfully held a levy of a hundred men at his house contrary to the king's Act.

'What a mad matter,' said the duke, 'for him to enterprise his one hundred against nine hundred.' However, he confessed he had imagined killing Northumberland, though meaning no actual harm. It was enough to convict him of felony but not of high treason. Innocent of the latter charge, the axe blade was turned away from him and everyone assumed he was acquitted of all. People cried in loud voices 'God save the Duke' over and over again, throwing their caps in the air. Orders to stop the shouting were made, but the news continued to be broadcast all over London before people realised they were deceived; he had been acquitted only of high treason, and sentenced to be hanged for felony. The people hope he will gain the king's pardon.

7 December 1551: *The Great Muster in St James Fields*

To his evident enjoyment the king was twice encircled by his new 'gendarmerie' displaying their arms, each man with 'his spear in his hand' and well horsed. Astride his own mount, the king watched with delight as the spectacle unfolded, beginning with four of his own trumpeters preceding Lord Bray in gilt armour bearing the royal 5-foot banner leading the king's pensioners, five in a line, riding on white and black horses in full camlet harness, followed by a hundred of their servants.

By degree came the nobles, each with their personal standard and one hundred men-at-arms, each section preceded by a trumpeter. First the Lord Treasurer, his standard a gold falcon, his men in red and white; then the Duke of Northumberland's men in black velvet, his standard a ragged staff and a crowned silver lion against red damask; the Lord Marquis of Northampton with his standard a crowned maiden's head, his men in yellow and black, carrying both javelins and flags; Lord John Russell, now Earl of Bedford, his men in red and white, his standard a white goat; the Earl of Rutland, his standard a peacock, while his men were in yellow and blue carrying pencelles; the baboon standard of the Earl of Huntingdon followed, his men in blue with spears; the Earl of Pembroke, Lords Darcy and Cobham, his men in black coats edged with white, and the Lord Warden of the Cinque Ports ended the show.

3 January 1552: King Edward's Lord of Misrule

In keeping with past tradition, King Edward sent his Lord of Misrule, George Ferrers, out of Greenwich to the city of London. He, wearing a furred gold gown, his retinue of young knights and gentlemen in baldrics of yellow and green, landed at Tower Wharf, some on foot, some on horseback, along with fifty tall men of his guard in red and white. On Tower Hill they arrayed themselves in procession, behind a standard of St George on yellow and green silk. Setting off squibs and merrily playing trumpets, bagpipes, drums and flutes, they Morris danced and rode around the city, throwing coins into the streets.

Misrule's Council, dressed like sage men in blue taffeta gowns, passed judgement at the Great Cross in Cheapside where they set up a gibbet and stocks to capture men. Trumpets blew. A herald and a 'doctor of law' made a proclamation setting out Misrule's progeny, household and dignity. This was followed by the taking of a hogshead of wine from a cart, from which everyone drank. Then the Lord Mayor invited everyone to dinner.

This Christmastide was the first time King Edward had kept open court and table, and the Lord of Misrule made the king laugh several times with witty and harmless pranks, comic jousts and a droll procession of priests and bishops parading through the court.

22 January 1552: *The Duke of Somerset Executed*

Despite the directive proclaimed the day previously that no one was to leave their houses before ten o'clock, by seven o'clock in the morning Tower Hill was crowded. People came to see the Duke of Somerset's execution from all round the city, outskirts and further afield. The duke was brought to the scaffold at eight o'clock, surrounded by a huge number of guards with their halberds, as well as the sheriffs and wardens of the Tower.

In his speech, the duke said each country and realm had its laws and statutes which all loyal subjects should obey. He affirmed he had never plotted against his nephew and asked them to pray for the king.

Suddenly, for no apparent reason, people began jostling each other, running away in all directions while some were pushed over and others fell into the Tower ditch. John Stow, who had gone to witness the execution, said that some of the guards who were supposed to attend were late. Seeing the duke already on the scaffold, the latecomers began to run, crying to each other to follow fast. Men running fast with bills and halberds made people think that 'some power' had come to rescue the duke and they rushed to get out of the way.

The duke, who had put his head on the block, rose, begging the people to calm down and not trouble him at such an hour. He put his head back on the block. The axe came down.

Somerset's head and body were coffined and carried in for burial on the north side of the choir in St Peter ad Vincula. The 'good duke' was deeply mourned by the people. Some put their hands in his blood, others dipped their handkerchiefs for a keepsake. The crowd that had assembled stayed all day, bewailing his death, dissatisfied that he, merely convicted of a felony, had been executed.

16 May 1552: *Muster at Greenwich*

To celebrate his recovery from bouts of measles and smallpox, King Edward rode into Greenwich Park to watch a second display of his gendarmerie. Once again Lord Bray led with the king's standard and pensioners, followed by the Lord Treasurer and the Duke of Northumberland. This time, Lord Grey, Duke of Suffolk was next, his standard a silver unicorn followed by the white goat standard of the Lord Privy Seal, who, as before, was followed by the Marquis of Northampton and the earls of Rutland and Huntingdon. They were followed by the green dragon of the Earl of Pembroke, his men in red, white and blue. The Lord Admiral's men wore black coats embroidered with white, his guidon the Cross of St George with a silver anchor. Lord Darcy's standard of a maiden with a flower in her hand floated across the park, his men wearing white-embroidered red coats. Lord Cobham and the Warden of the Cinque Ports once again brought up the rear, the last standard a red cross with a sunbeam revealing a half-rose, his men and spears all in black.

26 May 1552: Maypole Broken
The white and green maypole in Fenchurch was, by unanimous vote of the Lord Mayor's Council, taken down and broken up. This was a great disappointment to the people, who by custom enjoyed dancing around it, holding the silk ribbons extending from the castle in its middle.

1 November 1552: Second Act of Uniformity
Today, the Feast of All Saints, it was proclaimed that Cranmer's revised Book of Common Prayer must be used for all church services in England, which everyone must attend on Sundays. The Lord's Supper replaces the Mass, for bread and wine are natural substances representing Christ's body and blood. Communion tables replace high altars.

25 December 1552: New Children's Hospital
King Edward, on 23 November last, had Christ's Hospital opened at Greyfriars for poor and sick children to be given meat, drink, lodging and clothes.

On Christmas Day afternoon the hospital housed 340 children, all of whom stood to watch the mayor and aldermen ride to St Paul's for the service. The children were all dressed in russet cotton, the boys wearing red caps, the girls with kerchiefs on their heads. Between every twenty children stood a woman keeper. The masters, surgeons and physicians stood in front.

25 December 1552–1 January 1553: Christmastide Amusements

On Christmas Day, to begin his amusement for the king, the Lord of Merry Disports, taking for his armorial beast a seven-headed hydra, sent a solemn ambassador, a trumpeter, a drummer, a fifer, a boy playing a kettle drum and a herald speaking a strange tongue with an interpreter to the king. They were all dressed like Turks.

On St Stephen's Day, ships were wheeled into the hall. The main vessel, its poop covered with white and blue, disembarked the Lord of Misrule with his horse. He was dressed in an ermine-furred purple velvet gown braided with silver spangles. Pages of honour followed him carrying his helm, shield, sword and axe. Six councillors came down the gangplank representing a divine, a philosopher, an astronomer, a poet, a physician and an apothecary. In between their discourses were the antics of jugglers, tumblers, fools and friars.

On New Year's night, the Lord of Misrule devised a feat-in-arms: a challenge on plumed hobby horses, six challengers barded in white and blue, six defenders barded in black and yellow. A furious fight with mock lances ensued, which made king and court laugh.

10 January 1553: Lady Mary at Court

Although King Edward had not fully recovered from his cold and cough of a few days ago, he gave audience to Lady Mary in his chamber of presence. She rode from her house in St John's via Fleet Street to Westminster with a retinue of 200 lords, knights, ladies and gentlewomen of her household, and was accompanied to court by the duchesses of Suffolk and Northumberland, lady marquises of Northampton and Winchester, the countesses of Bedford, Shrewsbury and Arundel, the ladies Clinton and Browne, and many more. At the outer gate she was greeted courteously by the lords Suffolk, Northumberland, Winchester and Bedford, while the earls of Shrewsbury and Arundel led her to the king.

1 March 1553: Parliament Assembled at Whitehall

Unusually, the first day of Parliament took place at Whitehall. The king, dressed in his robes of parliament and sitting under his cloth of estate, looked pale. He was said to be a little 'diseased from a cold and it was not thought meet for his grace to ride to Westminster in the air'. Knights, burgesses of London, and those from the shires were all present as Parliament was opened. Once the king and lords spiritual and temporal had departed, the commons went to sit in the common house.

10–11 April 1553: King Edward Gives Away His Palace of Bridewell

King Edward, who has stirred very little of late from his chamber and looks weak and thin, received the Lord Mayor of London on 10 April. At audience the king revealed he was giving Bridewell Palace to the city to be used as workhouse for poor and idle persons, granting 700 marks of rent from the lands of Savoy and all the beds and bedding of the Savoy Hospital which his grandfather, Henry VII, had set up.

The day following, the king left Westminster for the healthier air of Greenwich. As his barge sailed past the Tower of London, guns and cannon were shot in noisy salute, alerting all the ships down to Ratcliffe to shoot their guns, including the three great ships being rigged for expedition to parts unknown under the direction of Sebastian Cabot.

28 April 1553: Mayday Jousts Postponed
The customary Mayday jousts held at Greenwich have been put off until Whitsuntide, it was announced. The king has only appeared in his garden once since his arrival at Greenwich. News from a 'trustworthy source' is that the king is becoming weaker and wasting away, coughing up matter, sometimes greenish-yellow, sometimes bloody. The doctors are perplexed but believe his health will improve as the weather warms.

20 May 1553: The Three Great Ships
There was much excitement and bustle when the three great ships came before the windows of the Palace of Greenwich, towed downriver before they departed to find a north-western passage through the Arctic regions for a direct trade route with Cathay. Unfortunately the king was too ill to see them. Courtiers ran out of the palace and crowds of common people flocked to the banks to see them. Even the privy councillors looked out of the window, while some of the king's servants ran to the roof and to the tops of the towers. The ships discharged guns and cannons, the air ringing with noise that echoed around the hills, while mariners shouted farewells to friends and others climbed the rigging to wave goodbye.

21 May 1553: Lady Jane Grey Marries Lord Guildford Dudley
Fifteen-year-old Lady Jane Grey, cousin of the king, married the fifteen-year-old son of the Duke of Northumberland, Lord Guildford Dudley, at his father's townhouse. To celebrate, great games and jousts were held with much feasting. As it was not thought expedient that the king 'should yet come to the open air and remain so long abroad', he sent presents of rich ornaments and jewels to the bride.

24 *June 1553: A Prayer for King Edward*

To the great astonishment of London citizens, the Privy Council have had printed and posted a prayer for the king, whom they believe cannot possibly live past tomorrow.

A source in the palace says the king 'no longer has the strength to stir, can hardly breathe, his body no longer performs its functions, his nails and hair are dropping off, and all his person is scabby'. Three days earlier it was said by the same source that the king himself 'has given up hope' and he feels so weak that he said he could 'resist no longer and that he is done for', and that he has signed his will, insisting the council sign it. He had ordered them to draw it up ten days ago after he was attacked by a hot and violent fever which left him still weaker and feverish. Since that time he has been unable to keep anything in his stomach and had to lie flat on his back though he could not sleep.

Since the end of May a source had said the king was wasting away, unable to rest unless he took medicine, and that his head and feet had become swollen. The rumour bruited was that the king has the same illness which killed his father's illegitimate son, the Duke of Richmond.

The city, nay, the whole realm, prays for King Edward that he may recover from the dreadful illness that is causing him so much hurt.

4 *July 1553: Is King Edward on the Mend?*

Today, rumours were flying about that King Edward's health was improving. For the first time in weeks, many saw him at Greenwich, but they also said that he looked so thin and wasted that they doubted anyone could 'foretell whether he will live an hour longer'.

The king has signed a will expressly appointing Lady Jane Dudley his successor, excluding Lady Mary on religious grounds, citing her disobedience to him, and Elizabeth on the grounds of her illegitimacy as enacted by his father.

6 July 1553: King Edward VI Dies at Greenwich

King Edward died at eight in the evening, held in the arms of his friend Henry Sydney. He was three months short of his sixteenth birthday and had reigned six and a half years.

QUEEN JANE
10–19 JULY 1553

Born at Bradgate Manor, Leicestershire, in 1537, Lady Jane Grey was the eldest daughter of Henry Grey, 1st Marquis of Dorset, later Duke of Suffolk, and Frances, daughter of Henry VIII's sister Mary. In his Act of Succession, Henry VIII had left the crown after Mary and Elizabeth to 'heirs of the body' of his niece. Frances had two other daughters, Katherine and Mary.

Jane, as studious and young as Edward, was respected by scholars all over Europe, for apart from being eloquent in Italian and French she was learned in Latin, Greek and Hebrew, and, as a result, knowledgeable in scripture. Visiting Bradgate once, the scholar Roger Ascham found Jane reading *Phaedo* in Greek. When asked why she was indoors when the rest of her family were out hunting, she told him that she thanked God for giving her 'sharp and severe parents' and 'so gentle a schoolmaster'.

Edward, in his device for the succession, left the crown to Jane in the belief that she was the only person who would not undo his godly work. Denying Mary's right to the throne meant he had to deny Elizabeth's. Jane was of his faith, similar in intellect and married; continuity of succession was served by inserting 'and her heirs male'.

Two days after Edward's death, at two o'clock in the morning, the council seized the Tower and discharged the constable, Sir James Croft, allowing Lord Clinton the opportunity to transport great guns into the Tower, especially to the top of the White Tower. Later that morning, the Privy Council commanded the Lord Mayor of London, six aldermen and merchants of the Staple to come to Greenwich. They revealed that the king had died and chosen Lady Jane Dudley as his successor. The following day, all the head officers and guards were sworn into her service.

When she arrived at the Tower on 10 July, her first warrant was to Sir Andrew Dudley, keeper of the wardrobe, for crimson velvet and Holland cloth to cover two chairs and two close stools. Her first letter was to the lieutenants of the shires announcing her rightful accession and commanding them to defend her and 'resist the feigned and untrue claim of the Lady Mary'. That same day, twenty-one privy councillors replied to Mary's letter of 9 July, rejecting her claim of being the rightful queen.

10 July 1553: Queen Jane Proclaimed

Queen Jane landed at Tower Wharf at three o'clock in the afternoon after sailing from Sion House, her home since she had married, and was met by a kneeling Privy Council. She was accompanied with a great company of lords and nobles, who entered the Tower first, the Duke of Northumberland leading. The ladies followed, then the queen, the train of her dress held by her mother. Her husband, Lord Guilford, with his hat in his hand, showed himself to be a handsome youth.

For an hour between five and six o'clock the Tower guns pealed, alerting the public of momentous changes. Once they fell silent, two heralds and trumpets, with the Lords of the Council, Lord Mayor of London and others, journeyed throughout London proclaiming the news of Edward VI's death and why Queen Jane was ascending the throne.

Very few in the sullen crowd called 'God save her'. Not one bonfire was lit. There was no feasting in the streets. Not one face showed any joy.

12 July 1553: *Lady Mary at Kenninghall*

Receiving word that Lady Mary had removed to Kenninghall Castle in Norfolk, with many nobles and gentry joining her, the council promptly ordered the Duke of Suffolk to muster a force to go and arrest her, but Queen Jane, weeping, said she did not wish her father to leave her. The Duke of Northumberland was requested to go, with the expectation that his fearsome reputation and his previous victory in Norfolk would ensure that nobody dared lift a weapon against him. The duke assented that he would go, trusting that the council was loyal to Jane, leaving her in their charge.

Lords, knights and gentlemen eager to go were commanded to muster at Durham Place. Great guns, bows, bills, spears, pikes, arrows, gunpowder and cannon balls, filling three carts, were taken to the Tower, along with a number of men-at-arms ready to move to Cambridge when commanded.

13–14 July 1553: *The Duke Rides Out*

After dinner, Queen Jane called the Duke of Northumberland into her presence, handing him her sealed commission as lieutenant of her army. As he passed through the council chamber, the Earl of Arundel said that he wished he could be with his grace 'in whose presence he could find in his heart to spend his blood'. Stopping to converse with the council, the duke said that he and those who accompanied him were going to 'adventure' their bodies and lives, leaving their families to the council's safekeeping, and if for any reason that trust was betrayed God would not count them innocent of their spilt blood. He reminded them they had freely given, and written in their own hand, their 'sacred and holy oath of allegiance' to Queen Jane. In reply, one of the councillors said that if the duke 'mistrust any of us in this matter, your grace is far deceived ... your doubt is too far cast'.

As the Duke of Northumberland and his men rode out of London, tidings were received by the council that besides Norfolk, Mary had been proclaimed queen in Buckinghamshire, Oxfordshire and Northamptonshire, with more men flocking to her standard. The sailors manning the fleet of six ships sent to Yarmouth to prevent any escape attempt by Mary had mutinied, threatening to throw their captains overboard if they did not support her.

19 July 1553: Mary Proclaimed Queen of England, France and Ireland and All Dominions

At the Cross in Cheapside, early evening, Mary was proclaimed Queen of England by heralds and trumpets, accompanied by the earls of Shrewsbury, Arundel and Pembroke, the latter throwing money into the crowd. Money also cascaded out of windows, thrown in delight. People wept for joy, caps were thrown into the air and the streets were so crowded with people crying 'God save Queen Mary' that the councillors could scarcely pass by as they rode to St Paul's for the *Te Deum*. Church bells rang until late and the crowds stayed in streets lit by bonfires all night, tables groaning with food. The people sang, shouted and laughed.

As soon as the Duke of Suffolk heard the tumult, he came himself out of the Tower, and commanded his men to leave their weapons behind them. Alone, on Tower Hill, he proclaimed Mary as queen.

Earlier that day, Edward Underhill, a gentleman pensioner on duty at the Tower, had asked Queen Jane to be godmother to his newborn son being baptised that day. Lady Throckmorton stood in for Queen Jane, the boy being named Guilford, and on her return was surprised to find the canopy of state removed and her lady, with her husband, now prisoners accused of high treason under guard in separate apartments.

25 July 1553: *Duke of Northumberland Imprisoned in the Tower*

The Duke of Northumberland, escorted by the Earl of Arundel and a number of light horsemen, bows and spearmen, was taken to the Tower of London. As he passed through the London streets, the people cursed him and called him traitor. Also arrested and taken to the Tower were his eldest son and heir, John, Earl of Warwick, his other sons Ambrose and Henry, and his brother Andrew. His wife was arrested earlier and is already in the Tower.

When the duke heard that Mary had been proclaimed queen by the council in London, he called for a herald and trumpets, rode to Cambridge marketplace and proclaimed her himself, afterwards allowing himself to be confined. When the Earl of Arundel arrested him for treason, the duke fell on his knees and desired the earl to be good to him, saying, 'Consider, I have done nothing but by the consents of you and the whole council.'

QUEEN MARY I
1553–1558

Misunderstanding that the people of England upheld her claim to the throne because they believed it was right and not for reasons of religion, coupled with her sanctimonious belief that God wanted her to restore England to the 'right path', led Queen Mary into blind self-righteousness and obstinacy. Although she had accepted Henry's will regarding the succession, she and other Catholics had always understood she was, and always had been, the legitimate heir, her mother being Henry's sole legal wife.

She set out conscientiously to be a good, hard-working queen, pushing herself when she should have delegated because she distrusted her ministers. Her heart, said to be more Spanish than English, caused her to rely heavily on Simon Renard, Emperor Charles V's ambassador, giving him all the letters of state to read and concealing her activities from her Privy Council.

As a woman ruler, and in her thirty-eighth year, the council soon began talking of marriage. On the advice of Renard, Mary insisted she would only marry the emperor's twenty-eight-year-old son, Philip of Spain, considered the greatest catch in Europe at that time. The council begged her to marry an Englishman. She told them she would not condescend to marry a subject. When pressed, she bluntly told them it was no business of theirs, and, more hysterically, if they forced her to marry elsewhere then she would die. Public opinion, however, had it that once Philip came to England the hated Inquisition would not be far behind. This led to an uprising against foreigners that scared Mary's sister Elizabeth, who worried that someone might try to either involve her as a figurehead or implicate her.

Mary treated Elizabeth honourably at first, giving her place of honour, but when Mary's first parliament refused to remove Elizabeth from the succession, her underlying hatred for Anne Boleyn's daughter was exposed. Insidious whispers by Renard of Elizabeth's supposed scheming and 'power of enchantment' and Gardiner's insinuation that Mary would only be safe if she executed her sister led the queen to publicly snub her and give precedence to her cousins Frances and Margaret Lennox. French diplomat Michel de Castelnau wrote in his memoirs that Elizabeth had thought her hopes of living were so small 'that she made a request of her sister, in case she was to be beheaded', that she might have an executioner brought from France.

In July 1554, Mary and Philip married. She was infatuated by his portrait and fell passionately in love with the man. Henri II of France, then at war with Philip, had said gloomily to the English ambassador that he anticipated Mary would soon discontinue peace with him, for it was too 'hard for a wife to refuse her husband anything he shall earnestly require of her'. Indeed, Mary would have done anything for Philip.

As soon as Mary reconciled England with the Pope, the burning of heretics began. The many burnings began to dent her popularity with the people, though neither she nor Cardinal Pole, the Pope's legate, could see it. At the end of August 1555, Philip left England, a month after Mary's 'pregnancy' proved to be no pregnancy, which she believed was God's way of telling her she was not fervid enough in rooting out heresy. Even more burnings ensued, now affecting those lower on the social scale such as labourers, maids and apprentices.

While Philip was overseas, Mary inundated her husband with letters and messengers. It was widely known she slept badly, was melancholic and cried constantly. Philip was in no hurry to return. Letters from members of his entourage show that Philip, being given no funds, had gone without food when not at court and was resentful at not jointly ruling.

Mary was in dreadful debt throughout her reign, endeavouring through the efforts of Thomas Gresham to pay her creditors while raising loans. At the beginning of 1556, in Flanders alone, she owed more than £100,000. When Philip returned in the spring of 1557, he only did to so to request more funds to help pay for the war he had persuaded her to declare on France. Soon after, he left again. But Mary, happy in undertaking activities to assist her beloved, was consoled by her belief she was now truly pregnant. But there was no baby.

Mary never saw Philip again, despite her constant and sorrowing messages for him to return to her. When she died, aged only forty-two years and nine months, Philip wrote that he 'felt a reasonable regret for her death'.

3 August 1553: State Entry of Queen Mary

Queen Mary entered Whitechapel around six o'clock in the evening, riding on a palfrey trapped in gold to its hooves. Her French-style gown, over a gold-embroidered purple satin kirtle adorned with great pearls, had sleeves of purple velvet. Rich jewels decorated her fore-sleeves and headdress.

All the gravelled streets were hung with arras and silk cloths while the citizens of London standing at the rails waved streamers and banners, weeping and shouting, 'Jesu, save your grace.' In gaps, musicians played and sang ballads. Cheers also rang out for twenty-year-old Lady Elizabeth, riding directly after the queen, followed by their ladies and gentlewomen.

With the tramping of hooves and feet from the 500 nobles in velvet jackets preceding Mary, her ladies and the guard fronting the men from the counties who had supported her – horsemen alone estimated to be around 10,000 – coupled with the Tower guns setting off peal after peal, it sounded and felt like an earthquake.

At the Tower entrance, the queen was met by three kneeling figures craving pardon: Thomas Howard, the old Duke of Norfolk; Stephen Gardiner, Bishop of Winchester; and Edward Courtenay, grandson of Katherine Plantagenet. All were granted their wish.

8 August 1553: *Burial of Edward VI*

With neither cross nor lights, Edward VI's burial procession to Westminster Abbey was led by children, clerks in surplices singing and crowds of commoners weeping, followed by the king's servants in black. In pairs, heralds carried the three standards: the Dragon, the White Greyhound wrought in fine gold, and the Lion. Norroy bore his helmet and crest, Clarencieux bore his target, garter and sword, and Garter carried his embroidered coat-armour. In between were his officers of the household.

The king's crowned effigy, dressed in gold robes, gold-embroidered coat and a great collar, with sceptre in his right hand and garter about his thigh, lay on the blue velvet-covered coffin. The chariot, draped in cloth of gold, was drawn by seven great horses, trapped in black velvet, their reins plaited black and purple ribbon, with a man in mourning black riding on each bearing a bannerol of the king's arms. Around them were banners of the Order of the Garter, the red rose and the arms of his mother and grandmother. His master of horse followed, leading the king's horse trapped in gold. The hearse in Westminster Abbey, shaped like an imperial crown, was without lights but hung with black velvet fringed with Venice gold.

High Communion was administered by King Edward's godfather, Thomas Cranmer, Archbishop of Canterbury, wearing a surplice and no cope. King Edward was then buried in his grandfather's chapel.

The dole of money was given within every ward, every poor household receiving 8*d*. The funeral expenses came to £5,946 9*s* 9*d*, which included the 9,376 yards of black mourning cloth issued to the king's household.

Queen Mary, for the sake of her brother's soul, held a High Requiem Mass in the Tower chapel, performed by Bishop Gardiner.

13 August 1553: Dagger Thrown at Dr Bourne

By order of the queen, her chaplain, Dr Gilbert Bourne, was ordered to preach at St Paul's Cross. When he said prayers for the souls of the dead and vehemently declared the recently released and reinstated Dr Bonner had been wrongfully imprisoned, his words caused a murmuring 'hurly burly' from an affronted congregation. From the crowd a dagger was thrown, hitting one of the posts of the pulpit.

The mayor and aldermen tried to calm and settle the crowd. Only Lord Courtenay being there stopped any great mischief being done while Dr Bourne, surrounded by fellows guarding him, was removed from the pulpit to the safety of the schoolhouse in St Paul's Churchyard. The queen, hearing of the fracas, sent for the mayor and aldermen and charged them to rule the city in peace and good order or 'have other rulers set over them'.

This incident followed an earlier one at St Bartholomew's two days earlier when an old priest began a Latin Mass and the people threatened to pull him to pieces.

18 August 1553: Arraignments at Westminster Hall

John Dudley, Duke of Northumberland, William Parr, Marquis of Northampton and the duke's son and heir, John, Earl of Warwick, were arraigned at Westminster Hall before the Duke of Norfolk. Dudley defended himself by asking whether a man was treasonous if he acted by the authority of the prince's council by warrant under the Great Seal of England and whether those of that council, equally culpable, could sit as judges at his trial. He was answered that his warrant was issued by a usurper and did not bear the Great Seal of the lawful queen. As regards members of the council, they, being 'unattainted', were in law able to judge unchallenged.

After this pronouncement, Dudley and the other prisoners said few words, merely confessing to the indictment. They were adjudged guilty. The duke humbly asked that the queen grant him a nobleman's death and to be gracious to his children, who acted only at their father's command. He also requested a learned man be sent to him for his instructions for the 'quieting' of his conscience.

The same day, the queen published a proclamation willing all men to embrace the religion she had always followed and meant, God willing, to continue. The queen instructed her council that she neither meant to compel nor constrain other men's consciences for God would put truth into their hearts.

22 *August 1553: Duke of Northumberland Executed*

All the Tower guard turned out, armed, at nine o'clock in the morning to escort the Duke of Northumberland from the chapel, where he had heard Mass and received the sacrament, to the scaffold. Meeting Sir John Gates at the garden gate, also to be executed that day along with Sir Thomas Palmer, they made obeisance to one another, saying they forgave each other.

The duke, on the scaffold first, wore a crane-coloured damask gown. Leaning on the rail, he confessed to promoting the new religion but saw the punishment of God in the deaths of Kings Henry and Edward and exhorted everyone present to return to the old faith. Ending his speech, he said he was 'worthy to die, he came to die, accusing no man'.

He removed his jerkin and doublet. As he finished praying, the hangman gave him a kerchief as a blindfold. He was beheaded with one stroke. Sir John Gates was not so fortunate. After speaking few words, it took three blows for his head to be severed. Sir Thomas Palmer, awaiting his turn, prayed. His head was taken off with one stroke. Their corpses with their heads were buried in the chapel in the Tower – the duke at the High Altar, the other two at the nether end.

John Dudley's father, Sir Edmund, had been executed on Tower Hill almost to the day forty-three years previously. In his few months' imprisonment in the Tower before his political execution by Henry VIII, Sir Edmund wrote a book of advice for the new king, *The Tree of Commonwealth* – its roots supporting godliness, truth, concord, justice and peace.

8 September 1553: *Lady Elizabeth Attends Mass*

Lady Elizabeth attended her first Mass, though feeling unwell with a stomach ache. At the beginning of the month, Elizabeth had requested a private audience with the queen. Granted, she was conducted to a gallery, with a half-door separating her from the queen. Weeping, Elizabeth came near to the queen and, falling to both her knees, hesitantly said she could clearly see her sister was not well disposed towards her, and she felt the only cause could be religion. She asked for books or a learned man to instruct her for she had been brought up in the way she had and had known no other.

30 September–1 October 1553: *Coronation of Queen Mary*

Travelling in a canopied chariot covered with cloth of tissue drawn by six horses, trapped in red velvet, Queen Mary wore an ermine-furred blue velvet gown. On her reddish-auburn hair was a circlet of gold set with many jewels over a close-fitting tinsel cap decorated with precious jewels and pearls, the two together so heavy that she had to support her head with a hand. Going before her in procession were lords, nobles and gentry and the thirteen newly created Knights of the Bath including Edward Courtenay, now Earl of Devonshire, and the young Earl of Surrey, grandson of the Duke of Norfolk. A second canopied chariot, drawn by six horses, both in cloth of silver, carried Lady Elizabeth and Anne of Cleves. Gentlewomen, all in red velvet, rode after.

The cheering crowds lining the tapestry-hung streets strewn with grass, flowers and sweet herbs chased away the queen's fears of religious revolt. They passed the four great giants set up at Fenchurch and singing children at Gracechurch corner to reach the Florentine Pageant, where a green-clothed angel puppet with a trumpet seemingly played a tune when the instrument was lifted to its mouth, a trumpeter secretly hiding behind a screen.

At the conduit in Cornhill were three pretty children, clothed as women: Grace held a sceptre, Virtue a cup and Nature an olive branch. In order they knelt and sang a ditty to the queen. At the little conduit the queen received a purse containing £1,000 from the aldermen, while at the schoolhouse in St Paul's Churchyard she listened for a while to the children singing. On the top of St Paul's steeple, a brave fellow stood by the weathercock, unfurling into the wind eight great streamers of the city's arms. Standing on one foot, he waved a little flag then knelt in reverence to her. At the dean's house and the conduit in Fleet Street, groups of children sang holding burning perfumed tapers.

The following morning, at eleven o'clock, the queen walked to the abbey upon blue cloth strewn with pretty flowers, the way railed on both sides. Slender, being sparing in her diet, the queen wore a blue velvet gown, lined with powdered ermine almost as white as her complexion. Her eyebrows, hardly visible, accentuated the largeness of her hazel eyes. At the abbey, there were so many ceremonies in anointing, crowning and other old rituals that it was almost five o'clock before she departed, now dressed in a crimson velvet gown, the crown on her head. Three sheathed swords and one naked were borne before her. In her hand was the gold sceptre, in the other the ball of gold which she twirled and turned. Her ladies followed, all in crimson velvet with gold coronets on their heads. Carried into Westminster Hall, the queen sat on a stone chair covered with brocade, resting her feet upon two of her ladies, while she dined by candlelight.

Outside, an 'ill scramble' took place for the carpet and rails for keepsakes. Boards were set up outside with all kinds of meat cast out of the kitchen. Afterwards there was 'no less scrambling' for the boards which were carried away.

5 October 1553: Mary's First Parliament

Parliament today had only one motion for the day: the repeal of the divorce between King Henry VIII and Katharine of Aragon. The marriage was declared good and lawful.

Lady Elizabeth was not removed from the succession despite the vehement wishes of the queen, who said that it was a disgrace to allow her to succeed, she 'being a heretic, hypocrite and bastard, born of an infamous woman' and unknown father; that Elizabeth had the face of Mark Smeaton, the lute player.

Parliament will this term repeal other statutes so the realm can be reconciled to the Pope's obedience and to allow Cardinal Pole, as the Pope's legate, into England with power to hold legatine courts.

13 November 1553: Arraignments at the Guildhall

Walking heavily guarded through the crowds, the axe going before them, Thomas Cranmer (who upheld Mary's right to the throne), Lord Guilford Dudley and his wife Lady Jane, accompanied by two of her gentlewomen, were taken from the Tower to the

Guildhall, to be arraigned of treason. Guilford's brothers, Ambrose and Harry, were with them. Lady Jane wore a simple velvet-edged and lined black gown and black French hood. A black velvet book hung from her girdle and she carried an open prayer book in her hand.

Returned to the Tower, the Lords Robert and Guildford, in an act of charity by the queen, were allowed the liberty of walking the leads on the Bell Tower; Lady Jane was granted the liberty of walking in the queen's garden, though the wedded couple were forbidden contact.

8 December 1553: Lady Elizabeth Leaves Court

After a recent outburst by the queen that Elizabeth had 'not a single servant or maid of honour who was not a heretic; that she talked every day with heretics and lent an ear to all their evil designs', Elizabeth asked to leave court to live at her house at Ashridge, near St Albans. Though she attended Mass, the queen accused her sister of only doing so in order to dissimulate, either out of fear or hypocrisy. Elizabeth had answered timidly, her voice trembling, that she went to Mass of her own free will, prompted and moved by her conscience.

Before she was allowed to leave, Lords Arundel and Paget, in a meeting with her, said that if she left 'the straight road' and intrigued with either heretics or the French, she would regret it' and she would be closely watched. Elizabeth responded she was attending Mass at the dictates of her conscience and would prove it by her way of living; she was no hypocrite and wished only to obey and please the queen.

A source at court said the queen has showed constant dislike for her sister, brooding upon the injuries she believes Elizabeth's mother inflicted on hers. Since the marriage of King Henry and Katherine of Aragon was declared legitimate, the hatred of the queen for the Lady Elizabeth has become common knowledge.

On her journey, 10 miles from court, Lady Elizabeth wrote to the queen asking if she could borrow a litter and be sent items such as chasubles, chalices, crosses and copes for her chapel.

14 January 1554: A Marriage Knot to Be Knitted

Bishop Gardiner made an eloquent speech to everyone assembled in the queen's presence chamber that Queen Mary intended to marry Prince Philip of Spain. Lords and nobles were informed that in the marriage contract Mary would receive a dowry of 3,000 ducats, any issue would be heir to England and Flanders, England would not be involved with Philip's wars and no Spaniard would be given a seat on the council, castles, titles or office in the queen's house or elsewhere. He ended that they should thank God that so noble and worthy a prince would so humble himself as to be like a subject leaving the queen to rule. He said the queen asked them, for her sake, to 'receive him with all reverence, joy and honour'.

The news of the marriage was already abroad before the proclamation as harbingers, preparing for the ambassadors' arrival for the 'knitting up' of the marriage contract, had arrived in advance on New Year's Day, and had been pelted with snowballs. When the Spanish ambassadors arrived the day after at Tower Wharf, the public showed their disgruntlement by keeping their heads down and remaining silent as they passed.

Over Christmastide, the queen blushed furiously when her ladies teased her on her coming nuptials. On Twelfth Night, Lord William Howard, seeing the queen pensive, pointed to the seat on her right and said that he wished that the prince was present to drive her care away, which made her blush very prettily.

The queen has often said she does not marry for carnal reasons and had thought she would remain a maid forever, so often had her father used her as a bargaining piece since she was three years old.

27 January–1 February 1554: Rebels and Turncoats

Rebels led by Sir Thomas Wyatt, son of the poet, marched into Rochester. Taking control of the bridge, he set on it three or four double cannon. Mr Cobham, Sir George Harper and other men had taken up arms in protest at the queen's forthcoming marriage. Meanwhile, Henry Grey, Duke of Suffolk had, with his brothers Lords John and Leonard, 'stolen from his house at Sheen and run away'. The queen, in response, had sent out the Duke of Norfolk, Earl of Ormond and Mr Jerningham, Captain of the Guard, with a great number of captains and soldiers towards Gravesend to subdue the rebels. At the same time, Francis Hastings, Earl of Huntingdon was sent to pursue Suffolk with 200 men

As the Duke of Norfolk set off, he requested a watch be set at every gate of the city by armed householders and sent ahead a herald into Rochester with a 'free and frank pardon' to any who would desist. The herald was told by the rebels that they had done nothing which required pardon, and that they would live and die in the quarrel.

At the outbreak of fighting, Sir George Harper turned coat and joined Norfolk's men while one of the captains of the duke turned himself about and ordered his men to fight for the rebels. His men turned their ordnance against their fellows, crying 'A Wyatt! A Wyatt!', which caused the duke, earl and captain to flee, leaving behind cannon, munitions and ordnance, their men running away without swords, arrows or strings in their bows.

When news reached the queen that Wyatt's rebels had passed Deptford and Greenwich unopposed, heading towards Blackheath, she proclaimed from Whitehall that Wyatt and his company were 'rank traitors'. The number of armed men at the gates and the drawbridge to London Bridge was doubled and the bridge broken down. Shopkeepers in Southwark were told by the Earl of Pembroke and Lords Cobham, Howard and Clinton to shut their shops and windows, pack their wares away and stand armed at their doors.

Early in the morning of 1 February, ministers implored Mary to move to the Tower for safety but she refused. Around three o'clock that afternoon, the queen rode to the Guildhall with her lords and ladies, heralds and trumpets blowing. There, she told all assembled that she was marrying by her council's consent and advice and 'that she would never marry unless all her subjects be content and would live as she had done hitherto'. Holding up her hand with the espousal ring on her finger, she said that she was wedded to her realm; as for the rebels, she said they should 'fear them not, for I assure you, I fear them nothing at all'. The queen, though short and delicately framed, has a surprisingly loud and man-like voice which can be heard at some distance.

True to her word, the queen returned to Whitehall, where she insisted on remaining, but her pensioners have been put on guard around her. One of them, Edward Underhill, reported that when he and his fellows came into the chamber of presence with their poleaxes in their hands, the ladies were very fearful, 'some lamenting, crying and wringing their hands'.

7 February 1554: Sir Thomas Wyatt Apprehended

After three days of constant bombardment from the Tower, Sir Thomas Wyatt, having no desire to see the householders of Southwark killed or their homes destroyed, moved his men to Kingston Bridge. Although the bridge had been 'plucked up', men swam over to fetch boats and they marched through Kensington, arriving at Hyde Park Corner in the afternoon of 7 February where the queen's men awaited them.

Under attack, the rebels were split into separate bands at Charing Cross. Some of the company ran down the old lane by St James to Westminster but found the gates being shut against them. After shooting arrows into the garden, they fled back the way they came to mingle with the queen's soldiers. Wyatt's band marched to Temple Bar, down Fleet Street, shouting 'God save Queen Mary' all the way to Ludgate, where he knocked at the gates thinking he would gain entry. The gates remained locked and, standing on the other side, Lord William advised him to go. With no aid from the city forthcoming, Wyatt retraced his steps. At Temple Bar he yielded after Master Norroy Herald advised, 'Sir, ye were best by my counsel to yield. You see this day is gone against you, and in resisting ye can get no good but be the death of all your soldiers to your great peril of soul.'

Sir Maurice Berkeley bade Wyatt to ride pillion behind him and took him to court, where it was seen that he wore shirt of mail with very fair sleeves, a velvet cassock with yellow lace, a velvet hat with broad lace and a pair of spurred boots. That night, he was sent by water to the Tower.

12 February 1554: Execution of Guilford and Jane Dudley

Ten o'clock this morning, the 'tall and comely' Lord Guilford Dudley was brought to the scaffold set up on Tower Hill. After a small declaration, not having been allowed a priest of his own faith, he knelt and prayed. Holding up his eyes and hands to God many times, he asked the people to pray for him before laying his head upon the block, which was taken off at one stroke of the axe. His body was thrown into a cart, his head wrapped in a cloth and placed alongside. As the cart conveyed his remains to the chapel, Lady Jane caught sight of his dead body on the way to her own scaffold on The Green. She remained calm, as she had when watching him walk to his death from the window of Partridge's at No. 5 The Green, where she had been lodged.

Although her two ladies wept the whole short journey, Jane's own eyes remained dry as she prayed. She wore the same gown in which she was arraigned and carried a prayer book in her hand.

On the scaffold she made a short speech wherein she declared she knew little of the law and titles to the crown, and as for coveting the crown she said, 'I do wash my hands in innocency' and asked them to pray with her. Kneeling, she read Psalm 51 aloud in English. Standing, she gave her book to the Lieutenant of the Tower. As she untied her gown, the executioner went to help her but she turned away, her ladies taking her gloves, gown, headdress and collar from her.

The executioner then knelt before her to ask her forgiveness, which she gave him willingly. He arose and told her to stand on the straw. Seeing the block, she said, 'I pray you despatch me quickly'. She then knelt down, tied a handkerchief about her eyes, and, feeling for the block, she said, 'Where is it? Where is it?' One of those on the scaffold gently guided her hands and she laid her head upon the block.

Neither Jane nor Guilford had attained seventeen years of age.

23 February 1554: *Lady Elizabeth Arrives at Whitehall*

Dressed all in white, her face pale, Elizabeth was carried by open litter to Whitehall Palace by way of the queen's garden, accompanied by a red-coated escort of guard. The queen refused to grant audience to her sister, who was lodged in the palace, allowed to retain only two gentlemen, six ladies and four servants, and 'neither she nor any of her suite can pass without crossing the guard'. Her arrival was expected ten days ago, after the queen had sent two of her physicians to ascertain whether she was as unwell as she claimed in response to the queen sending for her on the day of Lady Jane's execution. Had she been well, Lords Howards and Hastings and Sir Thomas Cornwallis had orders to arrest her and bring her to the Tower, but she was so unwell that the party have only travelled two or three leagues a day, she being unable to stand, eat or drink.

Lord Courtenay, on 12 February, was taken from the Earl of Sussex's house, arrested and imprisoned in the Tower. There are

Right: 1. King Henry VII. (From *Royal House of Tudor*, 1866)

Below: 2. St Paul's before 1561, from a drawing by Wyngaerde. (From *Mediaeval London*, 1901)

Left: 3. Queen Elysabeth of York. (From *Royal House of Tudor*, 1866)

Below left: 4. Perkin Warbeck. (From *Prisoners in the Tower of London*, 1866)

Below: 5. Prince Arthur. (From *Royal House of Tudor*, 1866)

6. Ludlow Castle. (Author's collection)

Above: 7. The Tower of London. (Courtesy of Ana Gic from Pixabay)

Right: 8. King Henry VIII in his prime. (From *The Wives of Henry VIII*, 1905)

9. Queen Katherine of Aragon. (From *Royal House of Tudor*, 1866)

10. Princess Mary, sister of Henry VIII. (From *Royal House of Tudor*, 1866)

Above: 11. *Harry Grace A Dieu* – Henry VIII's newly built ship of 1522. (From *Archaeologia*, vol. VI, 1779)

Right: 12. Queen Anne Boleyn. (From *Royal House of Tudor*, 1866)

13. Hever Castle, home of the Boleyns. (Courtesy of Nadin Lisa from Pixabay)

Above left: 14. Hampton Court Great Hall. (Courtesy of M. L. Knights)

Left: 15. Westminster, from a sketch by Wyngaerde. (From *Mediaeval London*, 1901)

Below: 16. The remains of Whitby Abbey, dissolved in 1539. (Courtesy of Dave Hostad from Pixabay)

17. Queen Jane Seymour. (From *Royal House of Tudor*, 1866)

18. King Henry VIII later in life. (From *Henry VIII*, 1902)

Above left: 19. Queen Anne of Cleves, Henry's fourth wife. (Courtesy of the Rijksmuseum)

Above right: 20. Queen Katheryne Howard, his fifth wife. (Courtesy of the Rijksmuseum)

21. Gainsborough Old Hall. Kateryn Parr once lived there, and Katheryne Howard visited on the long Northern Progress. (Author's collection)

Right: 22. Replicas of dress worn by Henry VIII and Katheryne Howard. (Author's collection)

Below: 23. Queen Kateryn Parr, Henry's sixth and final wife. (From *Royal House of Tudor*, 1866)

Below right: 24. King Edward VI, Henry's son and successor. (Courtesy of the Rijksmuseum)

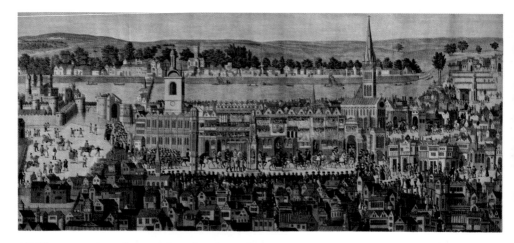

25. The procession of King Edward VI from the Tower to Westminster. (Courtesy of Yale Center for British Art, Paul Mellon Collection)

26. A woodcut of the murder of Mr Arden of Faversham. (From *Archaeologia Cantiana*, vol. XXXIV, 1920)

27. The Palace of Greenwich, drawn by Wyngaerde. (From *Mediaeval London*, 1901)

28. Queen Jane. (From *Royal House of Tudor*, 1866)

29. Lord Guilford Dudley. (From *Royal House of Tudor*, 1866)

Above left: 30. Queen Mary I. (From *Two English Queens and Philip*, 1908)

Above right: 31. Mary's husband, Philip II of Spain. (From *Royal House of Tudor*, 1866)

Left: 32. Winchester Cathedral. (Courtesy of Julia Schwab from Pixabay)

Above: 33. The burning of vicar John Rogers, condemned as a heretic by Bishop Gardiner. (From *Actes and Monuments*, vol. 6, 1838)

Right: 34. The inimitable Queen Elizabeth I. (Portrait of Queen Elizabeth I by Marcus Gheeraerts the Elder, © Portland Collection/ Bridgeman Images)

35. Lord Robert Dudley,
Elizabeth's favourite. (From
*Two English Queens and
Philip*, 1908)

36. Mary, Queen of Scots.
(From *Love Affairs of Mary
Queen of Scots*, 1903)

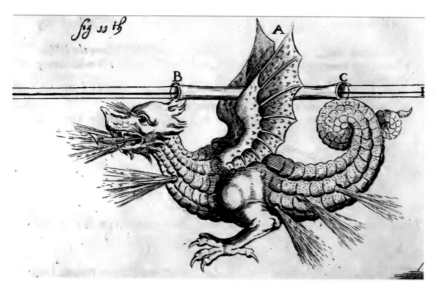

37. A diagram depicting a contemporary dragon firework. (From *Pyrotechnia*, 1635)

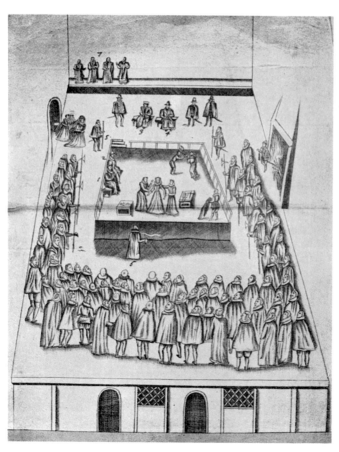

38. Robert Beale's drawing of the execution of Mary, Queen of Scots. (From *The Tragedy of Fotheringay*, 1895)

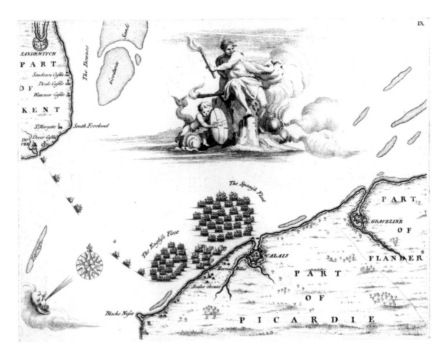

39. The launch of the fireships against the Spanish Armada in 1588, engraved after the tapestry hangings originally produced for Charles Howard. (Courtesy of the Rijksmuseum)

40. The Sylvan Fancy, an entertainment at Elvetham near the end of the Tudor era. (From *The Progresses and Public Processions of Queen Elizabeth*, 1823)

rumours that both Courtenay and Elizabeth will be executed. Allegations abound that Lady Elizabeth had intrigued with the French ambassador after the council found, in the seized pack of the ambassador's letters, a copy of a loving letter sent to Mary by Elizabeth in January from Ashridge in which she apologised for not writing for three weeks owing to 'such a cold and headache that I have never felt their like'. Mary, encouraged by Renard, believes this shows the two must be in league. Reasoned folk think the French would love to implicate the lady to pave the way for Mary, Queen of Scots.

15 March 1554: Sir Thomas Wyatt Arraigned

Sir Thomas Wyatt was arraigned at Westminster for treason and rebellion. He denied conspiring at the queen's death; he merely wanted to prevent Spanish strangers coming into the realm. He confessed to sending a letter to Lady Elizabeth advising her to move as far from the city as she could to be safe from strangers, but she had merely sent a messenger thanking him for his good will.

Six days ago, several children gathered in a field and, dividing into two bands, acted out the fight between the queen's men and Wyatt's, wounding each other in the process. The little fellow playing the part of the Prince of Spain was nearly hanged by his fellows but was cut down just in time to save his life. Most were arrested, whipped and shut up in the Guildhall.

18 March 1554: Lady Elizabeth Taken to the Tower

On Palm Sunday, Lady Elizabeth was taken to the Tower from Westminster by river accompanied by the Marquis of Winchester and the Earl of Sussex. She was expected at the Tower the previous day but Elizabeth begged to speak to the queen and when this was denied she asked if she could at least write to her. This was granted, and while she was writing the tide rose so high they could not safely shoot London Bridge. Queen Mary was so angry at the news that those responsible were told they would not have 'dared do such a thing' in her father's lifetime and that she wished he 'might come to life again for a month'.

The Lord Chamberlain, Sir John Gage, was at the Tower to receive Elizabeth at the drawbridge. As she entered, she looked up to heaven and said, 'Oh Lord, I never thought to have come in here as prisoner; and I pray you all, good friends and fellows' – looking at the warders and soldiers – 'bear me witness that I come in no traitor but as true a woman to the queen as any is now living, and thereon will I take my death.' Turning to the Lord Chamberlain, she asked if all the armed men were there for her. He said not but she said, 'Yes, I know it is so; it needed not for me, being alas, but a weak woman.'

Before he left the Tower, the Earl of Sussex, tears in his eyes, said, 'What will ye do, my lords? What mean you therein? She was a king's daughter and is the queen's sister … go ye no further than your commission.'

11 April 1554: *Sir Thomas Wyatt Beheaded*
Today, Sir Thomas Wyatt was beheaded upon Tower Hill.

With a book in his hand, he came to the scaffold and used his last words before the crowds to exonerate both Lady Elizabeth and Lord Courtenay, saying that neither was 'privy of my rising or commotion before I began, as I have declared no less to the queen's council. And this is most true.' Without saying anything further, he turned away, took off his gown, unfastened his points, removed his doublet and waistcoat and in his shirt knelt down upon the straw. He curled into himself awhile, raised himself onto his knees, prayed, put the blindfold on, and laid down his head, taken from him with one stroke.

His body was quartered upon the scaffold, to be set at different places. His head was taken away to be placed on a stake on the gallows beyond St James.

19 May 1554: Lady Elizabeth under House Arrest

Eighteen years to the day since her mother left to go to her execution, Lady Elizabeth was released from the Tower at three o'clock in the afternoon into the custody of Sir John Williams and Sir Henry Bedingfield to be taken to the manor of Woodstock. There she is to remain under house arrest at the queen's pleasure, lodged in the easily guarded gatehouse, in the apartment with the Irish oak roof painted blue and sprinkled with gold. The council found no sufficient evidence to condemn her.

For the last few weeks Lady Elizabeth has had the freedom to walk in the Tower garden, although consternation was caused when a child of five, son of one of the soldiers in the Tower, talked to her. The child was questioned as to whether messages had been passed to Elizabeth, but he said he had only given her some flowers.

Many people, unaware that she had not been set free, rejoiced at her departure. The Steelyard merchants shot off three cannons as a sign of their joy at what they believed was her liberation. They were scolded for it by both queen and council. People turned up to see her pass, crying out blessings and throwing cakes and flowers into her lap.

Stopping for the night at Richmond, the Lady Elizabeth's servants were ordered to leave and not attend her. As they took their leave, she sorrowfully desired them to pray for her: 'For this night,' she said, 'I think I must die.' While they wept, Elizabeth's gentleman usher accosted Sir John, Lord Thame and asked him outright if his lady was in danger of death that night. 'God forbid,' exclaimed Sir John, 'that any such wickedness should be intended, rather than it should be wrought, I and my men will die at her feet.'

19–23 July 1554: Arrival of Philip of Spain

Despite northerly winds, desperate seasickness and having to evade French warships, Prince Philip passed safely from his own ship, too large to sail into Southampton, onto Lord Admiral Howard's frigate. On board he was given a banquet and presented, by a herald, with the Order of the Garter, the collar a gift from the queen which cost between 7,000 and 8,000 crowns.

Once disembarked, Philip, walking very slowly with 'upright gait to lose no height', was greeted by nobles and a hundred English archers wearing his livery. Mounted on a white horse, with crimson gold-edged velvet trappings, he made a gallant figure as he rode to the church and on to his lodgings.

The Titian painting of Philip presented to the queen last November did not do him justice. He is grey-eyed, fair complexioned with a broad forehead and straight nose. He has since grown a beard.

As a gift for the bride, the Emperor sent with his son the most beautiful tapestries of his Tunis expedition and a quantity of very fine jewels.

After dinner on 23 July, Philip left for Winchester in a violent rainstorm. He arrived at the bishop's palace completely soaked and his finery ruined. After a change of clothes he went, by way of the gardens, to meet with Queen Mary for the first time. His manner was so gracious and gallant that he has left all her ladies aflutter, while the queen is as much in love with the original as she was with the portrait.

25 July 1554: *Mary and Philip Marry*

Philip and his Spanish nobles entered quietly through the west door of Winchester Cathedral, no sword borne before him. He wore, with the Collar of the Garter, a mantle of gold ornamented with pearls and jewels – another gift from the queen – over white doublet and breeches. Shortly after, the Earl of Derby bearing the sword before her, Queen Mary entered wearing a similar mantle. She had walked through the crowded streets from her lodging, her train borne by the Marquis of Winchester. The day for the wedding was considered auspicious by the Spanish, being St James's Day.

Just before the espousal, Bishop Gardiner, who was officiating, announced that the Emperor had bestowed the Kingdom of Naples upon his 'chief jewel and son and heir'; Queen Mary would marry a man equal to her in rank. To cheers and shouts for God to send the couple joy, the Marquis of Winchester and the earls of Derby, Bedford and Pembroke gave away the queen in the name of the whole realm. Laid upon the book, the wedding ring was blessed, while the king laid three handfuls of gold coins on top, scooped up by Lady Margaret Clifford, the queen's only attending female relative, who put them into the queen's purse. The king and queen clasped hands.

After Mass and the offering of jewels and tapers was finished, bride and groom walked hand in hand under one canopy to the bishop's palace, where they sat under one cloth of estate, dining sumptuously to music. Otherwise, all were 'admirably served in perfect order and silence'. Underhill, who was at the wedding banquet as a server, said that the meat of the second course was given to the bearers. He had carried a large, very delicately baked 'pasty' of a red deer on a great gold charger. The gold dish he had to give back to the kitchen but the pasty, which went untouched, he sent to his wife and her brother who shared it with friends.

In the chamber of presence afterwards, the king and queen danced together in the German fashion while the dukes and noblemen of Spain danced with the 'beautiful nymphs' of England. After supper, which they ate in private in their own chambers, the Bishop of Winchester blessed the marriage bed where the king and queen remained alone and only they know what happened that night. The ten days following will be filled with masques, banquets, singing and dancing while the city of London prepares the pageants for the king's entry.

2 October 1554: *Burial of Duke of Norfolk*

Thomas Howard, 3rd Duke of Norfolk, aged eighty-one years, who died at Kenninghall on 25 August after falling ill after the last council meeting on 7 May, was today buried in St Michael's Church at Framlingham. The wax hearse had a dozen bannerols and twelve-dozen escutcheons, three coats of arms and a banner of damask. His motto was 'By the grace of God, I am what I am'. Mourners, rich and poor, sat down after the burial to a great dinner at which forty-eight oxen, one hundred sheep and sixty calves were killed, served alongside venison, swans, cranes, capons, rabbits, pigeons, pikes and bread with a copious amount of wine and beer.

His grandson Thomas, son of the duke's deceased eldest son, the poet-earl Henry Howard, and Frances de Vere, was named heir to the duke's fifty-six manors and other estates and becomes the fourth Duke of Norfolk.

12 November 1554: *Queen Mary Pregnant*

To open Parliament, the king on horseback and the queen in an open litter travelled to Westminster Abbey, their majesties wearing mantles of crimson velvet with long trains and hoods, lined with powdered ermine. Two swords of power were carried before them. The crush of people in the palace, streets and abbey were such that it was almost impossible for anyone to move. Cries of 'Oh, how handsome the king is', 'how kind and gentle he looks' and 'look how lovingly he treats the queen' abounded to the pleasure of everyone.

The queen looked as if she was three months with child, affirmed by a person from court who said not only that her 'stomach clearly shows it and her dresses no longer fit her' but also that she has 'felt the babe' and suffers from morning sickness. A source said the queen believes the baby is due in April, and is a blessing and sign from God at the righteousness of her actions.

2 December 1554: *The Pope Restored to Primacy*

With a grave countenance, the Pope's ambassador and legate, Cardinal Reginald Pole, arrived at St Paul's Cathedral with great pomp, having borne before him a cross, two pillars and two poleaxes of silver. He was met by Bishop Gardiner who announced that the king and queen, repealing certain Acts, had restored the Pope to his right of primacy and revived the laws for punishment of heretics.

4 February 1555: *The First Heretic Burned*

John Rogers, ex-vicar of St Sepulchre and prebendary at St Paul's, condemned as a heretic by Bishop Gardiner and degraded of his titles by Dr Bonner, Bishop of London, was 'carried' from Newgate between ten and eleven o'clock in the morning to be burnt at the stake at Smithfield. The queen's pardon followed him but he declared he would not recant.

The crowd murmured discontentedly, watching in horror as Rogers was chained to the stake and faggots piled about him. As he burned, he recited Psalm 51, washing his hands in the flames. Onlookers wept and others prayed for God to give him strength, perseverance and patience to bear the pain. At the end, his ashes and bones were gathered by some, wrapped up in paper to preserve them while others made threats against the bishops, especially Bonner, who would not allow Rogers any last words with his wife or eleven children, one still 'sucking at her breast'.

There was more murmuring at the news Bishop Hooper, once Bishop of Gloucester and Worcester, will be burnt at Gloucester, for he is well loved and known for his daily provision of food to prevent starvation. A source says that the Spanish ambassador wrote to the king to say that he fears revolt if the bishops burn people at the furious rate they intend and that there are other ways of chastisement such as secret executions, banishment and imprisonment.

30 April 1555: Almost Delivered

At daybreak, the report received during the night that the queen had been delivered of a male child with 'little pain and no danger' had been made so public that everybody, with demonstrations of joy, shut up their shops, rang church bells and set up tables with spreads of food and wine and made bonfires in every street.

In the afternoon, people returning from Hampton Court to give their congratulations said that the report was false but that the queen looked well. They had seen her at the small window she sits at every morning to watch the procession, which, at her request, goes around the place so she can graciously bow her head courteously and cheerfully to all the personages, who in return salute her.

The Lady Elizabeth has been privately brought to the court, living in retirement with three or four of her women. None but their majesties have seen her, she visiting them via private stairs. It is rumoured that no one favours Elizabeth more than the king does.

1 June 1555: Physicians versus *Ladies*

The physicians announced that Queen Mary should give birth two days after the new moon. The queen's ladies disagree. They say she has not yet shown any sign of such a state of pregnancy as to 'bring forth speedily'. The king anxiously awaits the birth of a prince or princess as he is keen to leave for Flanders to attend the public obsequies for his grandmother Juana of Castile, who died on Good Friday. He has already given leave to his attendants to depart and await him overseas.

3 August 1555: Normal Business Resumes

Queen Mary and King Philip moved from Hampton Court to Oatlands Palace, giving many ladies leave to return to their homes, while officials resume their services and duties, for much business was left in abeyance when the queen retired. The move to Oatlands will help the queen ease back into business while giving tacit broadcast that, though in mid-June the king had openly said the queen had commenced labour pains, she was in fact not pregnant.

Yet physicians remain puzzled. The signs suggested the queen was in her seventh month: the child moving, 'increase of girth, hardening of the breasts which distilled'. Others had secretly professed that her pregnancy would 'end in wind'.

Leave to withdraw was also extended to Elizabeth, who had stayed with the queen throughout. She has been given complete liberty.

17 *August 1555: Move to Greenwich*

The court travelled from Hampton Court to Greenwich where Queen Mary will remain while the king goes 'beyond sea'. They rode through London, the queen conveyed in an open litter between her husband and Cardinal Pole, who will stay with her.

The king intends to leave as soon as the fleet – twelve ships and his own galleon, being outfitted in the Thames – are ready to sail to Dover. Her attendants say she is disconsolate at his leaving and that she travelled by litter to stay near to him rather than take the leisurely trip by water. When she supposes she is alone, tears flow down her face.

The crowds lining the streets were vast, some running from one vantage point to another to see the queen and cheer her.

29 *August 1555: The King Departs*

Queen Mary waved goodbye to King Philip at the riverside, returning after to her apartments to watch him from a window. The king, for his part, ensured that she could see him on the barge taking him to Dover, for when the barge approached the window from which she was watching, he waved his bonnet to her to demonstrate his affection. The queen remained gazing after him, giving vent to her grief with floods of tears, until she could no longer see him.

13 September 1555: Venetian Ambassador Visits Court

Queen Mary gave audience to the Venetian ambassador and afterwards talked with him about her husband's departure when, with tears in her eyes, she suddenly and passionately declared she had received no letter from him for seven days. The ambassador kindly comforted her, saying no doubt the king would be sure to make a speedy return and soon be with her again.

13 October 1555: 'Unbecoming to his dignity'

Since the beginning of the month, the queen had prepared for the return of the king, assuming he would return in time for the opening of Parliament on 21 October. To her sorrow, he has written to her that, though anxious to gratify her wish for his return, he feels he cannot continue residing in England in a form 'unbecoming to his dignity'. In Spain he rules absolutely in all things, but in England he is only allowed to take part in the affairs of the realm through her, when he would rather share government with her.

The Spaniards who had remained in England depart hourly, most of them hoping never to return, for the king wrote he needs his Spanish household and guards in Flanders, for the Emperor intends to imminently abdicate and sail afterwards to Spain.

Lady Elizabeth, who resided permanently with the queen at Greenwich, has been given permission to return to a house of her own. The queen will go to St James.

The execution of heretics has been resumed, and the ex-bishops Ridley and Latimer are to be burned at Oxford within a few days.

1 January 1556: New Appointments

Dr Heath, Archbishop of York, was appointed Lord Chancellor and given the Great Seal after the death of Bishop Gardiner on 12

November two hours after midnight. He had grown frail and was unable to go up or down stairs.

Gardiner's body was carried from his house at Southwark to St Mary Overy, where his bowels were buried and his body enclosed in lead and laid in a vault of brick made for it until the spring, for although in his will he requested to be buried in Winchester, his wishes will have to wait until the great flooding from the winter rains drains away. His effigy, with mitre on its head, a gold cope, gloves and rings on his fingers, had already been made.

25 January 1556: *Charles V Abdicates*

The queen received a messenger from her husband, Philip, informing her that she can in future style herself queen of many great crowns as the Emperor has inviolably renounced all the kingdoms of Spain, Sicily and his lands in the Indies, reserving only Burgundy. His assurance that he will be returning soon was the news that gave her most comfort.

The same day, Somerset Herald arrived from Rome with the bulls for Cardinal Pole to become Archbishop of Canterbury in place of the degraded Cranmer. He will sing his first Mass on Palm Sunday.

21 March 1556: *The Burning of Thomas Cranmer*

Dr Cranmer was burned despite having at first recanted. The queen decided his recantation was feigned only to save his life and deemed him unworthy to have her pardon. Hearing her pronouncement, Dr Cranmer retracted all that he had said and signed with his own hand. As he was chained to the stake and the faggots set alight, he pulled from his bosom a copy of his writing and threw it into the flames, asking both God and the people to pardon him for having consented to sign such writings, saying he had hoped that his future presence might have been of use to them. He prayed they would all persist in the new religion and absolutely denied the sacrament and supremacy of the Roman Catholic Church. Putting his right arm and hand into the flames, he said, 'This, which has sinned, having signed the writing, must be the first to suffer punishment' and burned it himself.

2 April 1556: Devotions of Queen Mary

Queen Mary entered the hall, where on benches either side sat forty-one poor women, their washed feet on stools. Around her neck was a towel and a linen apron over her purple gown. Lined with marten fur, its sleeves were so long and wide they reached the ground. She and each of her ladies carried a silver ewer and basin. Before each woman, the queen knelt on both knees. Each woman's right foot was washed and dried, then she made a cross and kissed it fervently as if something precious. Encircling the room several times, the queen gave each woman a large wooden platter filled with pieces of salted fish and two large loaves, a wooden bowl filled with hippocras, a piece of cloth for clothing, then shoes and stockings and, for the sixth and last round, leather purses containing forty-one pennies together with an apron and towel, all of this with her own hand. Her majesty quitted the hall for a short time and returned carrying the gown she had been wearing. Being short-sighted, she peered at each woman closely and gave the gown to the poorest and most aged woman she could see.

This was the queen's first public appearance since the discovery a few weeks ago of a plot to steal the Spanish bullion from the Exchequer. Rumour once again implicated Lady Elizabeth, saying the queen was to be assassinated and replaced with her sister, but it was, in fact, all to do with greed and a get-rich-quick scheme with the end aim of depriving the Spanish of their gold.

9 June 1556: Lady Elizabeth's Attendants Arrested

Mistress Kat Ashley, governess of Lady Elizabeth, along with three domestics and two gentlemen dependents, one of whom is Elizabeth's Italian teacher, were arrested and removed from Hatfield House, suspected on account of religion.

To console and comfort her sister, the queen sent members of her council to explain why her attendants were arrested so that she did not take amiss the removal of those who could bring suspicion down on her. She sent with them a ring as a token of her love.

Queen Mary replaced those arrested with people dependent upon her, and appointed Sir Thomas Pope as governor of the household, an honour he tried to decline. It appears Lady Elizabeth once again finds herself in ward and custody, albeit decorously and honourably, and even if her servants are found innocent they will not be allowed to return.

6 March 1557: Lord Stourton Executed for Murder

Charles, Lord Stourton was transported from the Tower to Salisbury, there to be hanged by a halter of silk for the murder of father and son William and John Hartgill of Kilmington.

Hostility arose between Charles and William when the latter refused to allow Lord Stourton to browbeat and cheat his mother out of money after her husband died. So angered was he by the interference that, Whitsunday last, Lord Stourton took a group of armed servants to accost William Hartgill at church but William's son, John, with crossbow and gun, drove them away and made a daring escape to fetch the sheriff. Much damage had already been done; while the Hartgill family sheltered in the church tower, their crops were destroyed, their livestock stolen and William's riding gelding killed.

Brought before the Star Chamber by the queen after his arrest, Lord Stourton was fined and ordered to pay compensation to the Hartgills. A meeting was set up in Kilmington church for Twelfth Day. Charles, accompanied by fifteen servants, tenants and gentlemen, sent word to the Hartgills in the church that he preferred the church house, a church being no place for business. Father and son demurred that if not the church, then in the open. Charles counter-proposed to set up a table on the village green, which was agreed. That done, he laid upon it a purse, saying, 'The council have ordered me to pay a certain sum of money, every penny of which they should have.'

Father and son emerged, and Stourton immediately ordered his men to arrest them for felony. Struggling against their captors, father and son were violently manhandled into the church house, bound and beaten severely while Stourton watched. As the lord left the building, John's wife, who had tried to see what was happening, was left dying on the ground as he near decapitated her with his sword.

John and William then disappeared. Stourton, again under arrest, denied knowing where they were, saying they must have escaped. Questioning of the servants revealed John and William had been taken to Stourton's house at Bonham in the night and beaten to death with clubs in the garden while Stourton watched. The bodies, as they thought, were carried to a cellar where, finding by groans the men were not quite dead, he ordered their throats to be cut, saying killing them was of no more account than killing two sheep. They were then tumbled into a pit already dug by the servants.

Sir Anthony Hungerford uncovered the bodies in the same apparel they were taken in, 15 feet down, covered with earth, two thick courses of paving, woodchips and shavings 'above the quantity of two cartloads'.

20 March 1557: Return of King Philip

King Philip returned to Greenwich at five o'clock, his ship coming up with the tide. As the ship came abreast of the court gate, it shot sixteen pieces to salute the queen.

7 June 1557: *War with France*

War with France, to join with King Philip, was proclaimed and a herald with trumpets sent to France to announce it to the King of France in accordance with English custom of never going to war without first declaring it.

8 July 1557: *Proclamation*

The queen today issued a proclamation for all seafaring English subjects to go to sea in their ships to act against the French and Scots. Two days ago, King Philip passed over the sea to Calais. Soon to follow him, the Earl of Pembroke was appointed as head of the army assisted by Lords Montague and Clinton, who are already at Dover.

25 July 1557: *Lady Elizabeth Received at Richmond*

Queen Mary invited Lady Elizabeth to Richmond. Lodging at Somerset Place, she was taken by water in the queen's barge, which was richly hung with garlands of artificial flowers, covered with a canopy of green sarcenet and embroidered with branches of eglantine with gold blossoms. Sir Thomas Pope and four ladies of her chamber accompanied her. The queen's barge was attended by six boats filled with her highness' retinue, all dressed in russet damask and blue embroidered satin spangled with silver. Their bonnets were cloth of silver plumed with a green feather.

Queen Mary received Elizabeth in the garden in a sumptuous pavilion made to look like a castle. Formed from cloth of gold, the walls of the pavilion were designed to alternate silver lilies with golden pomegranates. At the royal banquet there was a confectionery subtlety made in the shape of a pomegranate tree bearing the arms of Spain commemorating her marriage day. Minstrels played but there was no masking nor dancing.

3-4 August 1557: Death of Lady Anne of Cleves

Lady Anne of Cleves, who died at Chelsea on 17 July, was buried at Westminster Abbey by the high altar. The procession from Chelsea was long, with all the children of Westminster, three crosses, priests and monks. The Bishop of London and Abbot of Westminster rode together, before all the nobles and her officers and servants, all wearing black. The chariot, with heralds carrying eight banners of arms and four banners and 100 servants carrying burning torches, came by St James and Charing Cross. Watch was kept all night with lights burning.

Next day, a mitred and coped Bishop of London sang a Requiem Mass and censed the corpse while she was carried to her tomb. Her head officers broke their staffs, ushers their rods, and all were cast into her grave.

27 August 1557: Victory at the Siege of St Quentin

Since 12 August, King Philip with his army of English nobles and soldiers had continually battered the French town of St Quentin with twenty-nine cannons on the eastern and northern sides, levelling a great part of the walls and the towers, though at night men – and women – made new defences. English miners went under the moat and walls. Once the town was breached, it was taken by storm at vespers on 27 August.

The Earl of Bedford reported that the 'Swartzrotters', deemed masters of the king's army, showed much cruelty. Greedy for spoils, they set the town on fire, and women and children hiding in the cellars gave such pitiful cries as they were burnt that 'it would grieve any Christian heart'.

1–8 January 1558: England Loses Calais

The Duke of Guise, the general of the French army, 'under colour' of victualling Boulogne and Ardres, unexpectedly and swiftly crossed the border into the English-owned Calais Pale on New

Year's Day. He divided his army into two: one part battered and took the bulwark of Sandgate and Ruisbank fort in Calais harbour while the other took Newnham Bridge, leaving him strategically well placed to assault Calais town.

The assault on the town began on 4 January from five double cannon and three culverins placed on Ruisbank sand hills, which after three days' bombardment breached the wall next to the Water Gate. This was the duke's second unsuspected ruse. While Englishmen and Calais townswomen rushed to fortify that part of the town under cover of night, the duke planted fifteen double cannon against the castle, using low tide to wade over the haven. The English plan to blow up the castle with the French in it failed. French soldiers began trying to enter the town but were repulsed, its gates barricaded, the bridge burned down and a trench dug.

Lord Wentworth, aware that the town was no longer defensible, sent word he would surrender. The duke agreed so long as all the goods and fifty English prisoners remained. The next morning the French entered. Guarded by Scottish light horsemen, English soldiers left. The bruit is that taking Calais was the French king's revenge for the loss of St Quentin. Men, women and children of Calais were ordered out of their homes and herded into the churches and left without food or drink over that day and the next while the French ransacked their houses. The following afternoon, Guise had a proclamation made that, before they were expelled from the town, all money, plate and jewels held by those in the churches was to be left on the high altar on pain of death.

24 April 1558: Mary, Queen of Scots Marries the Dauphin

Mary, Queen of Scots, now in her sixteenth year, married the fourteen-year-old Dauphin Francois in the city of Paris. The marriage was consummated that night according to reports. A grand banquet was held with stately service, followed by masquerades and revels, although the usual jousts and tournaments will be held after the fighting ends.

17 November 1558: Death of Queen Mary

At midnight, in her bedchamber at St James, Queen Mary received extreme unction, but died before Mass was finished, between five and six o'clock, having been ill and melancholic for the last few months.

The late queen's physicians and surgeons opened her. Her bowels and heart were coffined separately, the latter in a small velvet-covered coffin bound with silver. The clerks of the spicery and chandlery covered the royal corpse with spices and waxed linen cloth, after which it was coffined, covered with purple velvet and the seam covered with lace, fastened with gilt nails. The coffin, covered in cloth of gold with a silver cross, was laid on a trestle table decorated with her arms in fine gold in her black-hung privy chamber, where her ladies will keep watch every night with lights burning.

Queen Mary made her will on 30 March when she believed herself to 'be with child' and with the consent of her husband. Her main wishes were for alms in the sum of £1,000 be distributed, for her mother to be removed from Peterborough to be buried near her, and for money to be given to her servants, religious houses and towards a hospital 'for the relief and help of poor and old soldiers', especially those hurt or maimed in the wars and service of the realm. Had she had issue, she left the crown to her husband but in a codicil written on 28 October she wrote that, God having given her neither 'fruit nor heir of my body' and feeling herself sick and weak in body, her husband had no further government, order and rule within this realm but it remains and descends to 'my next heir and successor'. She made no mention of Elizabeth by name.

QUEEN ELIZABETH I
1558–1603

Elizabeth, the people's princess, delighted the crowds by interacting with them at her coronation. Such charisma was observed by her subjects throughout her reign, as she charmed those she met while on her progresses, undertaken most years to communicate with people at all levels of society. Visits averaged one or two days, having dinner in one place, supper in another. Visiting small and large towns, she listened to economic problems, evaluated local economies and reviewed the fortifications of her ports as well as showing herself to her people. Martial displays became a covert way of training soldiers. Far from bankrupting the people with whom she stayed, Elizabeth's accounts showed she provided her own furnishings and paid for extra fuel, provisions, food, beer and wine, the latter supplied for her courtiers as Elizabeth ate sparingly and drank only beer. Unlike the rest of her family, she was very economical in her expenditure.

From the moment Elizabeth gained her throne, she was faced with problems. The French urged the Pope to declare her an illegitimate heretic, ineligible to wear the crown, so that Mary, Queen of Scots could claim it. She had to fight her own bishops just to be crowned. Unlike Mary, she was moderate in religion although deeply spiritual, as the prayers she composed show, but she did not wish to enquire too closely into people's beliefs. She disliked idolatry but was happy to allow some statuary to remain and was angered when those orders were disobeyed. She decreed all churches to hold services according to the Book of Common Prayer and have an English Bible. All her subjects were commanded to attend church on Sundays and holy days. Most people were accepting of this, except the most fervent Catholics who refused to attend church or attended with wool stuffed in their ears.

Elizabeth's first acts as queen were to turn the exchequer around and improve the coinage after it had been debased by Mary and Philip.

From early on, Elizabeth had unwaveringly decided she would only marry after considering the good of her people rather than her own private happiness, despite the unrelenting pressure on her to wed and produce an heir. Those who knew her best, though, even from the start of her reign, declared they knew she would never marry. Eligible princes and others sought her hand throughout the first twenty years or so, some even with the idea of converting her to save England or with the plan to rule over her; after all, a woman should submit to a man's authority. Elizabeth had been taught many lessons regarding men: they pretended love for gain, used women to advance their ambitions and believed women were inferior. Throughout her reign, Elizabeth used her own judgement, wit, intelligence, education and shrewdness to rule both court and realm. She knew who she was. Hers was the authority and she knew how to use it.

Family and friends were immensely important to Elizabeth. Henry Carey, son of her aunt Mary, was given a barony immediately for his loyalty and financial aid. His sister Catherine was made a lady of the privy chamber and her puritan-leaning husband, Sir Francis Knollys, was later made vice-chamberlain. In the domestic calendar there are entries that show she looked out for granddaughters of her uncle Sir Edward Boleyn. The friends she made during imprisonment and house arrest stayed loyal to her all their lives and she to them. William Cecil, who had looked after her interests, was made her chief councillor and later Lord Burghley. All her ministers were chosen for their ability, loyalty and honesty.

Elizabeth discretely cherished the memory of her mother, wearing a ring with her likeness on her finger all her life. In 1593, visitors to Hampton Court wrote home that they had visited the queen's bedroom with its bed and silk coverlet and nearby were shown a bed with a tester, embroidered by the queen's mother. Like her mother, Elizabeth enjoyed her leisure time writing poetry and music, playing the virginals when she wished to be solitary; and, if needing to be calmed, she made translations from Greek and Latin writers. She also studied political history, astronomy, mathematics, logic, philosophy and architecture. When wanting to be active, dancing was her delight; even in the year before her death she was reported as dancing galliards in the morning. She enjoyed plays and had her own troupe that went around the country. She put on jousts, public displays and pageants accessed by the general public and was shown much love and devotion by her subjects.

17 November 1558: Long Live the Queen

Between eleven o'clock and noon, Elizabeth was proclaimed Queen of England by heralds and trumpets, accompanied by the Duke of Norfolk, the earls of Shrewsbury and Bedford, the mayor and others. All afternoon, church bells rang, bonfires were lit and tables of food and drink were set out for everyone to make merry.

28 November 1558: Queen Elizabeth Rides to the Tower

On streets newly gravelled, Queen Elizabeth, dressed in purple velvet with a scarf about her neck, rode to the Tower. Cheering crowds sang and played instruments to show their great joy as she passed. She, in turn, delighted them by waving, smiling and giving words of thanks. The Earl of Pembroke bore the sword of state before her. Robert Dudley, a close friend from her 'Tower days' and newly made master of horse, followed.

10–14 December 1558: Full Catholic Rites for Queen Mary

Mid-afternoon of Saturday 10 December, eight gentlemen carried Queen Mary's coffin to the four-square hearse made in the black-hung chapel of St James. The high altar was covered in purple velvet. Crowns and roses decorated the posts of the hearse. Inside black-cloth-covered rails, fifteen purple-cushioned black stools with footstools were placed for the comfort of chief mourners while at vigil, and forty-six great tapers burned day and night, their flickers glittering on the church ornaments.

After dinner on Tuesday, heralds created an order of procession. The coffin, with crowned life-sized effigy on top, wearing crimson velvet robes with many beautiful rings on its fingers, was placed into a chariot for its journey to Westminster Abbey, drawn by five horses trapped in black velvet. Two porters with black staves led the procession. Priests in surplices carried the cross in front of the singing gentlemen of the chapel. The standards followed, trumpeters for each: foremost dragon, then greyhound and in between them two by two the knights, chaplains and officers of the household. The lion led the barons, bishops, viscounts and chief officers and the Archbishop of York with the Count of Feria. Last in the procession were the chief mourners and all the queen's ladies on horseback, all in black, with their horses trapped to the ground in black.

Twelve gentlemen carried the coffin through the abbey, the floor covered with black cotton, to the double-storey hearse decorated with wax angels and 432 escutcheons in gold and silver shining in the light of a thousand candles. A wax archangel was on each post which upheld her canopy of estate, inside of which painted in fine gold in each corner were the four evangelists. '*Dieu et Mon Droit*' was embroidered in gold on the black silk-fringed valance. All-night watch was kept by 100 black-gowned poor men holding long torches, while guards held staff-torches. Chandlers waited quietly, handing out new torches to those whose torches had burnt out.

Mass was sung on Wednesday, executed by mitred bishops. After the offering, including all her royal habiliments, banners and standards by knights and heralds and a poleaxe by Lord Sheffield, Queen Mary was buried and, Cardinal Pole having died the day after her, the Archbishop of York cast earth on her coffin, after which her officers broke their staves over their heads and cast them in.

Once everyone had gone to dinner, the common people tore at the black cloth to take away any piece they could.

1 January 1559: Proclamation

The Lord Mayor, by virtue of the queen's proclamation of 30 December, gave notice to all London churches that henceforth the Litany was to be read in English and likewise, at Mass, the Epistle and Gospel of the day.

12–15 January 1559: Coronation of Queen Elizabeth

On the afternoon of Thursday 12 January, travelling via her private corridor in Whitehall to the river stairs, Queen Elizabeth entered her tapestried barge to 'shoot London Bridge at the still of the ebb'. With music playing, towed by a long galley rowed by forty men in their shirts, she set off for the Tower, accompanied by the barges of her nobles and others.

Saturday was a cold day with little flurries of snow in the morning. From every house and shop window hung banners and streamers, while crowds lined the way waving flags and pennants.

The parade began with a thousand horse, lords and ladies all in crimson velvet, with heralds in coat armour and trumpeters in scarlet gowns. The queen dazzled in a gold robe, travelling in a gold-brocade litter pulled through the sanded and gravelled streets by two mules. It was open so everyone could see her. On her head she wore a gold coif with a plain gold crown like a princess but covered with jewels. In her hands she held a pair of gloves. Around her walked bareheaded footmen in crimson velvet jerkins, a white and red rose on their breasts and backs, the letters 'ER' in relief, alongside pensioners of the axe dressed in crimson damask. Then came the queen's chief officers and lords.

At her passing, the citizens cried out prayers, wishes and tender words to which Queen Elizabeth held up her hands and smiled, waving to those who stood far off and thanking those nearer with all her heart. Moved by her responses, the people cheered longer and louder and were enchanted when she stopped her litter to accept a bunch of flowers or listen to a child speak.

In Gracechurch Street, in front of The Eagle, set across the street was a three-storey stage with musicians playing sweet music. A red-robed Henry VII sat next to Elizabeth of York on thrones on the lowest platform. Roses sprang from them leading to the second stage where Henry VIII and Anne Boleyn were seated. In front of them a white gold-crowned eagle with a branch of little roses ascended to an image of Elizabeth. At Cornhill, the queen was represented sitting on the 'Seat of Worthy Governance' supported by the Virtues. The Soper Lane pageant bestowed blessings on her from St Matthew's Gospel, blessings echoed by the people around her. Passing trumpeters, singers and musicians, the pageant at the Little Conduit was called 'Time', at which the queen commented, 'Time has brought me hither.' Old Father Time, with his daughter

Truth, appeared from a hollow and presented her with 'The Word of Truth', a Bible that she promised to diligently read.

When she entered into Westminster there was no less shouting and cheering of people than when she started her journey.

On Sunday, all the bells in London rang, as Queen Elizabeth walked to the abbey upon purple cloth, which, for souvenirs, was cut up once she had passed. Her long train was carried by the Duchess of Norfolk. She was solemnly crowned in a tapestry-bedecked Westminster Abbey by the Bishop of Carlisle. Mass and ceremonies concluded, and having twice changed her apparel, the queen came out of the abbey wearing a royal robe of cloth of gold, carrying in her hands the sceptre and orb. She smiled at the crowd and gave them all a thousand greetings before leaving to dine in Westminster Hall. The crowds were delighted, but a foreign visitor, one Schifanoya, said in his opinion she 'exceeded the bounds of gravity and decorum'.

The motto the queen has taken is one her mother used: '*Semper eadem*' – 'Ever the same'.

25 January 1559: *The Queen's First Parliament*

After service in the abbey, Queen Elizabeth opened her first parliament. She wore a close-fitting ermine-lined crimson robe fastened up to her throat, with a lace trimming around the top. She wore no customary hood but a cap of beaten gold, covered with fine Oriental pearls. The populace knelt as she passed, shouting, 'God save and maintain thee.' She turned to one side and to the other answering, 'Gramercy, good people' smiling sweetly at everyone.

1 May 1559: *Pinnaces A-Maying*

To the hullabaloo of trumpets, drums and guns, two pinnaces, with streamers, banners and flags wafting in the breeze, sailed on May Day evening to the queen's palace at Westminster. While the queen, lords and ladies watched from the windows, the two ships fought with squibs while the 'mariners' threw eggs and oranges at each other. By mischance, a squib fell on a bag of gunpowder. Some men set alight jumped into the Thames, but no one was hurt and hundreds of small boats watching the sights pulled them out.

8 May 1559: Decrees of Parliament

Parliament determined God's word should be in the tongue of the people and services resume according to the Book of Common Prayer. Bishops were ordered not to leave London until they had taken the oath acknowledging Queen Elizabeth as Governor General of the Church, renounced all foreign jurisdiction and promised to be faithful to her, her heirs and successors.

24 May 1559: Peace with France

The French ambassadors, in England to confirm the peace, were invited to supper at Whitehall. At six o'clock, led into the garden by a private gate, they met the queen, looking beautiful in a dress of purple velvet covered with jewels and pearls. She took them into her private orchard, conversing with them eloquently in French, which she speaks as readily as Italian, Latin or Greek.

At the sound of trumpets, she took them through a door created from flowers, leaves and roses into a sweet-scented flower-wreathed gallery. A table of estate was placed in the centre and the queen invited the Constable of France, M. de Montmorency, to sit with her. The French lords and gentlemen sat on one side of a large table, the ladies on the other side. Owing to the farthingales the ladies wore, there was not room for them all to sit so some of the Privy Council gallantly gave up their seats and sat on the rushes on the ground so all the ladies could sit. The delicious banquet lasted two hours, followed by a masque of red-robed astronomers, with torchbearers in green damask. Afterwards, the company danced until eleven o'clock.

Many presents were gifted of gold and silver, plus dogs – mastiffs for wolf hunting, hounds and setters – and horses. To the young brother of the constable, as a signal mark of favour, the queen gave him many valuable clothes which had belonged to her brother, King Edward, who had been of a similar age.

29 May 1559: The Queen's Avowals

Conversing with the queen about matrimony, the Spanish ambassador, the Bishop of Aquila, was taken aback when the queen vowed she would marry no man whom she had not seen, nor would she trust portrait painters. When he teased her for such nonsense, she declared more firmly that she was resolved not to marry except to a man of worth to whom she had spoken. Further, she would like for at least half a year to associate with him and acquaint herself with his manners and mode of life. She stated that one of the qualities her husband must possess is that he 'should not sit at home all day amongst the cinders but should in time of peace keep himself employed in warlike exercises'. The bishop turned to Sir William Pickering, whom rumour had named a prospective bridegroom, but he replied that if he asked the queen for her hand she would just laugh for he knew she had every intention of dying a maid.

25 June–10 July 1559: Plays and Shows at Greenwich

Everyone vies to provide the queen with entertainment, from plays with a queen, a giant and St George and the dragon to the escapades of Robin Hood in the greenwood with Little John, Maid Marian and Friar Tuck.

The London crafts mustered men at arms in coats of velvet and chains of gold, with guns, touch-boxes, Morris-pikes and halberds, swords, daggers and flags at St George's Fields in preparation for their show at Greenwich, which, on 3 July, the queen watched from the gallery over the park gate. The Lord Admiral and Lord Dudley set up two battles in array to skirmish before her: 400 gunners in shirts of mail and open helmets, 200 halberdiers in Almain rivets and 800 pikemen in fine corselets. Drums beating, mingling with flutes and trumpets, 'three onsets' in every battle, the two battles marched towards each other, guns shooting powder, Morris-pikes clacking noisily and soldiers pretending to fight in close combat, skirmish after skirmish.

The show over, the queen thanked all the participants. They – and the thousands of people who had come to watch – cheered and hurled their caps into the air. Provision had been made for the soldiers: beer and cheese, butter and saltfish, beef, venison, geese, capons, rabbits, chickens, sturgeon and pastry items as well as cherries and cream.

The following day the queen visited Woolwich to see the launch of her new ship, the *Elizabeth Jonas*, and had a banquet on board.

In Greenwich Park a tourney of lance and sword was put on and her gentlemen pensioners ran at spears. Kitchen tents had been set up providing wine, ale and beer. Enjoying her subjects' love of show, the queen had a banqueting house erected in the park, constructed of fir poles, plaited with birch branches and all manner of flowers – roses, gillyflowers, lavender and marigolds – with herbs and rushes. She and the ambassadors supped there.

26 July 1559: *French Ambitions*

Newly ascended to the French throne, fifteen-year-old Francis II, husband of Mary, Queen of Scots, was proclaimed King of Scotland, England and France and had emblazoned the arms of England with those of France. Mary's Guise uncles advised him to send French troops to Scotland, saying that once he had crushed the rebellious subjects fighting his mother-in-law he would be able to invade England – the only barrier between the kingdoms being a fordable 'little rivulet' – and claim the English crown.

23 October 1559: Mary of Guise Deposed

The lords and barons of Scotland openly proclaimed the regent, Mary of Guise, and all Frenchmen as enemies and traitors to Scotland. They have asked Queen Elizabeth to take James Hamilton, Duke of Châtellerault and heir apparent, under her protection and help establish 'this island in perpetual unity and concord'.

5 November 1559: A Suitor for the Queen

The Prince of Sweden and Duke of Finland, who recently came in person to woo Queen Elizabeth, was honoured with a joust. One of many suitors, he is the first foreign prince come to court her to visit England. Lord Robert Dudley and Henry Carey, Lord Hunsdon, the queen's cousin, wearing scarfs in the queen's colours of white and black, were the challengers. Defenders Lord Ambrose Dudley and others, with heralds, trumpets and footmen, all wore scarfs of red and yellow.

5 December 1559: Funeral of Frances, Duchess of Suffolk

Frances, Duchess of Suffolk, who died on 20 November, was buried at Westminster Abbey in a chapel in the south side of the choir. Mother of Lady Jane Grey, she died with her other daughters, Katherine and Mary, by her bedside.

24 March 1560: Proclamation

To provide for the surety of her kingdom and her subjects, Queen Elizabeth has sent out forces by sea and land, without hostile intent, to defend against the French invading by way of Scotland. Safe conduct was offered to any French man-of-war returning to France.

8 September 1560: Death of Lady Amy Robsart Dudley

Lady Amy Dudley, twenty-nine-year-old wife of Lord Robert Dudley, was discovered dead of a broken neck at the foot of the circular stone staircase descending into the hall from the elegant apartments above in Mr Foster's house of Cumnor Place, 3 miles from Oxford.

That Sunday morning, Lady Amy rose early and commanded everyone in the household to visit the fair, arguing with the widow Mrs Odingsell, who refused, saying it was 'no day for gentlewomen to go'. Lady Dudley told Mrs Odingsell, 'she might choose and go at her pleasure, but all hers should go' and leave her alone. When asked who would keep her company if they all left, Lady Amy replied she would sit with one Mrs Owen at dinner. The maid, Pinto, confirmed this, but when asked if she thought the lady suicidal, Pinto said that her mistress virtuously prayed daily upon her knees, and although she had heard her pray to 'God to deliver her from desperation' said her words should not be misunderstood.

Lord Robert immediately sent his friend Thomas Blount, Amy's stepbrother Mr Appleyard (who is also the Sheriff of Norfolk) and her brother Arthur to investigate the 'suddenness of the misfortune' and thoroughly, to their utmost 'travail and diligence to learn the truth', whether it be by 'evil chance or villainy'. Staying away so no one could say he influenced the investigation, he enjoined them 'by order of law by jury and coroner' to ensure the body was fully examined, for he knows what public rumour will say: that he murdered his wife.

22 September 1560: Funeral of Lady Dudley

In pairs, the procession began with eighty poor men and women, university men by degrees, house officers, choir and minister. Led by two conductors, the body of Lady Dudley was brought from Gloucester College where she had lain since 14 September to the 14-foot-tall hearse, decorated with escutcheons and pennons, in the black-clothed church of Our Lady at Oxford. Heralds in coats of arms carried standards and pennons of arms: Rougecross and

Lancaster first, followed by Mr Appleyard, who carried the great banner of arms, while Garter and Clarencieux preceded the coffin, which was borne by eight tall yeomen.

Mrs Margery Norris, whom the queen calls 'her crow', was chief mourner, the daughter and heiress of Lord Williams of Thame, who died last October, both of whom became great friends of the queen when she was under house arrest at Woodstock. She was followed by gentlewomen in black, then the yeomen, and lastly the Mayor of Oxford with his brethren. The cost of the funeral was thought to be more than £2,000.

21 November 1560: The True Ruler of England!

Francis II refused to ratify the Treaty of Edinburgh, made in July, in which France and England agreed that all their land and naval forces would withdraw from Scotland and that he and Mary would not use the arms of England in their heraldry. Francis insisted that he and Mary are the true rulers of England.

5 December 1560: Death of Francis II, King of France

A little before midnight, Francis II died. He leaves the crown to his ten-year-old brother, Charles, Duke of Orleans, now Charles IX, said to be handsome, gracious and high-spirited. The king will be guided by his mother, Catherine de Medici, until he attains fourteen years.

Mary, the young, beautiful and graceful widow of Francis, now dispossessed of the crown of France and fearful of ever recovering that of Scotland, has been constantly crying with doleful lamentations, inspiring universal pity for her plight.

26 March 1561: Funeral of Lady Jane Seymour

One of the best-loved maids of the queen, nineteen-year-old Lady Jane Seymour, daughter of Edward, Duke of Somerset, who died on 20 March, was brought from the queen's almonry and buried in the same chapel as the Duchess of Suffolk. In attendance were all the choir of the abbey, two hundred of the court and eighty mourners, gentlemen and women, lords and ladies, all in black, and the queen's privy chamber.

4 June 1561: St Paul's Flaming Crown

Thunder and lightning had threatened London all morning. Between one and two in the afternoon, people in boats on the Thames and working in neighbouring fields saw lightning, like a long, pointed dart, pierce and break through the steeple of St Paul's. Those near the cathedral at the time said they had felt a violent force of air like a whirlwind and noticed a great smell like brimstone. Two hours later, smoke started seeping out from under the spire of St Paul's, and suddenly it was ablaze, the flames like a crown, and within quarter of an hour the brass eagle and cross, and the glittering globe admired by so many, plummeted from the top. On the south side, all the vaulting of the church was consumed, with the lead, timber and bells. People came running from all sides: courtiers, nobles and commoners arranged themselves in lines to carry buckets of water hand to hand but the fire would not be stopped. It finally abated by itself about ten at night.

The queen, starting a fund, contributed 1,000 marks and a warrant for timber to be taken out of her woods to repair St Paul's with all speed once materials and workmen are gathered.

24 June 1561: A Fight on the River Thames

At Greenwich, a barque with two top castles was prepared for the queen. She invited Lord Robert and the Bishop of Aquila to view the show of soldiers in small pinnaces assaulting a castle on the river, defended by a garrison of soldiers with guns and spears. It started with a great shooting of guns and ended with the hurling of balls of wildfire.

Mischievously, the queen and Lord Robert teased the ambassador that as the latter was a bishop he could marry them. The bishop pretended for a while to enjoy their joking but at last snapped that he would be glad to marry them if it would help extricate her from the tyranny of her councillors and reinstate religion.

12 August 1561: Lady Katherine Grey 'big with child'
Lady Katherine Grey, no longer able to hide being pregnant, revealed that she and Edward Seymour, Earl of Hertford, married secretly just before Christmas last, after her mother gave consent on her deathbed. She said the ceremony took place when the queen was away from court hunting and was witnessed by Jane, the earl's sister, who died in March. Nor can the priest be found who married them, and without witnesses the ceremony will be held illegal and the child illegitimate. Lady Katherine was committed to the Tower, while the earl was ordered home from France.

22 September 1561: Gathering of 10,000
Queen Elizabeth's subjects, knowing she was returning to St James from her house at Enfield, cut down hedges and ditches from Islington to make way for her. Ten thousand people waited to see her and show their affection, but she was late and, it being night-time, came via St Giles-in-the-Fields.

10–17 October 1562: Queen Ill of Smallpox
At midnight, Sir William Cecil was hastily summoned from London to Hampton Court where Queen Elizabeth was very ill with smallpox. People in the palace were in mourning as if she had already died. The queen began feeling unwell on 10 October. Thinking it would make her feel better, she took a bath, but afterwards, as she came into the cold air, she came out in a violent

fever. Lady Mary Sidney, who nursed the queen throughout her illness, was also infected and, much to the repugnance of her husband, Sir Henry Sidney, will be disfigured by it.

During discussions regarding the succession – whether it should be Lady Katherine or the Earl of Huntingdon – the queen started to recover from the crisis which had kept her unconscious and speechless for two hours.

5–9 August 1564: The Queen Visits Cambridge University

The bells of King's College chapel rang, a signal for all the bells in Cambridge to add their chimes to herald the queen's arrival on horseback, her trumpets resounding and declaring her approach on the main lane 'strawed' with rushes and flags, coverlets and boughs. All the other lanes were boarded to stop anything other than the queen's train entering through the great gate. As she passed, everyone knelt and called out '*Vivat Regina*'.

Queen Elizabeth was dressed in a black velvet gown, a caul of pearls and pretty jewels on her red hair, with a feathered hat on top spangled with gold. Two scholars stepped out. Kneeling, they welcomed her in verse and prose. At the west door a kneeling Sir William Cecil greeted her, while kneeling beadles kissed their staves and handed them to Cecil to give to the queen, who said, laughing, she could not well hold them all. In response to the Latin oration, she commended the speaker for his memory, saying she dare not answer in Latin for fear they would laugh at her if she spoke it false. She prayed privately in the chapel, listened as the choir sang an English song of gladness and marvelled at the beauty of both the building and the singing. A *Te Deum* was sung in English, in pricksong with organs playing, followed by evensong. After the service the queen was shown to her lodging after being presented with four pairs of Cambridge double gloves edged and trimmed with fine gold laces, six boxes of sweets and other conceits.

The next day, a Sunday, after listening to the Latin sermon, she stayed in her lodging until evensong, and during the evening watched a play her surveyor had written, *Aulularia Plauti*, lit by guards holding torch-staffs until the play ended around midnight. After dinner on Monday and Tuesday, the queen listened to disputations and in the evening watched the play *Dido* on Monday and on Tuesday Mr Udall's *Ezechias* written in English.

After visiting all the colleges on Wednesday and knowing she was taking her leave on the morrow, she was invited to give a Latin address. She at first demurred, citing womanly shamefacedness in the presence of so many learned men. Giving in, she spoke at length in Latin, encouraging them to more diligently follow their learning for now they would be able to see the 'difference between true learning and an education not well retained' as she had made them all witnesses thereto and would 'release their ears from the pain of it'.

29 September 1564: Lord Dudley Created Earl of Leicester

After the service at St James on Michaelmas Day, Lord Robert Dudley was led by the earls of Sussex and Huntingdon into the queen's presence chamber. He wore a black gown edged with lace with nineteen pairs of gold aglets on the sleeves. Before him, his brother Ambrose, Earl of Warwick bore his sword, Garter bore his patent and Lord Clinton, Lord Admiral, his cap and coronal. All made obeisance to the queen three times. Lord Robert knelt before her.

Garter gave the patent to Cecil, who read it out aloud. The Earl of Warwick presented the sword to the queen, who put it about the neck of her new Earl of Leicester, putting the point under his left arm and then, while putting his cap and coronal on his head, with a mischievous smile, tickled his neck. Solemn-faced, the new earl gave the queen his humble thanks and arose and went to the council chamber to dinner, trumpets sounding before him.

Cecil, knowing how dear Dudley is to the queen, was pleased at the honour for, as he had said earlier in the month to a friend, she loves him like a brother, which is the impediment to the earl ever becoming her husband, although he is worthy of such an honour.

31 December 1564–1 January 1565: Football on the River Thames

A frost, which began on 21 December, turned the Thames to ice from London Bridge to Westminster. So deep and firm was it that on New Year's Eve, a game of football was played on the river as boldly as if it had been on dry land. The court, being at Westminster for the Christmas season, shot at pricks set upon the Thames. Men and women walked on the river in greater number than in any street of the city of London, which will soon be flooded when it thaws.

29 July 1565: Mary, Queen of Scots Marries

Early in the morning, Queen Mary married nineteen-year-old Lord Darnley, son of the Earl of Lennox and Margaret Douglas, daughter of Henry VIII's sister Margaret, erstwhile Queen of Scotland, in Holyrood chapel according to the Catholic rite. Mary wore mourning dress until after the ceremony when she put on wedding finery for the marriage entertainments. Darnley glittered in an outfit studded with jewels.

17 August 1565: Queen Elizabeth Visits Coventry

The queen was met on horseback by the sheriffs of Coventry in scarlet cloaks accompanied by twenty young men in a livery of fine purple velvet to escort her to the mayor and his brethren in their scarlet gowns waiting to welcome her to the city. The mayor, kissing the mace, delivered it into the queen's hands and knelt before her. The city recorder came forward and presented her majesty with a purse containing £100 in angels. The queen accepted it, saying, 'It is a good gift, £100 in gold.'

The mayor said boldly, 'If it please your grace, there is a great deal more in it.'

'What is that?'

'It is the hearts of all your loving subjects,' he said.

'Indeed, a lot more,' she replied.

21 August 1565: Clandestine Marriage of Lady Mary

Lady Mary Grey, the 'smallest lady in the court', secretly married Henry Keys, the sergeant porter, who is the biggest gentleman in the court, a widower, with several children. Upon the discovery he was committed to Fleet Prison while the lady was put under house arrest. Her sister, Katherine, and her husband, the Earl of Hertford, are still in the Tower for a similar offence, both kept more strictly since the gaolers had allowed them to be together, which had resulted in the birth of another son to the couple.

14 October 1565: Death of Sir Thomas Challoner

Lately returned as ambassador in Spain, Sir Thomas Challoner, a close friend of Cecil, died in Clerkenwell. Sir Thomas was born in London, brought up at Cambridge and knighted at Musselburgh in 1549. In his younger days, Thomas went on an expedition to Algiers under Charles V and was shipwrecked. He swam until the strength in his arms began to fail and then took hold of a cable by his teeth and hung on grimly, thus saving himself, though losing his front teeth as a result.

23 March 1566: Murder at the Scottish Court

News arrived from Scotland of the murder on 9 March, by order of Darnley, of one of Queen Mary's principal secretaries, David

Riccio, who was at supper with the queen and the Countess of Argyll. A terrified Riccio clung to Mary's dress but was dragged from the room by a fully armoured Lord Ruthven. He and his men stabbed the secretary fifty-six times in an adjoining gallery. Although proclaimed throughout Scotland that Mary's husband had taken no part in the murder, Queen Elizabeth said she knew differently because the conspirators had the king's own signature to the act and that he had claimed David had 'more company of her [Mary's] body than he', accusing his wife of allowing Riccio to influence her into not giving him the crown matrimonial. Queen Elizabeth told the Spanish ambassador that if she had been in Queen Mary's place, she would have taken her husband's dagger and stabbed him with it.

31 August–6 September 1566: Comedy Turned Tragedy

Visiting Oxford University while on her summer progress, Queen Elizabeth, after attending lectures and disputations, was set to watch the comedy of *Palamon and Arcyte* written by Mr Edwards of her chapel. But tragedy befell them as stairs and a piece of wall broke from the press of people, killing three men and injuring five others. The queen sent her physicians and surgeons to assist.

When the play was put on a second night, the actors performed their parts so well they made the queen laugh heartily, especially when during the play there was a cry of hounds in the quadrant as if upon the train of a fox, when young scholars in the window thought it truly was a hunt and cried out 'Now, Now! There, there! He's caught, he's caught!' Laughing, the queen said, 'Oh, excellent! Those boys are, in very truth, ready to leap out of the windows to follow the hounds.'

One of the actors, performing as a lady prettily gathering flowers in a garden, sang so sweetly, the queen gave eight angels in gracious reward.

18 December 1566: *Prince of Scotland Christened*

The Prince of Scotland, born on 19 June, was christened in Stirling Castle's chapel royal, conducted by Archbishop Hamilton with full Catholic rites, and given the names Charles James, after the King of France who is his godfather, along with Philibert of Savoy. Queen Elizabeth, as godmother, sent a beautifully wrought gold font, large enough to immerse the prince, weighing 333 ounces, amounting in value to £1043 19s, which was presented by the Earl of Bedford. It was of exquisite workmanship with many precious stones. Three days of banquets, masques, ballets, pageants and firework displays followed.

10 February 1567: *Lord Darnley Murdered*

Two hours after midnight, a massive explosion woke the whole of Edinburgh. It had blown up the house Lord Darnley was lodging in while he recuperated after an illness. A way away from the house, his body was found in the orchard alongside the body of his page, Taylor. To everyone's amazement there was no mark on either of them: no burns, marks of strangulation, violence, fracture, wound, or bruise. Among the debris strewn around were a slipper, a chair, a dagger and Darnley's furred purple velvet nightgown. The Earl of Bothwell was commanded to conduct an investigation; yet the people murmur against him and Queen Mary, saying they themselves had murdered him.

15 May 1567: *Marriage of the Scots Queen*

Queen Mary married the hastily divorced Earl of Bothwell just before dawn according to the rites of the Reformed Church. The Bishop of Orkney performed the service, with only three nobles present. After the nuptials, when she and Bothwell were in her closet, the queen was heard to scream aloud that she wished for death and asked for a knife with which to stab herself. Yet only the day before she created the earl Duke of Orkney, placing the coronet on his head with her own hands. Five days before the marriage, the Scottish lords informed her that if she married Bothwell they would consider making her son king.

29 July 1567: Charles James Crowned King of Scotland

Prince Charles James, after a sermon by John Knox, was crowned King James VI at Stirling Church after his mother signed the abdication on 24 July at Lochleven Castle and authorised her half-brother, the Earl of Murray, as regent until her son attains the age of seventeen years. In Edinburgh they made 'near a thousand bonfires', the people dancing and cheering, while the castle shot off twenty pieces of artillery.

13 September 1567: First State Lottery

By command of the queen, a general lottery was held at the house of Mr Dericke, goldsmith, in Cheapside containing a good number of prizes. The first prize of £5,000 was made up of £3,000 in ready money and the rest in plate, tapestries, covers and linen. Tickets were 10s each. The money raised was earmarked for the repair of the ports and other public works.

27 January 1568: Lady Katherine Grey Dies

All night, Lady Katherine listened to her ladies saying psalms, and as soon as one was finished she would call for another, all the time whispering the prayers said at the hours of death. Her ladies attempted to comfort her, saying she was yet still young, but she said, 'No, no life in this world, but in the world to come I hope to live for ever; here is nothing but care and misery.' Around six in the morning she asked Lady Hopton to send for her husband. As he came into the chamber, Lady Hopton's husband asked Lady Katherine how she did. She replied, 'Even now going to God, Sir Owen, as fast as I can.'

She asked him to honour her deathbed requests. Firstly, he was to beg the queen, 'even from the mouth of a dead woman', to forgive her displeasure for her offence and to be good to her children for 'in my life they have had few friends, and fewer shall they have when I am dead', and to free her husband to lighten his heart for 'my death will be heavy news to him.' Next he was to deliver her rings to her husband; the first was a ring with a pointed diamond.

'Your wedding ring?' asked Sir Owen.

'No, Sir Owen, the ring of my assurance unto my lord. Here is my wedding ring.'

She gave him a gold ring comprised of five links, four of which contained a love poesy written by the earl. She lastly gave him a third ring with a death's head, saying, 'This is the last token that ever I shall send him; it is the picture of myself.' Around the death's head were the letters 'While I live yours'. She then perceived her fingernails looked purple and said joyfully, 'Lo, here he is come, welcome Death.' She closed her eyes with her own hands and said, 'O Lord, into thy hands I commend my soul, Lord Jesus receive my spirit.' She died that moment, aged twenty-seven years.

Perhaps the words of her sister Jane, written in the end of her Greek New Testament on the night before her execution, came to her: 'Even at midnight be waking, lest when death cometh and stealeth upon you as a thief in the night, you be, with the evil servant, found sleeping.'

2–28 May 1568: Mary, Queen of Scots Escapes to England

Neither waiting for passport nor welcome, Mary ignored all advice and crossed the River Solway in a fishing boat, landing at Workington on 16 May. She requested asylum in England rather than France, not wanting those who had once seen her in splendour to see her as an exile and fugitive. She was conducted to Carlisle Castle for her safety.

Mary had escaped from Lochleven Castle on 2 May. Imprisoned for just under a year, there had been many ideas for escape attempts from that castle, sited on an island in a lake: leaving disguised as a laundress; being snatched while on one of the pleasure excursions on the lake, or while hawking on one of the other islands; or even being carried out in a box of papers. Her escape was engineered by Orphan Willie, a page of her captor, Sir William Douglas, half-brother to the Earl of Murray. He snatched the castle keys in a napkin when serving Sir William a glass of wine. Mary had captivated him alongside lovelorn George Douglas, who awaited with horses to carry her away. At the ensuing Battle of Langside on 13 May, 6,000 men flocked to her banner to fight for her but they were beaten by the Earl of Murray's army, despite her solemn avowal to the lords fighting for him that her abdication was extorted and she the rightful ruler of Scotland.

Lord Scrope and Sir Francis Knollys arrived at Carlisle Castle on the evening of 28 May. As gently as possible they broke the news that Queen Elizabeth was unable to receive her until she was proved innocent of her husband's murder, 'whereupon she fell into some passion with the water in her eyes'. Her tears forcing him into comforting her, Sir Francis told her that his queen would be the gladdest in the world to see her purged of the crime. He also sent word that the Earl of Northumberland had complained at not being allowed to take Queen Mary into his own custody, having been told he had had no warrant to do so.

Problems Exacerbated: 1568–1603

Mary, Queen of Scots had left Elizabeth in a quandary. She did not want the Catholic claimant to her throne in her country, but nor could she force the Protestant Scots to take her back. Allowing her to take refuge in either France or Spain was a guaranteed way for her to foment mischief against England, for she had consistently refused to renounce her claim to the English crown. Given the options, Elizabeth had little choice but to effectively keep her under honourable house arrest with a trusted noble. She chose the Earl of Shrewsbury for the task.

Mary was allowed her own domestic staff, never fewer than sixteen. Her chambers were decorated with fine tapestries and carpets, while she embroidered her cloth of estate herself. She had her own chefs who prepared a choice of thirty-two dishes daily, and had, until she proved herself untrustworthy, been allowed to hunt and walk in the surrounding countryside. Unfortunately, Mary loved being the authoress of her own dramas, taking the lead as the romantic heroine. In October 1568 she wrote to Philip II that she knew well how to 'ingratiate herself' and had 'already won over Sir Francis Knollys', although she was mistaken in that instance. However, she continued to use her tears and self-made misery to captivate anyone who came into contact with her, devising plot after plot, not caring how she used or ruined others. Letters streamed from her to the Pope, her relatives and nobles in France, to Philip II in Spain, the Duke of Alva in the Netherlands and others claiming ill treatment, danger to her life, and that Elizabeth meant to kill her or act prejudicially to her son. As a result, the Pope encouraged the Catholics of England to rebel against the queen, which culminated in Elizabeth's excommunication in 1570.

Mary lied and plotted incessantly, saying again and again that the English throne was hers by right, and that as a prisoner she had every right to participate in plots against Elizabeth. It was generally the same plot with different players. There were the 1569 northern uprising, the Ridolfi plot of 1571, the Spanish-funded Francis Throckmorton plot in 1583 for the invasion of England with the Duke of Guise and the Babington plot of 1586. Elizabeth's councillors determined that Mary would not escape the consequences of her actions and, with this last plot, they finally had proof that Mary had assented to Elizabeth's murder.

At first, Elizabeth had tried to get Mary restored to her throne. All that changed when she was forced to execute her kinsman, Thomas Howard, Duke of Norfolk for his involvement in the Ridolfi plot. After this she vowed never to liberate Mary, and buttressed Mary's son on the Scottish throne. Gradually, Elizabeth listened to her ministers and became suspicious of her Catholic subjects in general and priests in particular, especially those groomed to assassinate her with the support of the Pope and Philip II.

Spain, an ever-growing problem, dominated Europe and was cruel to its Protestant subjects in the Low Countries. Further, Philip II decided only Spain had the right to control the seas in the Atlantic and Pacific despite the discovery of lands by other nations, including England. His galleons were full of New World gold and jewels, giving him the riches to overrun Portugal, send troops to the Netherlands and to build an armada to invade England. Elizabeth allowed her ships to scupper his plans and tried to ruin him economically, which worked until 1588, when the Spanish Armada managed to reach England. Elizabeth also sent an army to help the Dutch Protestants fight against Spanish rule. She did not like war but was determined to defend England against Spanish attempts to use the Netherlands against her.

Then there was Ireland, dubbed 'the Englishman's grave' by the Venetian ambassador, and to which Philip II and the Pope continually sent troops to cause trouble.

It was not all bad, however. This was the age of the great playwrights and poets – Shakespeare, Bacon, Webster, Marlow and Spenser – and the blood-stirring seamanship of Drake, Raleigh, Hawkins and Frobisher, together with the exploration, discovery and colonisation in 1584 of new lands. There was also increased trade with Russia, Constantinople and other far-flung places.

Elizabeth's godson, John Harington, reminiscing about her three years after she died, wrote that 'when she smiled, it was pure sunshine that everyone chose to bask in if they could'.

17 May 1569: Tragic Accident?

Nine-year-old George, son and heir of Thomas, Lord Dacre and ward of the Duke of Norfolk, was tragically killed at Thetford when leaping over an unsecured wooden vaulting horse. The horse fell on top of him and 'bruised the brains out of his head'. His great northern inheritance descends by law to his three sisters, who are all married to the duke's sons.

15 September 1569: Death at Sussex's House Party

An accidental death occurred at the house party in Cawood where Thomas, Earl of Sussex was entertaining lords and ladies, among them Northumberland, Westmoreland, Talbot, Herbert and Wharton. The guests had been hunting and shooting all week, and while the nobles were playing bowls in an adjoining field, one of the earl's men, shooting at the butts, accidentally hit his own servant in the head with a 'prickshaft'. The arrow was well shot, but the servant moved too close to the butt to see his master win.

11 October 1569: Duke of Norfolk Imprisoned in the Tower

Thomas Howard, 4th Duke of Norfolk, the queen's cousin, was lodged in the Tower, in the same chamber his grandfather, the third duke, had occupied, arrested for treason by Sir Henry Neville at Windsor.

During the conferences held at York the previous year to examine the 'casket letters' and causes of Queen Mary's abdication, the duke began courting her with letters and gifts, thinking to marry and be the keeper of her. Catching the rumour, Queen Elizabeth took the duke aside when he was at court, and asked what news of marriage he had brought to her, giving him the opportunity to confess. He replied that it was merely an idle rumour and that he despised the thought of a match with the Scots queen and preferred to sleep safe upon his pillow.

On her progress in September, at Titchfield, the queen heard the rumour anew. She invited the duke to dine with her privately, advising him that 'the bee who reposed and rested himself upon a pillow, should take heed and look to himself' – a gentle admonition the duke ignored. It was another opportunity for him to confess to his actions, and a watch was set upon him when he did not. Many of his letters were intercepted, as were those of the Bishop of Ross and the northern lords. One such letter revealed that, once free, Mary, forced to 'sail with the wind', intended to force her country into submission, discard the duke and send her son to Philip II to raise.

Queen Elizabeth had her own shrewd idea of the gusts swirling around. In mid-September, the court now at Windsor, she alerted the Earl of Shrewsbury, sending the Earl of Huntingdon and Viscount Hereford to remove Mary to Tutbury Castle and guard her well for there was a plot afoot for her to be forcefully carried away. She also commanded the duke to come to court.

Elizabeth received two letters: one from Mary, complaining that she believed the Earl of Huntingdon was a rival claimant to the English throne and should have no care of her; the other from the duke claiming he was ill in bed with stomach trouble, though he managed to precipitously leave his house in London to gallop to

Kenninghall Castle. Fearing he meant to raise a rebellion, knowing that he had been communicating with the Catholic northern lords, Elizabeth wrote to him again, firmly commanding him to present himself, reaching the court in short journeys by litter if need be. That same day, Mary wrote to him to 'behave valiantly' for God would protect his life, and Shrewsbury wrote to Cecil to tell him that before Mary was removed from Wingfield Manor she had burnt many papers.

The Earls of Pembroke and Arundel, with Lord Lumley, arrived at court on 30 September. Being known partisans of the duke, they were put under house arrest, in readiness to be examined along with the Bishop of Ross, a Florentine banker called Ridolfi, and others arrested after being implicated in the letters. That day, the duke sent a messenger to the Earl of Westmoreland not to stir or his head would be put in danger, and wrote to the queen that although he was very ill, he was on his way to throw himself on her mercy. The queen then wrote to Shrewsbury and Huntingdon that they could stand down as Norfolk was 'coming in quietly', otherwise the 'world had seen some effects of the authority God has given us'.

It was a puzzle why Mary had fomented such trouble. She was well aware that, up to the end of July, Elizabeth had been negotiating with the Lords of Scotland for her release until they, at the Convention of Perth, had said they did not wish her return.

8 November–20 December 1569: Northern Lords Rebel

Two days after Queen Elizabeth ordered Thomas Percy, 7th Earl of Northumberland and Charles Neville, 6th Earl of Westmorland to appear at court, she sent an order to the Earl of Sussex to 'assemble, levy and arm our good subjects'. The queen's summons scared the earls. They assumed they would be joining the Duke of Norfolk in the Tower. As they had already dashed the plot to free Mary through a letter of hers to abort the rising and secret intelligence from the duke via bottles of beer, they were unsure what to do.

In the middle of a cold November night at Topcliffe, the church bells were rung in reverse to sound the alarm. Hearing shouts that the castle was surrounded, the Earl of Northumberland fled to the Earl of Westmoreland at Brancepath Castle. Though the alarm had been false, they decided their only choices were to fight or end up on the scaffold. Avowing their unshaken allegiance to Queen Elizabeth, the earls commanded their tenants, retainers and commons to muster in defence of her person to remove evil councillors, re-establish the religion of their ancestors and free Mary and the Duke of Norfolk.

Informed of the rising, the Earl of Sussex sent to the rebel earls asking them to surrender before being outlawed. Their answer was to enter Durham on 14 November. In the cathedral, they, with their wives, tore up and trampled underfoot English bibles and prayer books, destroyed the communion table and replaced it with altars to celebrate Mass. In the meantime, Mary was moved south to Coventry and lodged in the gatehouse by St Mary's Hall.

Within days, the rebels, with forces amounting to 4,000 foot and 1,600 horse, mustered on Clifford Moor. Their first thought was to march on York, but they soon heard that an army captained by the earls of Essex, Rutland and Cumberland was marching north to join forces with Lords Scrope and Sussex, the latter having shown himself utterly loyal despite his brother, Egremond, being one of the rebels. Against the size of men and weapons advancing towards them, the rebels fled north towards Hexham, using unbeaten paths and creeping under hedges to come unseen to the castle of Naworth, where they were refused shelter by Leonard Dacre, enemy soldiers almost at their heels.

The two earls, losing their courage, left their company without a farewell, fleeing into Scotland. The rest of the rebels were arrested without resistance and martial law decreed some 600 men, cursing their leaders, were hanged.

19-20 *February 1570: The Charge of Lord Hunsdon*

The aforementioned Leonard Dacre, believing he was safe and his part in the Northern Rising unknown, received news that confessions had revealed his involvement. Calling Dacre that 'cankered subtle traitor', Queen Elizabeth sent Lord Hunsdon north. Expecting the castle to be besieged, Dacre fortified Naworth Castle and gathered a force of 3,000 borderers. When his spies informed him Lord Hunsdon was on the road to Carlisle, he decided to waylay him, sending out 1,500 footmen and 500 horse, who were ready in battle array before Lord Hunsdon had entered the moor.

Seeing them, Hunsdon commanded his footmen to 'keep themselves in breath' and the main body of horse rearward to back the footmen. Then he, his three sons and 100 horsemen breasted the hill and charged, a hail of arrows flying around them. Within a short time the battle was over. Some 400 to 500 of Dacre's men were slain and he, with 500 horsemen, fled into Scotland, chased for 4 miles by Hunsdon and his small company. Lord Hunsdon interceded with the queen for pardon for the bewildered borderers left behind.

5 *March 1570: Queen Elizabeth Excommunicated*

A bull excommunicating Queen Elizabeth was fixed to the gates of the Bishop of London's palace. Issued by Pope Pius V, it releases English subjects from obeying her. Catholics fear that the queen, who so far has granted them mostly free exercise of their religion in their houses so long as they attend services held in parish churches, will be forced to enact sterner measures against them.

4 *August 1570: Duke of Norfolk Released*

The Duke of Norfolk was removed from the Tower but remains under house arrest at his house of Charterhouse near Smithfield.

He was released at the personal clemency of the queen after his personal submission to her.

31 January 1571: New Suitor for the Queen

The French ambassador, La Mothe Fenelon, was invited to a banquet and seated with Queen Elizabeth. Broaching the subject of a marriage to the twenty-year-old Henry, Duke of Anjou, brother of the French king, the queen replied she would rather be loved for herself than because she was Queen of England. He gallantly replied that the prince would both love and honour her, and would in due time make her the mother of a fine boy. The queen became so full of the subject, consulting Ladies Clinton and Cobham and discussing it with her other ladies, that the court was filled with feminine tittle-tattle about Anjou's personal charms and supposed gallantries.

Two weeks earlier, the Earl of Leicester had written to Walsingham asking for a description of Anjou: the reply was he was 3 inches taller than Walsingham, with a good-shaped body and well proportioned, though his legs were long and thin; that he was haughty at first approach but affable afterwards. Other intelligence said women found him charming and he was skilled in fencing, disliked war and hunting and preferred to read.

7 September 1571: Duke of Norfolk Arrested

The Duke of Norfolk, arrested at eight in the morning at Charterhouse but kept close in his chamber, was taken to the Tower in the evening around five o'clock. Two servants were allowed to attend upon him, with officers to provide and dress his meat. His servants Charles Bailly and John Sinclair, the steward of Charterhouse, have also been arrested. The latter was implicated in a plot to take the Queen of Scots away from Chatsworth. On that day the duke was to have gone away 'leaping on horseback at his back gate' with a message for Queen Elizabeth that he was gone and she would not be able to fetch him again and that he was assured of marrying the Scottish queen.

Letters between the duke and Mary had been conveyed by the Bishop of Ross. He too has been arrested. It is said he was to go to Chatsworth and measure a certain window to see if she, with one woman and one man of her chamber, could escape through it, be set upon a horse and ride away while a distraction was made. Another plot foiled.

1 January 1572: New Year Gifts

Some of the New Year gifts received by Queen Elizabeth were remarkable: from the Earl of Leicester a gold bracelet, a clock in the clasp, decorated with rubies; from the Earl of Warwick a gold branch with a white enamelled gold rose with six red roses, each with a lozenge diamond. In the top of the white rose was a spider with a lozenge diamond back, and under it a bee with two diamonds. John Harington, a friend from her 'Tower days', gave her a gold heart decorated with rubies and small pearls, rising from its centre a branch of red and white roses with smaller jewels of two diamonds, three rubies, two emeralds and two pearls.

16 January 1572: 'Ridolfi plot' Revealed

Thomas, Duke of Norfolk entered Westminster Hall with the fatal axe, edge forward, borne before him. The platform held George Talbot, Earl of Shrewsbury as Lord High Steward with twenty-six nobles arrayed either side.

Silence was commanded in court, while the duke was charged with attempting to deprive the queen of her crown and life, raising via the Duke of Alva troops of men to land at Harwich, and treating secretly to marry the Scottish queen contrary to his promise under hand and seal. In evidence, the court saw letters found hidden under roof tiles of his house: correspondence to and from Ridolfi and the Bishop of Ross; one from the Countess of

Northumberland thanking him for his financial aid to her and her husband; and a letter to the Pope dated 20 March 1571. In this last letter the duke had requested the Pope to aid his and Mary's 'just enterprise' by gaining Philip II's aid in furnishing 6,000 harquebusiers, 4,000 guns, field artillery and 'a person experienced in leading an army'. The duke thought it even better if 10,000 men could be raised as 2,000 could be sent to Scotland and 2,000 to Ireland. He closed with the promise that he was resolved to 'hazard a battle; and essay to rescue her by force' while possessing himself of 'the person of the Queen of England by way of pawn'.

Mary reinforced Norfolk's instructions, adding in her letter that she was in jeopardy of her life, 'menaced with poisoning and other violent deaths', and that when plots are discovered men are imprisoned, losing their goods and their lives. She told the Pope to inform Philip II that Elizabeth had 'many a time been on the point of compassing my death' and accused the queen of ordering one of her guards to assassinate her. The court were shown the deciphered reply by the Pope dated 16 May approving of their design, confirming he had sent Ridolfi to Philip II with his approval and a request for the aid sought.

The duke said his memory faltered, that he was unable to remember such an intricate variety of matters, and denied everything except for sending money to Scotland to aid his friends, the northern earls. As for the rest of the charges, the evidence was provided only by those who were his inferiors.

The verdict of guilty by his peers was unanimous.

4 June 1572: Duke of Norfolk Executed

At seven in the morning, the Duke of Norfolk was brought to a scaffold newly built upon Tower Hill. Wearing a black satin doublet, a long gown of black raised velvet, velvet nightcap and felt hat, he looked about him, and, the noise being great, begged the people to quieten. In his speech he confessed he had dealt secretly with the Queen of Scots, which he should not have done, but with regard to any conspiracy against Queen Elizabeth he said there was no intent; his dealings with Ridolfi were only in respect of his accounts and reckonings, and though he had received letters from the Pope, he never gave consent. He sang a psalm or two, then asked the Dean of St Paul's to entreat the people to pray with him and then be silent so 'that his spirit be not disturbed'.

The duke forgave his executioner as he asked pardon of him and gave the man 40s in gold and 18s 6d in silver along with his hat, gown and doublet. Standing now in a white sleeveless fustian shirt, he at first refused to put the handkerchief over his face, saying 'he would lie quiet ... with his face open', but was entreated not to add more horror to himself. Kneeling, he stretched his neck over the block, chin downward, while the people, shedding tears, prayed for him. His head was cut off with one stroke. His body was buried in the Tower chapel.

The queen mourns for her cousin. Three times she had stayed his execution until Parliament forced her hand in May. She has absolutely refused to take action against the Queen of Scots but has sworn she will never suffer her to have liberty.

18 August 1572: Fireworks at Warwick

Staying at Warwick Castle with Lord Ambrose, Earl of Warwick, and his wife, Queen Elizabeth was entertained after dinner by country people dancing in the courtyard while she, smiling with delight, watched them from her chamber window. For the evening a fireworks show was put on. In Temple Field ditch a fort was made of timber and canvas, inside of which men dressed as soldiers cast out squibs, fireworks and balls of fire in mock battle against an enemy castle, captained by Edward de Vere, Earl of Oxford.

Brought up from London, twelve-score short cannon and twelve or thirteen battering pieces were fired to add to the noise and mayhem. Both bands fought valiantly, shooting harquebuses and casting balls of wildfire into the River Avon, which flashed and flamed, making the queen laugh. Then the grand finale: a dragon flew overhead with flames shooting from its mouth, setting the fort alight, while men threw squibs into the air, some of which were cast so high they flew right over the castle into the town, on to houses, courts and streets, almost to the church.

A ball of fire, by mischance, set a house on fire at the bridge end wherein the miller and his wife were in bed. They were saved but their house and possessions perished. Others houses that were set alight were rescued by the nobles and townsfolk working together. Another house had a ball go through both sides, leaving a hole as big as a man's head, but did no further harm. The next day, the miller and his wife were brought to the queen who, with her courtiers, gave them comfort and recompense. To help the losses of others the sum of £25 15s 8d was given.

29 August 1572: Massacre in Paris

Queen Elizabeth, out hunting, received urgent letters from France. So distressed was she by the news they contained that she returned immediately to Woodstock Palace. Assembling the court, she revealed that in Paris, on St Bartholomew's Day, Huguenot nobles and their families who had gathered for the wedding of the French king's sister to the King of Navarre along with Protestant citizens – husbands, wives and their children – had been dragged from their lodgings and houses and slain in the streets, with many of the bodies thrown into the River Seine.

The French ambassador arrived with a letter from Charles IX regarding the death of Admiral Coligny and the nobles. As she read that the French king cited the reason for the slaughter was the discovery of a plot against his person and the conspirators punished, the queen said, with a stern countenance, that her news of what had passed was quite sufficient to prevent her from being deceived, or giving entire credit to the letter she was holding. She continued in angry tones that even if everything had happened as the king said, she would like to know what 'blame was attributable to the women and children who were murdered'.

19 March 1573: *The Queen's Maundy*

At Greenwich, Queen Elizabeth entered into the hall and, after singing and prayers, washed the feet of thirty-nine ladies. In rounds, she gave to each woman broadcloth to make a gown, a pair of shoes, a wooden platter with half a side of salmon, six red herrings and two cheat loaves with a dish of claret wine. Each poor woman received the towel and apron used for them, a small white purse with 39d and then red leather purses containing 20s, after which, it being sunset, she and her company withdrew.

31 August–3 September 1573: *The Queen's Reception at Sandwich*

At seven o'clock in the evening, Queen Elizabeth reached Sandwich and was welcomed by the mayor, principal town officials and 300 musketeers, all dressed in white doublets with black-and-white ribboned sleeves over black hose with white garters, who discharged their guns. She rode between the gilded lion and dragon posts set at the bridge end onto newly gravelled streets strewn with rushes and herbs, leaves and flowers on cords hanging across the streets, past houses, every one of which was painted white and black.

The next day, the town put on an entertainment. It started with men trying to knock each other into the water from two boats. On the other side of the haven, a fort had been built for an assault: a shooting battle between two captains to the enjoyment of both bands of men.

The following day, it was the turn of the town's wives, who made a banquet on a table 28 feet long, housing 160 dishes, of which the queen sampled many (without a taster) and merrily asked for some to be reserved and carried to her lodging.

On Thursday, just before she left, 120 English and Dutch children at the schoolhouse showed off their skills, spinning fine bay yarn.

20 *February 1574: Storming the Castle*

At Hampton Court, Sir Francis Walsingham told the French ambassador, La Mothe Fenelon, that he had never seen the queen so well disposed towards marriage. The ambassador, in England to arrange a private visit by Francis, Duc d'Alencon, brother to Charles IX, favoured Walsingham's suggestion that the duke should regard his queen's heart as a strong castle which he might boldly carry by storm.

30 *May 1574: Death of Charles IX*

King Charles IX of France died of tuberculosis at his Chateau de Vincennes. Since the massacre of St Bartholomew's Day, the twenty-three-year-old king said he often heard the screams of murdered Huguenots ringing in his ears as his health declined.

9–27 *July 1575: Earl of Leicester Stops Time*

Arriving at Kenilworth tilt yard at eight o'clock in the evening, Queen Elizabeth was greeted by a sibyl dressed in white silk and a tall, large-limbed porter dressed as Hercules. Holding a club and large keyring, he complained he had never seen such uncouth trudging to and fro, such din and talk, when suddenly in mock surprise he spied the queen and fell on his knees. Six trumpeters, with a tantara from their 5-foot silver instruments, sent the queen forward to the Lady of the Lake, sitting on a moveable island lit by blazing torches. Floating from the middle of the pool to land, the lady said that although she had kept the lake since King Arthur's day, she relinquished her office, lake and power to the queen.

Music played against the sound of guns and fireworks as the queen rode over a bridge to the inner court, one person saying it was 'as though Jupiter himself was coming to show himself'. Noise and flames were heard and seen 20 miles away. Dismounting, the queen was conducted to her lodgings.

John Laneham wrote that, after a quiet Sunday occupied in divine service and prayer, Jupiter displayed his power with a 'blaze of burning darts flying to and fro, beams of stars coruscant, streams and hails of fiery sparks, lightnings of wildfire on water and land, flight and shooting of thunderbolts, all with such continuance, terror and vehemency ... that the heavens thundered, the waters surged, the earth shook' and, hardy as he was, it scared him.

On Monday, the queen hunted the hart until nine o'clock in the evening and rested on Tuesday, walking through the chase listening to music. The following days she went hunting or was entertained by bear-baiting, acrobatic feats by an Italian and another fireworks display. Friday and Saturday were windy and rainy, tempering the drought and heat caused by the fair weather and sunshine that her majesty had brought with her.

Sunday dawned fair, and in the afternoon a bridal play took place, in the tilt yard where a quintain had been set up. Sixteen lusty lads on Morris horses entered with the bridegroom, all dressed in holiday clothes, some wearing 'boots and no spurs', others wearing 'spurs and no boots', some in a hat, some in a cap, some a coat, some a jerkin, but all wearing a blue bride lace on a sprig of broom tied around their left arms, holding an alder sapling for a spear in their right hands.

In came the bridegroom wearing his father's large tawny worsted jacket, a high-crowned straw hat, harvest gloves on his hands to show good husbandry, inkhorn on his back to show he was bookish and lame of one leg. The ugly, brown-complexioned bride, demurely simpering and foul smelling, said she would dance before the queen for she would 'foot it finely as the best' with her dozen damsels for bridesmaids. The bridegroom took the first course at the quintain, broke his spear and nearly fell off his unruly mare; then, keeping clean the handkerchief his mother had given him, he blew his nose on the 'flappet' of his father's jacket. The rest of the band ran: some toppled down right, others to the left; two horses fell in love with one another; another man missed the quintain and hit it with his head, before they decided to run at one another, tumbling to the ground. 'A man would have laughed even if told that his wife lay dying', and the queen laughed appreciatively, as she also did at the Coventry Play afterwards, followed by a banquet of 300 dishes and a masque.

It was too hot for any activity on Monday except for hunting in the cool of the evening, and on the queen's return a mermaid greeted her to ask her to aid the Lady of the Lake, for her mere presence would force the cruel knight, Sir Bruce Sans-Pitie, to flee. Thus rescued, the Lady of the Lake came to shore with Arion riding on a 24-foot dolphin whose stomach played music. Contrived from a boat, its oars resembled fins. The Coventry Play was shown again at the queen's desire, for it made her laugh heartily.

With the weather breaking the day after, the grand supper and other spectacles were laid aside and the queen and party enjoyed the exquisite gardens. The queen rested until her departure on 27 July, listening to a last speech by Silvanus, who bade her farewell as she passed through the forest. It was said the revels cost the earl £60,000. The whole time the queen stayed the clock was stopped, its bell silenced for the conceit that time had stood still.

4–8 November 1576: Sacking of Antwerp

Philip II's soldiers, in cold blood, massacred 17,000 men, women and children. Piles of dead carcases in many places exceeded the height of a man. The killing continued days after, and the goods and merchandise of English merchants was seized, with some hanged as well. The Inquisition has also been invited into the Low Countries by the Duke of Alva, not content with the excess of blood already spilt.

On 8 November, the Pacification of Ghent, with its avowal to drive out the Spaniards, was signed.

16–22 August 1578: The Queen Visits Norwich

Sixty handsome, stalwart young men in black satin doublets and hose, with yellow-banded black taffeta hats, escorted Queen Elizabeth from Hartford Bridge for her welcome by the mayor. At Town Close, King Gurgunt, the mythical builder of Norwich Castle, before he could begin his speech, was stopped by the rain, while the queen proceeded past the pageant of women and children spinning and weaving to the musicians in the marketplace and on to the cathedral, where a *Te Deum* was sung.

Unsettled weather stopped most activities, including the water entertainment. Instead, the queen was treated to a masque and gifts from the gods: from Jupiter a riding wand made from whale fin; from Juno a purse; from Mars a pair of knives engraved 'to hurt your foe' and 'help your friend'; and from Venus a white dove which sat upon the table before the queen. Apollo serenaded her, playing an Italian guitar, while Pallas presented her with a Book of Wisdom and Neptune an artificial fish with a great pike in its belly. From Diana came a bow with silver-tipped arrows and from Cupid an arrow of gold. To every speech the queen listened graciously and gave her thanks to everyone.

As she departed on Friday, the queen thanked them all for the great cheer they had made her and also for the open households given to her servants. She knighted the mayor, shook her riding staff and said with tears in her eyes, 'I shall never forget Norwich. Farewell Norwich.'

21–23 *September 1578: Earl of Leicester Marries*

The summer progress ended at Wanstead House, Queen Elizabeth arriving during the marriage celebrations for the forty-six-year-old Earl of Leicester and the widowed Countess of Essex, the queen's cousin, thirty-four-year-old Lettice Knollys. She brought with her some of the council and the French ambassadors.

A love match, it had been known for at least a year they intended to marry once the countess' period of widowhood ended. The two have flirted ever since the countess was twenty years old and have been so close that there had been friction between Leicester and Essex, causing scandalous talk, though unfounded, that Leicester had poisoned her husband when he died in Ireland of dysentery in September 1576.

The Earl of Leicester's chaplain, Humphrey Tindall, performed the ceremony at around seven o'clock in the morning, after which followed a great feast. The bride wore an informal morning dress. Other attendees were Leicester's brother, Ambrose, and his friends Lord North (whom the queen visited towards the beginning of the month), the Earl of Pembroke and on the bride's side her father Sir Francis Knollys, vice-chamberlain of the queen's household, and her brother, Richard.

The queen has long been close to both parties of the marriage, the countess often attending the queen when she visited Kenilworth, including the nineteen-day festival in 1575 after which the Countess of Essex was hostess to the queen and the earl at her home in Chartley.

On Sunday and Monday, everyone was feasted, the queen at the earl's own table paying great courtesy to them.

22 *January–14 February 1579: Visit of John Casimir*

Despite a sharp winter of snow, John Casimir, son to Frederick III, Prince Elector Palatine of the Rhine, voyaged over the sea from the

Low Countries. He was lavishly received at the Tower of London and conveyed by cresset light and torchlight, by trumpets, drums and fifes, to Sir Thomas Gresham's house to await an audience with the queen at Westminster.

Three days later, the queen graciously received him, giving him permission to hunt at Hampton Court. On Sunday 1 February, and for two days after, he was honoured with a joust, running at the tilt, and barriers with swords on horseback. The queen honoured him on 8 February with the Order of St George, tying the garter about his leg with her own hands.

Such an abundance of snow fell on the morning of 5 February that at its shallowest it was 2 feet deep, at its worst 5 feet, with deeper drifts outside the city in which many men, women and animals died. It continued to snow for three days then froze for two, followed by rain and thaw. The floods rose so high that in Westminster Hall fish were discovered after the thaw.

The prince took his leave on St Valentine's Day.

17-21 *July 1579: Queen Nearly Shot*

The queen, in her barge on the Thames, was talking with the French ambassador, Earl of Lincoln and Sir Francis Knollys. Thomas Appletree, a young manservant of Lord Hunsdon, with two or three children of her majesty's chapel, was rowing up and down nearby while randomly and recklessly shooting a harquebus. By misfortune, a bullet shot clean through both arms of one of the watermen, a mere 6 feet from her highness. Bleeding profusely, the queen bid him to be of good cheer for he would want for nothing to his ease. Thomas was quickly arrested and condemned to death.

On 21 July, he was brought to the waterside at the same place where a gibbet had been set up. The hangman put the rope about his neck, then removed it. Thomas had received a pardon from the queen.

10 March 1580: *The Queen Visits the French Ambassador*

Nine o'clock in the morning the queen went on a river excursion in her barge to the French ambassador's house accompanied by Lords Clinton and Howard with their wives and daughters. The ambassador, told he had a visit from the lords, came downstairs in his nightgown and was much surprised to find Queen Elizabeth, gay and laughing, walking up and down his garden. She told him she had never before visited an ambassador's house, but thought it a good way to show her affection for France, their majesties and, more particularly, Francis, made Duke of Anjou now that his brother Henri was king.

6 April 1580: *The Great Earthquake*

A great and sudden earthquake occurred throughout the kingdom which lasted an hour, signalled by the great clock bell in the Palace of Westminster, which rang by itself. In Kent and on the coast, the land not only quaked but 'the sea so foamed that the ships tottered' and the earthquake moved the land three times in the night. People left their beds and ran into the churches.

4 April 1581: *The Queen Visits the* Golden Hind

Queen Elizabeth dined in the cabin of Captain Drake's ship, the *Golden Hind*, at Deptford, where it was kept in the dockyard as a national monument after Drake's feat of circumnavigating the globe. A huge crowd of people assembled for the occasion, at least one hundred piling onto the wooden plank between the ship and shore, which broke under their weight. Fortunately, no lives were lost. After dinner, the queen conferred a knighthood on the captain.

Originally named the *Pelican*, in August 1578 Drake renamed it the *Golden Hind* in respect of his friend and sponsor of the voyage, Sir Christopher Hatton, whose armorial crest is a golden hind, and perhaps in appeasement for executing Hatton's personal secretary for mutiny.

Drake had set sail from Plymouth on 13 September 1577 with a small fleet and sailed first to the Cape Verde islands off the coast of north-west Africa, where Spanish and Portuguese ships with their treasure were captured. They crossed the Atlantic and reached Brazil, to travel through the Strait of Magellan in 1578, which took sixteen days. Encountering fierce storms, the fleet was separated. Now in the Pacific, Drake attacked Spanish ships and ports for treasure then continued north, probably landing in California to repair the ship, before continuing across the Pacific to the East Indies and Java, and then around the Cape of Good Hope, arriving back in Plymouth laden with treasure on 26 September 1580.

8–9 May 1581: *Beauty* versus *Desire*

The French ambassadors, in the midst of negotiating marriage between Queen Elizabeth and the Duke of Anjou, more commonly called Monsieur, were honoured by gentlemen of the court with a triumph. The Four Foster Children of Desire were the challengers; the queen's viewing gallery was the Fortress of Perfect Beauty.

On the day, a high mound of earth (a frame of canvas on wheels with musicians hidden inside), the Rowling Trench, was brought in. Gunners, in crimson satin, fired realistically painted wooden cannon, sweet powder from one and sweet water from the other, as the challengers entered and rode around the tilt. Scaling ladders were placed against the mound and footmen threw flowers and fancies against it until the defenders entered: one was dressed in armour hung with apples and fruit, another had hair hung over his helmet to signify Eve, and the four Knollys brothers were present, with a page dressed as Mercury to give their speech. In the middle of the running, Sir Henry Leigh entered as Unknown, broke six staves and went out again.

For the meal, the queen had caused a banqueting house to be built using masts and canvas painted to resemble stone and glass windows. It was decorated with ivy, holly, herbs, flowers, gold spangles and fruits – pomegranates, oranges, cucumbers and grapes – and between them clouds, stars and sunbeams.

On the second day, the foster children entered in a horse-drawn chariot so large there was room within for musicians and a woman representing Desire. Towards evening, after a 'noble shivering of swords', Mercury, in ash-coloured garments and olive branch in hand, knelt before the queen and declared that the children were sorry for allowing Violence to accompany Desire, submitting themselves wholly as bondsmen to her.

17 November 1581: Queen Elizabeth Betrothed?

Monsieur, the queen's suitor whom she has affectionately nicknamed 'her Frog', has visited with the queen since the beginning of the month. While they were attending the festival of her accession, they had a long and intimate discourse and the queen took a ring from her own finger and put it upon his. Speculation was rife that the queen was promising to marry him.

2–7 February 1582: Monsieur Goes to Fight in Flanders

Accompanying Monsieur on his departure from England, the queen stopped at Rochester to show him all her great ships, saying all her ships would give him service whenever he needed them. The French lords with him said that it was no wonder she was called 'Lady of the Seas'.

At Canterbury, the queen openly feasted all the French nobility. Then as the queen and Monsieur took their personal leave of each other, 'she loath to let him go and he as loath to depart', he promised to return in March. The duke travelled on to Sandwich where on 7 February he boarded the great warship *Discovery* with the Earl of Leicester and Vice Admiral Howard. The previous night, the ship was nearly fired by powder when a fire occurred in the gunroom, but one of Howard's men laid himself flat in the flame and stayed the fire until water came. He was scorched on the face and hands, and his garments burnt, but will be well rewarded by the queen.

While the ships were still at anchor, there came a post that Antwerp had risen. Monsieur sailed away with fifteen ships to go to Flushing.

24 February 1583: *The Archbishop and the Innkeeper's Wife*

Dr Edwin Sandys, Archbishop of York, wrote to Lord Burghley regarding an extortion plot made against himself. In May 1581, the archbishop had lodged in Doncaster at an inn kept by one Syssons. When the archbishop was in bed, Syssons got his wife to slip naked next to him while he was sleeping and then, with dagger in hand, 'made forcible entry', with Sir Robert Stapleton acting as witness. They asked for hush money and the archbishop gave Syssons £500, and to Stapleton £200 and a valuable lease. Their greed in blackmailing the archbishop further has led to their imprisonment and fines.

26 July–18 August 1584: *Feuding Families*

In court, the Earl of Shrewsbury complained his wife, Elizabeth, has removed many things from Chatsworth and carried them to the house of her son, William Cavendish, at Hardwick. He also claimed that his stepsons, Sir Charles and William Cavendish, forcibly stopped him from entering Chatsworth House, the latter threatening him with sword and pistol (for which he had a short spell in prison), and the countess had induced his son, Gilbert, to take her side.

The countess responded that they were her belongings and that the earl had turned her own son, Henry, against her. Furthermore, she said the earl was seeking to take Chatsworth away from her, though she and her previous husband, Sir William Cavendish, had built it on the land they purchased for £600 in 1552.

Intervening, the queen tried to effect a reconciliation. The countess said she no longer wished to live with her husband and even wanted to end her life. The countess and the earl had married in 1567 as a love match and not so long ago 'his Bess' was the earl's sweetheart.

11 February 1585: Using Treason to Murder

Today, in the Star Chamber, Thomas Lovelace was found guilty of counterfeiting a traitorous letter about a plot to assassinate the queen to implicate his cousins Thomas, Leonard and Richard, by throwing it on an open highway to be discovered. He hoped they would be questioned, imprisoned and executed so he would receive their goods and leases. His punishment was to be paraded on market days at pillories in London and Kent and to have both his ears cut off.

29 June 1585: Armour Lottery

A lottery for marvellous, rich and beautiful armour was drawn in St Paul's Churchyard, a house of timber and board erected for the purpose.

7 July 1585: School for Thieves

A man named Wotton, a gentleman born and sometime merchant who had fallen into decay, kept a struggling alehouse at Smart's Quay near Billingsgate. Deciding to set up a new venture, he established a schoolhouse within the inn, where he taught young boys how to cut purses by hanging up two devices: a pocket and a purse, both filled with coins and hung about with many hawks bells. He that silently took a coin out of the pocket graduated as a 'public foyster', and one that took a silver silently out of the purse was adjudged a 'judicial nipper'.

15 August 1586: The Babington Plot

Church bells all over London pealed at the joyful news of the capture of the traitors who had conspired to assassinate Queen Elizabeth. Psalms were sung, bonfires lit and banquets set up in the streets. In an effort to evade capture, Anthony Babington, the twenty-four-year-old leader, had cut his hair and used husks of green walnuts to darken his fair complexion, but after ten days of hunger he and four of his companions were driven out of hiding to beg for food.

The plot began in April in Paris, when a priest, John Ballard, met with Don Bernardino de Mendoza, the Spanish ambassador deported from England for his previous plotting against the queen. They decided they would recruit someone within England to aid Philip II to invade England, free Mary, Queen of Scots and assassinate Elizabeth. Ballard said he knew some sympathisers to Mary and on his arrival in England immediately recruited Babington and his friends, telling them that, being Catholics under an excommunicate queen, it was lawful and right for them to murder her.

Various plans were discussed. Ballard told them that there were men around her in court who had discussed whether to poison her or kill her by steel or shot, either in her garden or in her coach, perhaps on St Bartholomew's Day. The priest then told them that one man, John Savage, was already in England to undertake the deed. Babington mused that surely six, rather than one alone, would better ensure no miscarrying of the deed so that the assassination, liberation of Mary, rising and rebellion should occur simultaneously.

The plotters, already under suspicion, were watched and letters between Mary and Anthony were intercepted, copied, resealed and sent on. Those letters, together with notes, memorials, three-score ciphers, many amorous letters and compliments from great men of England, were disclosed when Mary's closet and desks were broken and searched on 11 August. Mary, out hunting that day, suddenly found herself under arrest and taken to Chartley under the custody of the stern Sir Amyas Paulet.

The court were informed that Babington wrote enthusiastically on 6 July to Mary with details of the plot, telling her there would be an 'invasion of sufficient strength, deliverance of her and the despatch of the usurping competitor' and that his friends, 'six noble gentlemen' zealous in the Catholic cause, would undertake the 'tragical execution'. Mary did not reply until 17 July, saying he should heed the advice of Mendoza and to be careful of the details; once everything was prepared and in readiness, then it would be 'time to set the six gentlemen to work'. She advised that with no certain date appointed the said 'gentlemen had about them or at court four stout men with good and speedy horses, for so soon as the said design shall be executed ... so she may be transported away before her keeper can know it or fortify the house'. She described three methods by which she could be delivered. She iterated he should not stir before being assured of foreign aid so she could be set in the midst of a good army, for if she was caught she might be enclosed 'for ever in some hole' from which she would never escape.

Babington replied to Mary on 3 August that what 'they have vowed they will perform or die', and ended with the wish that 'God grant her a long and prosperous reign'.

The plot had distressed and angered the queen, for Savage and Barnwell, members of Babington's group, had been to her court many times, and three of the others, Tilney, Abington and Windsor, had been gentlemen of her guard.

8 September 1586: *Spanish Fleet at Brest*

The Earl of Sussex advised the council that Spanish warships had arrived at Brest, anchored in a small harbour at the western extremity. The earl mustered men, skiffs and small boats for reconnoitre and sent out a barque to watch whither the fleet goes and prepared signals so their intent and purpose could be quickly disclosed.

4–6 December 1586: *Proclamation against Mary, Queen of Scots*

Importuned on all sides to carry out the sentence of death on Mary, Queen of Scots for the safety of her person, which she had so far stoutly resisted, Queen Elizabeth sank to her knees in Parliament, saying she took it hard that she, 'a woman, and the most tender-hearted on earth, should be called upon to take the life of her own kinswoman'. The sentence of death was given by the nobility under the Great Seal of England on 4 December.

The news was proclaimed by the Lord Mayor of London with earls, barons, aldermen and principal officers of the city, eighty of the gravest citizens in coats of velvet and chains of gold and a great number of gentlemen, all on horseback. At the sound of four trumpets, citizens in every lane rejoiced at the news, showed by ringing of bells, bonfires and singing psalms.

The trial was held in mid-October in front of a commission of forty-five nobles. The Queen of Scots gave no defence except a bare denial that nothing could be plainly and directly proved against her.

7 February 1587: *Execution of Mary, Queen of Scots*

The earls of Shrewsbury and Kent and the sheriff of Northamptonshire accompanied Mary to the black-covered scaffold, 2 feet high by 12 feet wide, set up in the hall of Fotheringhay Castle. Two executioners awaited her, who offered to pray with her. She refused, preferring to pray by herself. Her prayers ended, the executioners knelt and asked her forgiveness, which she gave, saying, 'I hope you shall make an end of all my troubles.'

They and her two women helped her up. Her women began to undress her and took off her rosary while she laid her crucifix on a chair. She began to help them herself as if she longed to be done, saying that she had never put off her clothes before such a company of knights and gentlemen. Her outermost gown was of black satin with a train, long hanging sleeves cut showing purple velvet beneath and trimmed with acorn buttons of jet and pearl. Below she wore a crimson satin bodice unlaced in the back and a crimson velvet skirt.

One of her women kissed a Corpus Christi cloth and put it over Mary's face and pinned it to her cap. She knelt upon the cushion, spoke aloud a psalm in Latin, then, groping for the block, laid down her head. Putting her chin over the block, she laid a moment quietly then stretched out her arms and cried, '*In manus tuas Domine.*'

Between ten and eleven o'clock, Mary, Queen of Scots was beheaded. It took two strokes, she making very little noise but not stirring at the first, and a third to sever a sinew so the executioner could lift up her head. Her cap of lawn and wig fell off; underneath, her cropped hair was as grey as if she had been seventy years old.

Her little dog, Geddon, had crept under her dress and refused to leave the corpse but lay between her head and shoulders until by force he was carried away and her blood washed off him. Her remains were conveyed into the great chamber to be embalmed ready for burial.

19–21 April 1587: Drake Burns the Fleet at Cadiz

Having been advised that the King of Spain over the last year had been busy preparing to assemble a great army at Lisbon and an invincible navy to invade England, Sir Francis Drake, arriving at

Cadiz on 19 April just before sunset, found more than sixty large ships and other smaller ships, among them thirty-two ships laden with provisions for the king's navy.

As Drake entered the harbour, he sunk one argosy with thirty brass pieces. Before night fell he had disabled thirty-eight great ships, their sailors diving overboard. Before burning the ships, he took their ordnance and used their provisions to fully stock his own fleet. Leaving during the night of 21 April, Drake sank a further argosy and two other great ships and brought away four ships of provisions.

Drake wrote to the council that there will be no invasion of England this year but that King Philip is unquestionably gathering supplies and ammunition throughout his dominions for a very great fleet and army to invade England.

23 December 1587: *Prince Arthur and His Knights*

Hugh Offley, a rich citizen of London and member of the Leather-sellers' Company, hosted this year's show of Prince Arthur and His Round Table Knights, a fraternity created in honour of Prince Arthur, son of Henry VII. The archers, 300 personable men dressed in black satin doublets and black velvet hose, each one holding a yew longbow and waxed arrows, marched in array, three together, and every three a bow-length from the other, from Merchant Taylors' Hall to Mile End Green. There were appointed certain stages, forts and marks for them to shoot at, with liberal rewards to them that won prizes, and plenty of food and drink to eat.

Queen Elizabeth, at the sight of the 'stately company of archers', stopped her chariot so she could watch. As they passed the queen, they knelt and wished that God would long prosper and preserve her. In her turn she graciously bowed to them, giving them most hearty thanks, and prayed God to bless all her good subjects.

19–20 July 1588: Armada! First Sighting

Spotted at dawn, the beacons were lit as the stately armada, commanded by the Duke of Medina-Sidonia, slowly passed, looking like a town of high towers and castles against the skyline. Under full sail, they laboured as if the wind was against them or the 'ocean sighed under their burden'. Reconnaissance by a pinnace observed 160 vessels, comprising seventy-seven galleons and large ships, the rest being caravels, pinnaces and galleys set in six or seven squadrons.

Receiving notice the Spanish had entered the Channel near the Lizard, Lord Admiral Charles Howard mobilised his own fleet. Although the wind was against the English navy still in port, the mariners, with great difficulty and industry, brought the fleet into the open sea, the admiral pulling at the hawser alongside them. Comprising twenty great galleons and fifty large ships, the fleet, manoeuvring windward, allowed the enemy to pass by so they could harry their ships from behind, the English ships being lighter and more manoeuvrable.

21–29 July 1588: Skirmishes between the Fleets

To provoke the Spaniards to fight, on 21 July Howard commanded the *Defiance* to discharge her ordnance, while he thundered upon the Spanish admiral's ship from the *Ark Royal*. Hoisting Philip II's standard, the duke put about and formed order of battle to protect his rearguard, which was being fired upon by Hawkins and Frobisher, separating the squadrons. Ordered not to get to close quarters – a disadvantage to the lighter English ships – they had to break off when the wind turned against them, allowing the armada to regroup and resume its journey at full sail. Drake in the *Revenge* had captured two galleons, crippling their rigging and masts with his cannon, and captured Don Pedro de Valdes, third in command, and Vice Admiral Ricaldo, whose ship had blown up, rent in both bow and stern.

For a day both fleets were becalmed in sight of each other, but an easterly arose in the dawn of 23 August, favouring the Spanish who steered towards the English on the attack, the latter skipping in and out of the slower ships. Using sail and oar, Spanish galleasses crept up on the English rearguard but were spotted in time to prevent them boarding as the ships swiftly sheared away from them. Both fleets, fiercely firing broadsides directly at each other, passed by, a ferocious lightning and thunder heard miles away, but Spanish shot flew sheer over the English ships which were deftly moved into the open sea.

The following day the armada, now abreast of the Isle of Wight, was bombarded until the wind fell, the attack resuming at dawn next day. The *Ark Royal* attacked the flagship, which, although severely damaged, managed to attack Howard's rudder and leave his ship drifting, quickly supported by English ships and towed by longboards until the rudder was repaired and he could again move with the wind. Spanish ships gave chase but in comparison to the English craft looked as if they were standing still. English and Spanish ships intermingled, cannonading each other, but as soon as a fresh wind favouring the armada sprang up, it indomitably resumed course for Calais, until the wind ceased that day. The day after, both fleets were stuck motionless in sight of each other, the French coast on one side and the English coast on the other.

On the morning of 27 July the wind freshened and fresh English ships joined the fleet, bringing the sail to 160. Skirmishing between the fleets was the hottest yet, continuing until four o'clock, many ships hidden from view by the smoke. Then the wind veered, favouring the Spanish, who arrived at Calais and anchored, now seven leagues away from Dunkirk where the Duke of Parma was ordered to wait for the armada so they could assist him in getting his troops across the Channel and up the Thames. The English fleet dropped anchor a league away.

In the night, Lord Admiral Howard sent eight ships, daubed on the outside with Greek pitch and resin, filled full of sulphur and other combustibles, among the ships of the armada, their flames shining over all the sea. The Spanish fleet weighed anchor, cut their cables, hoisted sail and the ships scattered. In half-moon formation the English ships chased after the great force, both sailing northwards out of sight, Spanish feathers plucked 'by little and little'.

8–9 August 1588: Queen Elizabeth: 'The heart and stomach of a king'

To counter the Spanish threat of invading England via the Thames, an army was assembled at West Tilbury, opposite Gravesend. Across the Thames a boom of ships' cables, chains and masts was erected. No news had come of the opposing fleets since 28 July, when Howard had deployed the fireships. To raise morale, on 8 August Queen Elizabeth sailed down the Thames to visit her troops, landing at midday. She was met by an escort of 1,000 horse and 2,000 foot, the soldiers lining both sides of the road to call out blessings to her as she moved to her lodging.

Conducted by the Earl of Leicester, the queen walked through the camp the following morning and took the stand to watch the march-past of her troops. Holding her command staff in her hand, she spoke to them when they assembled: 'My loving people, we have been persuaded by some that are careful of our safety, to take heed how we commit ourselves to armed multitudes, for fear of treachery. But I assure you, I do not desire to live to distrust my faithful and loving people. Let tyrants fear. … I have placed my chiefest strength and safeguard in the loyal hearts and good will of my subjects.' She continued that she had come to them resolved to live or die amongst them, for though she had the body of a weak and feeble woman she had 'the heart and stomach of a King, and of a King of England too, and think foul scorn that Parma or Spain, or any prince of Europe should dare to invade the borders of my realm; to which, rather than any dishonour shall grow by me, I myself will take up arms'. The soldiers cheered, their hearts so enflamed that the weakest soldier would fight the proudest Spaniard that dared land in England.

Just before the queen was due to leave that afternoon, despatches arrived and the first news that on 29 July the English had fired on Spanish ships for a solid nine hours, and so tremendous was the English artillery that the Spanish flagship sails and hull had over 200 cannonballs shot into it and was leaking, while another galleon was so riddled with holes it sank. When the English offered them surrender at fair terms and rescue, the Spanish refused, shouting that the English were 'Lutheran hens' and daring them to come to close quarters and fight them.

Other Spanish ships blundered onto the sandbanks around Flanders, wind and tide being against them, and to lighten their loads had thrown overboard large numbers of horses and mules. Skirmishing continued the following day as the ships left sailed northwards while English ships chased them, continuing to cripple and scatter them, following them past the outer isles of Scotland. The Lord Admiral wrote he had laid off further pursuit both for the terrible storms that arose and for want of powder and victuals, he and his men having only beans to eat and 'many of the men drinking their own water'.

The Holland fleet, commanded by Admiral Nassau, was patrolling, keeping watch alongside Captains Seymour, Winter and Palmer, while the Lord Admiral, arrived at Margate, was refitting his ships. In the meantime, Captain Henry White wrote from Margate to Walsingham to say that as his ship was used as a fireship, he was like one who had had his house burnt and asked for his favour for 'being in her majesty's service had almost beggared him'.

8 September 1588: Death of the Earl of Leicester

The Earl of Leicester, on his way to Buxton to take the waters, died unexpectedly. His body was conveyed to the castle of Kenilworth. Queen Elizabeth, grief-stricken at the death of 'her sweet Robin, her Eyes', locked herself in her chamber holding the letter he wrote to her on 2 September, adamantly refusing to unlock the doors and admit anyone into her presence.

15 September 1588: Victory Parade

Six hundred banners taken from the Spanish armada were carried in parade around London to show them to the people, and as the queen rode through the city she was received with great applause. Medals of commemoration have been struck. One with pictures of Spanish ships refers to the Duke of Medina-Sidonia with the words, 'He came. He saw. He fled.'

News from Rome is that the Pope, on hearing the English had triumphed, said, 'The King trifled with this Armada of his, but the Queen acts in earnest; were she only a Catholic, she would be our best beloved, for she is of great worth.' In France the Spanish ambassador, Bernardino de Mendoza, told the French king and his court that England had been defeated before the opposite was revealed, to the amusement of the Venetian ambassador whose verdict was that the English are 'the skilled mariners which rumour reported them to be, for while they have always been on the enemy's flank they have not lost a single ship', and their queen never once lost her presence of mind: 'Her acuteness in resolving on her action, her courage in carrying it out, shows her ... resolve to save her country and herself.'

10 July 1591: The Queen Visits Lord Burghley

The queen visited 'her spirit', Lord Burghley, lying sick of the gout at his fair brick-built house on the north side of the Strand. His servant, perceiving Elizabeth's fashionable and high attire upon her head, asked her as he conducted her through the door, 'May your highness be pleased to stoop.' The queen replied, 'For your master's sake I will stoop; but not for the King of Spain's.'

15–21 *August 1591: Visiting the Montagues*

Arriving mid-evening, Queen Elizabeth was greeted by Anthony, Lord Montague holding a gold key, standing between two porters carved from wood. He said there was a prophecy that the walls would shake and the roof totter until the fairest of all came and, by a glance of her eyes, made all sturdy. Gesturing to the porters, he said they had fallen asleep waiting, looking now more like posts than porters, but he would have cut off his eyelids to miss the end. Presenting the gold key to her, he said, 'The tongue of the lord who owns the house is the key of his heart, his heart the lock of his soul, in duty and service to you he is second to none.' Taking the proffered key, the queen alighted and embraced Lady Montague and her daughter, who took her to her chamber to rest as she did the following day, that being Sunday.

Having shot at deer early on Monday, the queen went for a walk after dinner where she was met by a pilgrim, dressed in russet velvet hat and coat decorated with silver scallops, who led her to an oak tree. Her arms were carved in its trunk with those of all the gentlemen of Sussex. A 'wildman clad in ivy' pointing to them said, 'The whole world is drawn in a map; the heavens in a globe; and this shire is shrunk in a tree', an oak which represented her strength.

The next day, dinner was laid on a 72-foot table in the garden. Afterwards, walking near a fishpond, the queen came upon a fisherman sitting motionless. As if talking to himself, he said that for two hours he had sat there and had not caught even an oyster, and if he fished all day would not catch a frog. Not looking at the queen, he mused, 'There is something beautiful which stays the very minnows and if the shadow of a man turns back the fish, what then the sight of a goddess?' Then he drew his net, and all the fish in it were laid at her feet.

For dinner next day, the table was doubled in length and Lord and Lady Montague danced with the country people to tabor and pipe. Afterwards the queen retired early for her departure the next day.

20–24 September 1591: A Sylvan Fancy

Edward, Earl of Hertford escorted the queen into Elvetham Park where a poet dressed in green and wearing a laurel garland welcomed her in Latin. Flower-garlanded maidens, the Three Graces and Three Hours, threw sweet herbs and flowers from baskets across the queen's path as she rode to the hall door. The Countess of Hertford, on her knees with her ladies and gentlewomen, awaited her arrival. The queen embraced the countess in her rising and kissed her.

A quarter of an hour later, a volley of chamber and brass pieces came from a Snail Mount, built of privet hedges, a fort and the 'Ship Isle' on the newly dug half-moon lake. For her comfort Hertford had also built canvas and board offices to house the scullery and kitchens, one with five ovens 14 feet deep, one a great kitchen with four ranges and another with a long range to serve all comers.

Though the following morning was wet and stormy, it eased off mid-afternoon and the queen was brought to a seat made for her by the lakeside. Over it was a green satin canopy of estate, every seam covered with silver lace. Its four pillars were silver and on its top four white plumes spangled with silver sparkled in the breeze. In front of her, Nereus, in red silk and cornered cap on his curly hair, swam towards her leading five Tritons with grey hair and beards sounding trumpets, heralding the Gods of the Sea. Inside the pinnace they towed sat Neara, the imprisoned love of Sylvanus, God of the Woods. Behind them swam mermen each armed with a huge 'wooden squirt'.

Wading ashore, Nereus presented the queen with a green-rush woven purse with a jewel inside, while the fort was suddenly surrounded by armed men. The Snail Mount, given horns of wildfire, looked like a monster. To the sound of trumpets, Sylvanus ran from the woods while a sea-god somersaulted from the ship's prow into the lake. Dressed from his middle to his knees in goatskin, bare skin and face dyed with saffron and two little horns protruding from his forehead, Sylvanus argued with Nereus, who threw him over his head into the water. Crying out, 'Revenge, revenge' as he waded from the water, Sylvanus and his followers threw paper darts; Nereus and his followers squirted water. When Sylvanus ran at the country people watching, they ran away shrieking and laughing. He retired into the wood while Nereus presented the queen with a sea jewel in the form of a fan.

The queen was so pleased with the entertainment the actors were given a double reward.

On her third day, Elizabeth listened to the pastoral song of *Phyllida and Corydon* from a casement window in the morning, and in the afternoon was entertained by an exhibition game of 'board and cord ', a tennis court squared out in cord. Stripped to their doublets, ten men played five-to-five handball. In the evening a banquet of a 1,000 dishes was set out in the garden, all the dishes glass and silver, accompanied by a fireworks display: a castle of fireworks, a globe as big as a barrel and rockets, firewheels and balls of wildfire cast on the water.

On the fourth morning, Aureola, the fairy queen, and a round of dancing fairies sang 'Elisa is the fairest queen that ever trod upon this green'.

As the queen departed, a farewell ditty of 'Come Again' was sung by hidden musicians at the park gate. The queen courteously stopped and listened to it all despite heavy rain.

28–30 *September 1592:* Visiting the Crow's Nest

Sir Henry Norris, dressed as an old soldier, said to Queen Elizabeth on her arrival at Rycote that old as he was he would give all his armour and weapons to serve her but could give only his heart, for his boys, fighting in her service, had stolen his equipment. He told her that his wife, her crow, was often frightened by rumours of their death for her own birds are to her the fairest and dearest. He ended that 'though nothing be more unfit to lodge your majesty than our crow's nest, your highness will make of it a phoenix nest'.

On Sunday, the queen walked in the garden and was met by the old soldier, who handed her a letter: 'Some news out of Ireland.' Inside was a gold dart set with diamonds with the motto 'I fly only for my sovereign'. A skipper from Flanders came with a letter and a gold key, with the motto in Dutch 'I only open to you'. In came a French page, and the queen received a sword with diamonds and rubies and in French the words 'Drawn only in your defence'. Last came a truncheon with a motto in Spanish: 'I do not command but under you.' The old soldier knelt before her and said his sons had remembered their duty.

28 *February 1594:* Poison Plot

The queen's own physician, Roderigo Lopez, and two retainers of Don Antonio of Portugal were on trial charged with attempting to poison the queen at the behest of the Pope and Philip II. Lopez, believed to be loyal, confessed that he had received a rich jewel and been promised the sum of 5,000 ducats and honours and preferment for his children if he poisoned the queen. His defence was that he never intended any hurt against the queen and had presented the jewel to her, meaning to merely deceive the Spaniard and take his money. All three were condemned to die, Lopez affirming he loved the queen as well as he loved Jesus Christ, but with Lopez being a man of the Jewish persuasion, this raised laughter rather than pity.

3 April 1598: Punishment of God

A fire raged in Tiviford in Devon for most of the afternoon and consumed 409 houses, £150,000 worth of plate, merchandise and household stuff. Fifty persons were burnt, although an almshouse in the middle of the town was preserved. It was caused by a poor woman frying pancakes with straw for lack of other fuel. The fire was seen as a punishment from God for the rich in the town have had small regard for the poor daily seen to perish in the streets for lack of relief.

29 August 1598: Funeral of Lord Burghley

Sir William Cecil, Lord Burghley, Master of the Wards, High Treasurer of England and councillor to the queen all her reign, died at his house by The Strand on 4 August. His coffin was conveyed to Westminster for a solemn funeral attended by heralds, the mourners numbering above 500, but his body was brought to Stamford and buried there among his ancestors.

Robert Devereux, Earl of Essex was seen to look exceedingly sorrowful, and rumour says it is because his last words with Burghley were in argument on whether or not to pursue peace with Spain. Burghley had argued for it, Essex against. The Lord Treasurer said he breathed nothing but war, slaughter and blood. This was the earl's first public appearance since retiring to Wanstead after his argument with the queen about the best course to take in Ireland, when, in temper and forgetting himself, he gave her a scornful look, swung on his heels and turned his back on her. The queen boxed his ears, bidding him, 'Go and be hanged.' He put his hand to his sword, but the Lord Admiral stepped in before he could draw it. Essex gave a great oath and shouted that he would not put up with such an affront and indignity, nor would he have taken it at her father's hands. He then left the court.

The queen said that Essex had 'played long enough upon her' and she meant to 'play awhile upon him and to stand as much upon her greatness, as he has done upon his stomach'. His friends have tried to make him see sense, saying 'there was no equality between a prince and subject' and to sue humbly for her favour, which he has refused to do in angry letters to them.

16 January 1599: Funeral of Edmund Spenser

Edmund Spenser, who died on 13 January and who surpassed all the English poets except Chaucer, was buried near to him at Westminster today. His funeral, paid for by the Earl of Essex, was attended by fellow poets. Their elegies and mournful poems, with the pens that wrote them, were thrown into his tomb.

Born in East Smithfield around 1552, Spenser was educated at Merchant Taylor's School and became 'a poor scholar' at Pembroke College, Cambridge. He first won acclaim with his poem *The Shepheard's Calendar* in 1579, and when his poem *The Faerie Queene*, with Queen Elizabeth as the chief heroine, was published in 1590 it was an instant success. Spenser had only just arrived in London, bringing despatches from Sir Thomas Norris in Ireland as the Irish, under the Earl of Tyrone, had rebelled. Spenser, his wife and four children had barely escaped with their lives when rebels set fire to his castle, which, surrounded by woodland, was an idyllic setting for his writing.

27 March 1599: Essex Leaves for Ireland

Robert, Earl of Essex, Lord Lieutenant, Earl Marshal, departed from Seething Lane on his way to St Albans en route for Ireland with a great train of noblemen and gentlemen on horseback before him, his coaches following. The queen had desired Charles Blount, Lord Mountjoy to take on the Irish expedition, but the earl had countered that Mountjoy was of too mean estate and bookish; that

Ireland required an experienced general like himself who could see it was 'not so much the young sprigs to be cut off as the root to be stubbed up' and that Tyrone should be attacked in full force, not parleyed with as previous lord deputies had.

The queen, tired of his constant importunity, finally agreed, sending him to Ireland with the largest expeditionary force ever seen – 16,000 foot and 2,000 horse – with instructions to prosecute and conclude the war, not to liberally confer knighthoods as he had done before except on well-deserving and worthy persons, to bypass other rebels and bend his whole force against the arch-rebel, the Earl of Tyrone.

The earl left under a clear sky sundered with great claps of thunder presaging the heavy rain and hail that followed but which did not deter people in the streets and fields coming to see him, even from 4 miles away, crying out blessings to him. Tyrone, busy with fortifications, recently received four ships out of Spain with a great store of money, men and munitions to help him continue his fight against the English.

29 September 1599: Essex under House Arrest

The Earl of Essex, without warning of his arrival, pushed into the queen's bedchamber at Nonesuch before she was up and dressed. Presenting himself on his knees, the unsmiling queen allowed him a short conference to justify himself against the sharp letters she had sent to him. She wanted to know why, when she had pressed him to go into Ulster against Tyrone, he had attacked other rebels, wasting time and so many men that he had to ask for more, and then when they were sent said he could do no more this year. Why, with so strong an army, in so long a time, at so great expense, had he done nothing? Why, when his army was whole, strong and complete, had he not fought Tyrone? If spring was not fit for war, why had he neglected summer? Autumn? Was no time of year fit? The queen was incensed at his leaving Ireland without her leave, for making a private truce with Tyrone, a truce easily broken by the rebels, when it had been in his power to overwhelm them and later pardon them for their treasons.

Common bruit has it that men marvelled how Essex had spent so much time and done so little except make new knights, the last count being fifty-nine, and heard that the rebels joked that Essex 'never drew sword but to make knights'. The nobility say that if he had been allowed to carry on he would shortly bring in 'tag and rag, cut and long tail' and draw the order into contempt.

Essex was committed to custody, though not to prison. He is being kept in the Lord Keeper's house without liberty.

31 May 1600: Essex Given Private Hearing

For eight months the Earl of Essex, in custody at the Lord Keeper's house, had made a great show of patience, modesty and humility, his last letter to the queen saying it was making him ill not being forgiven by her. The queen, pacified with his submission and humble letters, arranged for the earl to be heard in a private hearing before the council rather than the Star Chamber. The earl confessed his errors with tears, saying that the tears of his heart had quenched all the sparkles of pride that had been in him.

When he gave his justifications, the Lord Keeper said he had shown little obedience in his actions though he pretended obedience in his words. The judgement was that he should be discharged of his keeper, to keep to his house and have all his offices removed other than that of master of the horse, which everybody judges means he will soon be 'cockhorse' again as the queen is known to be easily appeased and because she had intended the earl's amendment, not his ruin.

23 June 1600: *The Queen Attends Lord Herbert's Wedding*

The queen honoured Lord Herbert by being present at his marriage to Mrs Anne Russell at Blackfriars. The bride met the queen at the waterside. Six knights carried her in a litter while the bride was led to the church by Lord Cobham and Lord Herbert of Cardiff, and escorted back by the earls of Rutland and Cumberland. The occasion was honoured by a wedding masque with a strange new dance by eight ladies. Each wore a skirt of cloth of silver with a rich silk gold-and-silver waistcoat, a mantle of carnation taffeta and their hair loose about their shoulders, curiously knotted and interlaced. After supper, the eight ladies came in and danced again, choosing eight more ladies to dance the measures. One of them went to the queen and asked her to join them. The queen asked her who she was.

'Affection,' replied the lady.

'Affection,' said the queen, 'is false.' Rising, however, she danced some measures.

10 October 1600: *All Is Not Gold That Glisters*

The Earl of Essex has been hoping for the renewal of his licence for sweet wines, which brings him great profit. The queen has not yet regranted it to him, saying, 'Benefits are not to be bestowed blindfold.' Despite the earl sending humble messages to her at which she rejoices, she said, 'Would God his deeds would be answerable to his words ... all is not gold that glisters.' The answers the queen gives are vexing the earl, who is on fire with indignation; he says the queen and council are resolved to thrust him into poverty.

6 January 1601: Twelfth Day Dances

Queen Elizabeth, as is customary, danced on Twelfth Day: this year, with the Earl of Essex still under house arrest, she danced in the presence of the ambassador from Muscovy, Gregory Invanovich Meklin, both measures and galliards, to show she is 'not so old as some would have her'. Courtiers believe this to be a reference to the hurtful reference of the Earl of Essex, who from his house has been letting slip angry words and letters, saying that the queen 'being an old woman, was no less crooked and distorted in mind than she was in body'.

Those that love Essex continue to advise him to be patient and humbly sue for her favour but such counsel falls on deaf ears. He says that instead of reaping a harvest a tempest has fallen on him; that he would not serve with base obsequiousness having done nothing amiss; that he had been unjustly committed to custody; and that princes have not an infinite power and may err as well as others. Such rash words are coming to the ears of the queen, along with knowledge of the letters the earl is writing to the King of Scotland.

Sunday 8 February 1601: A Rebellion Fizzles Out

At ten o'clock in the morning Robert, Earl of Essex, with his friend the Earl of Southampton and sundry other noblemen, all armed, departed from Essex House by The Strand, passing Fleet Street shouting, 'For the queen, For the queen.' Elsewhere, his friends cried out that Cobham and Raleigh wanted to murder the Earl of Essex 'in his bed'. The earl entered an armourer's shop in Fenchurch Street and tried to obtain munitions, which were denied him. He also called for citizens to arm themselves, but they ignored his command.

The Lord Mayor of London, warned in advance by the queen of a potential uprising, had ordered all the city gates shut and carts and coaches overset to bar many of the streets. While Lord Thomas Burghley and others proclaimed Essex and his men traitors in the queen's name, his band of followers slowly began to slink away. Up until then, no blood had been spilt.

At Ludgate, pikes and musketeers awaited. The earl drew his sword and commanded Sir Christopher Blount to set upon them. He did, and was sorely wounded and taken prisoner. The earl's hat shot through, he turned aside to Queenhithe to catch a boat to return to his house. Once home, he fortified his house and cast papers in the fire, saying he was determined to die. Later that evening, seeing the great artillery with which the queen's men surrounded his house, he and the other noblemen came out and fell upon their knees, surrendering their swords.

Sir John Harrington's verdict on the enterprise was that Lord Robert 'shifted from sorrow and repentance to rage and rebellion so suddenly he proved himself devoid of good reason or right mind ... and the queen well knows how to humble the haughty spirit but the haughty spirit knows not how to yield'. Knowing her authority as queen comes from God, he is sure it will not be taken away by any man.

25 February 1601: *Execution of Earl of Essex*
At eight this morning, Ash Wednesday, the Earl of Essex was executed within the Tower of London. He wore a gown of wrought velvet, a black satin suit, a black felt hat and a little ruff about his neck. His chaplain with two priests accompanied him.

Making obeisance to the lords, the earl gave a long speech asking them to be witnesses of his 'just punishment' and that his sins numbered more than the hairs on his head, continuing, 'I have bestowed my youth in wantonness, lust and uncleanness ... been puffed up with pride, vanity and love of this world's pleasures.' In closing, he said that he 'never meant violence towards the queen's person'. Taking some deep breaths, he prayed privately and ended with the Lord's Prayer.

The executioner then knelt and asked his forgiveness, which was given. Essex recited the Creed. He took off his doublet, revealing a scarlet waistcoat. He laid flat along the boards, put down his head upon the block and stretched out his arms, saying, 'Lord into thy hands I commend my spirit.' His head was severed from his body by the axe at three strokes; the first was deadly, depriving all sense and motion. The sheriffs of London had to rescue the headman, who was beaten by the crowds and who would have murdered him.

27 June 1601: *Death of Baron Norris of Rycote*

Sir Henry Norris has died, having outlived his wife and all of his children except his third son, Edward, with whom he had been living. All his sons, 'spirited, martial men', had distinguished themselves as soldiers, fighting in France, Ireland and the Low Countries.

16 February 1603: *The Queen Gives Audience to the Venetian Ambassador*

The Venetian ambassador, permitted audience with the queen, was led into the Presence Chamber where she awaited him. She wore a silver and white taffeta gown trimmed with gold and covered with gems and pearls, even under her stomacher. Around her neck was a long necklace of pearls and rubies, with great pearls around her forehead, and bracelets of double rows of pearls. On her head was a coif, on top of which she wore the crown imperial.

Although seated under her canopy of estate, on a platform with two steps, when the ambassador went to kneel and kiss her robe, she raised him up with both hands and allowed him to kiss her right hand. She listened and replied to the commission in Italian, standing and smiling all the while, until the close of the audience.

24 *March 1603: Death of Queen Elizabeth*

Today, at three in the morning, on the Eve of the Annunciation of the Virgin Mary, the queen died at Richmond Palace, having reigned forty-four years and four months, dying in the seventieth year of her age. She had been ailing for a few weeks after a cold, but had worsened on 15 March when she had felt unwell, sad and sorrowful, mourning the death of the Countess of Nottingham. Her second-cousin Robert Carey said she was melancholy and sighing, something he had only known once before, when the Queen of Scots was beheaded, and then she had wept many times, repeating she had not given her consent.

She asked for cushions to be laid in the privy chamber near the chapel and remained on them for four days and nights, no one being able to persuade her to eat or go to bed. Lord Charles Howard was sent for, who was absent because of the death of his wife, and no one knows how he got the queen into her bed. She still refused food and all the remedies offered.

The day before she died, unable to speak, the Archbishop of Canterbury was sent for and prayed with her until she passed, the queen making signs that it gave her comfort to hear him.

BIBLIOGRAPHY

Arnold (attributed to), *The Customs of London otherwise called Arnold's Chronicle* (London: 1811)

Bartlet, Aldred Durling, *An Historical and Descriptive Account of Cumnor Place* (Oxford & London: John Henry Parker, 1850)

Bentley, Samuel, *Excerpta Historica or Illustrations of English History* (London: 1831)

Breverton, Terry, *Henry VII: The Maligned Tudor King* (Stroud: Amberley Publishing, 2016 and 2019)

Brewer, J. S., J. Gairdner and R. H. Brodie, *Letters and Papers, Foreign and Domestic of the Reign of Henry VIII, 1509–1547,* 21 Volumes and Addenda (London: 1862–1932)

Brooke, Ralph (York Herald), *A Catalogue and Succession of the Kings, Princes, Dukes, Marquesses, Earls and Viscounts of this Realm of England* (London: William Jaggard, 1619)

Brown, Rawdon, *Calendar of State Papers Relating to English Affairs in the Archives of Venice* (London: 1873, 1877 and 1890)

Brown, Rawdon, G. Cavendish Bentinck and Horatio F. Brown (ed.), *Calendar of State Papers Relating to English Affairs in the Archives of Venice, Volumes 2 to 9* (London: 1867–1897)

Camden Society, *The Camden Miscellany Volume the Fourth* (1859)

Camden Society, *Chronicle of the Grey Friars of London, Volume 53* (1852)

Camden, William, *Annales, The True and Royal History of the famous Empresse Elizabeth* (London: Benjamin Fisher, 1625)

Camden, William, *The History of the most renowned and victorious Princess Elizabeth* (London: R. Bentley, 1688)

Campbell, Rev. William, *Materials for a History of the Reign of Henry VII from Original documents preserved in the Public Records Office* (1873)

Castelnau, Michael de, *Memoirs of the Reigns of Francis II and Charles IX of France* (London: 1724; originally published in Paris, 1659)

Cavendish, George, *The Life of Cardinal Wolsey* (London: Harding & Lepard, 1827)

Chambers, E. K., *The Elizabethan Stage* (Oxford: Clarendon Press, 1923)

Collier, J. Payne, *The Egerton Papers* (London: Camden Society, 1840)

Corporation of London, *Analytical Index to the Series of Records known as the Remembrancia 1579 to 1664* (London: E. J. Francis, 1878)

Crosby, Allan James, *Calendar of State Papers Foreign: Elizabeth, Volume 10* (London: 1876)

Ellis, Henry (ed.), *Original Letters Illustrative of English History*, (London: Harding, Triphook and Lepard, 1825 and 1827)

Feuillerat, Albert, *Documents relating to the Revels at Court in the time of King Edward VI and Queen Mary (The Loseley Manuscripts)* (Louvain: 1914; reprinted by Kraus Reprint Ltd, 1963)

Furnivall, Frederick J. (ed.), *Ballads from Manuscripts Vol I* (London: The Ballad Society, 1868–72)

Gairdner, James (ed.), *Letters & Papers Illustrative of the Reigns of Richard III and Henry VII* Volumes I and II (London: Longman, Green, Longman & Roberts, 1861 and Longman, Green, Longman, Roberts and Green, 1863)

Gayangos, Pascual de (ed.), *Calendar of State Papers Spain, Volumes 4-6* (London: 1879–1895)

Gairdner, James (ed.), *The Spousells of the Princess Mary to Charles Prince of Castile* (Camden Society, 1893; originally printed in Fleet Street by Pynson, 1508)

Goldsmid, Edmund (ed.), *The Maner of the Tryumphe of Caleys and Bulleyn and the Noble Tryumphant Coronacyon of Quene Anne by Wynkyn de Worde 1532–33* (Edinburgh: 1884)

Grafton, Richard, *Grafton's Chronicle: History of England 1189 to 1558* Vol II (London: 1809; originally called *A Chronicle at Large and Meere History of the Affayres of England and Kinges of the Same* (1569))

Green, Mary Anne Everett (ed.), *Calendar of State Papers, Domestic Series* (London: Longmans, Green, Reader & Dyer, 1867)

Green, Mary Anne Everett (ed.), *Calendar of State Papers, Domestic Series* (London: Longman & Co., 1871 and 1872)

Green, Mary Anne Everett, *Lives of the Princesses of England* Volume V (London: Longman, Brown, Green, Longham & Roberts, 1857)

Grose, Francis and Thomas Astle, *The Antiquarian Repertory: A Miscellany* (London: 1780) and (London: Edward Jeffery, 1808)

Hall, Edward, *Hall's Chronicle containing the History of England* (1809; originally called *The Union of the Two Noble and Illustre Families of Lancaster and York* (1548 and 1550))

Halliwell, James Orchard (ed.), *Letters of the Kings of England* (London: Henry Colburn, 1848)

Hayward, Sir John, *The life, and raigne of King Edward the Sixt* (London: John Partridge, 1630)

His Majesty's George IV Commission, *State Papers of King Henry the Eighth Volume I* (London: John Murray, 1831)

Historical Manuscripts Commission, *Calendar of the Manuscripts of the Marquis of Bath* (Dublin: Eyre & Spottiswoode, 1907)

Historical Manuscripts Commission, *Calendar of the Manuscripts preserved at Hatfield House (also known as the Cecil Papers)* (London: Eyre & Spottiswoode, 1883)

Holinshed, Raphael, *The Laste Volume of the Chronicles of England, Scotland and Ireland* (London: John Hunne, 1577)

Hume, Martin, *Calendar of State Papers relating to English Affairs in the Archives of Simancas* (London: Eyre & Spottiswoode, 1892)

Hume, Martin and Royall Tyler (ed.), *Calendar of State Papers, Spain, Volumes 9 to 13* (London: 1912-1954)

Kemp, Thomas, *The Black Book of Warwick* (Warwick: Henry Cooke & Son, 1898)

Kingsford, Charles Lethbridge, *Chronicles of London* (Oxford: Clarendon Press, 1905)

Leland, John, *Collectanea* Volumes III and IV (London: Richardson, 1770)

Lemon, Robert (ed.), *Calendar of State Papers 1547 to 1580* (London: Longman, Brown, Green, Longmans & Roberts, 1856)

Lemon, Robert (ed.), *Calendar of State Papers, Domestic Series* (London: Longman, Green, Longman, Roberts and Green, 1865)

Lodge, Edmund, *Illustrations of British History, Biography and Manners* (London: John Chidley, 1838)

MacFarlane, Charles, *The Cabinet History of England*, Volume VII (London: Charles Knight & Co., 1845)

Madden, Frederick, *Privy Purse Expenses of the Princess Mary* (London: William Pickering, 1831)

Martin, Thomas, *The History of the Town of Thetford* (London: J. Nichols, 1779)

Mumby, Frank A., *The Girlhood of Queen Elizabeth* (London: Constable & Co. Ltd, 1909)

Mumby, Frank Arthur, *The Fall of Mary Stuart: A Narrative in Contemporary Letters* (London: Constable & Co. Ltd, 1921)

Nichols, J. G., *Literary Remains of King Edward the Sixth* (London: J. B. Nichols & Sons, 1857)

Nichols, J. B., *London Pageants* (London: 1837)

Nichols, John, *The Progresses and Public Processions of Queen Elizabeth* (London: John Nichols & Son, 1823)

Nichols, John Gough (ed.), *Chronicle of the Grey Friars of London* (London: Camden Society, 1852)

Nichols, John Gough (ed.), *The Chronicle of Calais* (London: Camden Society, 1846)

Nichols, John Gough (ed.), *The Chronicle of Queen Jane and of Two Years of Queen Mary and especially of the Rebellion of Sir Thomas Wyat written by a resident in the Tower of London* (London: Camden Society, 1850)

Nichols, J. G. (ed.), *The Diary of Henry Machyn, Citizen and Merchant Taylor of London: 1550–1563* (London: Camden Society, 1848)

Nicolas, Nicholas Harris, *The Literary Remains of Lady Jane Grey* (London: Harding, Triphook and Lepard, 1825)

Norton, Elizabeth, *Anne of Cleves: Henry VIII's Discarded Bride* (Stroud: Amberley Publishing, 2009)

Park, Thomas, *Nugae Antiquae being a Miscellaneous Collection of Original Papers* (London: Vernor & Hood, 1804)

Pettigrew, Thomas Joseph, *An Inquiry into the Particulars connected with the Death of Amy Robsart (Lady Dudley)* (London: J. Russell Smith, 1859)

Pollard, A. F., *The Reign of Henry VII from Contemporary Sources Volumes I and II* (London: Longmans Green & Co., 1914)

Pollard, A. F., *Tudor Tracts 1532 to 1588* (Westminster: Archibald Constable & Co. Ltd, 1903)

Pote, Joseph, *The History and Antiquities of Windsor Castle and the Royal College and Chapel of St George* (Eton: 1749)

Rayner, J. L. & G. T. Crook, *The Complete Newgate Calendar* (London: Private Printing for Navarre Society, 1926)

Rigg, J. M. (ed.), *Calendar of State Papers Relating to English Affairs in the Vatican Archives 1558–1578* (London: 1916 and 1926)

Roper, William, *The Mirrour of Vertue in Wordly Greatnes or the Life of Sir Thomas More Knight* (London: De La More Press, 1903)

Royal Historical Society, *Camden Miscellany XXXI* (London: University College London, 1992)

Society of Antiquaries, *Archaelogia or Miscellaneous Tracts Relating to Antiquity* (London: J. Nichols, 1796)

Stow, John, *Annals of England* (London: 1605)

Stow, John, *Three Fifteenth-Century Chronicles with Historical Memoranda and Contemporary Notes of Occurrences* edited by James Gairdner (Camden Society, 1880)

Strickland, Agnes, *Letters of Mary, Queen of Scots* (London: Henry Colburn, 1845)

Thompson, C. J. S., *Poisons and Poisoners* (London: Harold Shaylor, 1931)

Thorpe, Markham John, *Calendar of State Papers relating to Scotland 1509 to 1589* (London: Longman, Brown, Green, Longmans & Roberts, 1858)

Turnbull, William (ed.), *Calendar of State Papers, Foreign Series, of the Reign of Mary, 1553–1558* (London: Longman, Green, Longman & Roberts, 1861)

Tyler, Royall (ed.), *Calendar of State Papers, Spain* (London: HMSO, 1916)

Tytler, Patrick Fraser, *England under the Reigns of Edward VI and Mary* (London: Richard Bentley, 1839)

Vergil, Polydore, *The Anglica Historia* (1555)

Williams, Sarah (ed.), *Letters written by John Chamberlain during the Reign of Queen Elizabeth* (Camden Society, 1861)

Wood, Mary Anne Everett, *Letters of Royal and Illustrious Ladies Vol. II* (London: Henry Colburn, 1846)

Wright, Thomas (ed.), *Queen Elizabeth and her Times, a Series of Original Letters* (London: Henry Colburn, 1838)

Wriothesley, Charles (Windsor Herald), *A Chronicle of England during the Reigns of the Tudors* edited by William Douglas Hamilton (Camden Society, 1875 and 1877)

Ziletti, Giordano, *Lettere di Principi* (Venice: 1577)